Activities for
Elementary School Science

James W. Stockard, Jr.
Louisiana State University

Michael R. Gilchrist
Auburn University at Montgomery

Illustrated by
Gerald McCarter, Stuart Daniel, and Rachel DeRamus
Auburn University at Montgomery

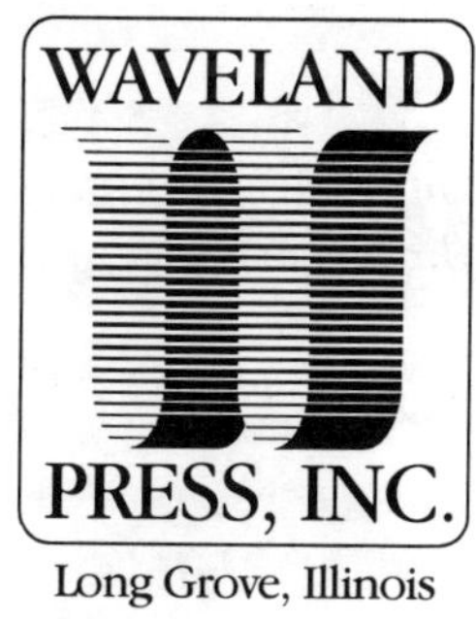

Long Grove, Illinois

For information about this book, contact:
Waveland Press, Inc.
4180 IL Route 83, Suite 101
Long Grove, IL 60047-9580
(847) 634-0081
info@waveland.com
www.waveland.com

ISBN 0-88133-998-9

Printed in the United States of America

9 8 7 6 5 4 3

This book
is dedicated to the authors' families,
to their students, and to their fellow faculty members
in the School of Education, Auburn University at Montgomery.

About the authors:

Dr. James W. Stockard, Jr., is a Professor in the School of Education, Auburn University at Montgomery. He served for many years in the public schools of Shreveport, Louisiana, as an elementary teacher, an instructional supervisor, a curriculum director, and an assistant superintendent for curriculum and instruction. Dr. Stockard has written books on elementary school social studies, elementary school math, elementary curriculum methods, and children's books on science, mathematics, and social studies. He received his doctorate at Louisiana State University.

Dr. Michael R. Gilchrist is an Associate Professor in the School of Education, Auburn University at Montgomery. He served for many years as a science teacher in Alabama and has conducted numerous science workshops for teachers. Dr. Gilchrist received his doctorate at Auburn University.

About the illustrators:

Gerald McCarter, Stuart Daniel, and Rachel DeRamus are art education majors at Auburn University at Montgomery. Gerald is a native of Montgomery, Alabama, and is interested in teaching and pursuing opportunities as an illustrator. Stuart was born and raised in Tuskegee, Alabama, and wants a career in the field of education. Rachel is a native of Prattville, Alabama, and wants to teach art in the schools.

Table of Contents

Part 2 — Life Science Activities

CHAPTER THREE

Animals

CHAPTER FOUR

Plants

Part 3 — Earth Science Activities

CHAPTER FIVE

Dynamic Changes in the Earth

CHAPTER SIX

Space

CHAPTER SEVEN

Water Investigations

CHAPTER EIGHT

Weather

Part 4 — Physical Science Activities

CHAPTER NINE

Chemical Properties

CHAPTER TEN

Physical Properties

RESOURCES

Overview
and Rationale

Science educators are currently engaged in designing curriculum reform initiatives that focus on learning as a constructive process as opposed to a transmitted process. For too long, science instruction has reflected an emphasis on drill and practice of procedures and the recall and accumulation of facts rather than as an activity-oriented, collaborative process. There is a new appeal to view the elementary science pupil not as a passive recipient of knowledge but as an active learner, working cooperatively and collaboratively with others on activities and projects where knowledge can be constructed.

Pupil-participatory, activity-oriented instruction has been advocated for the elementary school since shortly after the Civil War in America which ended in 1865. This book provides abundant opportunities for hands-on, activity-oriented, collaborative experiences in elementary science.

Real, hands-on materials, associated with a theme or topic of study, are the essence of developing interest, motivation, meaning, and true understanding in science classrooms. Higher-order thinking skills have their bases in activities involving concrete manipulation and observation.

The activities in this book are wide-ranging and can be adapted for many grade levels by increasing or decreasing the complexity of the activity. While the activities are categorized for convenience, they can also be fused with other subjects in an integrative, interdisciplinary format.

Each activity employs the same easy-to-follow sequence, making the transition from one activity to another smoother and less troublesome. The key elements of each activity plan are:

- Topic (a descriptive title)
- Grade Level (usually adaptable for a span of grades)
- Activity Time (the time it normally takes to complete the activity)
- Materials Needed (a list of all materials required to conduct the activity)
- Objectives (the resultant behaviors you want the children to exhibit)
- Introduction (starting the activity in an attention-getting way)
- Major Instructional Sequence (what you do, step-by-step)
- Closure or Evaluation (how you bring the activity to a conclusion)

By engaging your pupils in meaningful, worthwhile science activities, you are emphasizing the *processes* of learning rather than the *products*. The experience should be enriching to pupils and teacher alike!

CHAPTER ONE
Ecological Principles

The study of the surrounding air, water, and land relative to individual organisms or communities of organisms is called environmental science. The study of environmental science can range from a small area on the Earth to the Earth's entire biosphere, that part of the Earth and its atmosphere where organisms live or where life is possible. In recent years, environmental science has embodied the study of the impact of humans on the environment as well.

Ecology, the science of the relationships between organisms and their environments, is often erroneously used as a synonym for environment. The term ecology comes from the Greek *oikos* or "house" and *logos* "study of," and was originated in 1869 by scientist Ernst Haeckel. A branch of biology, ecology involves the observation and analysis of systems of living organisms and how they interact with their environment. Ecological studies look at communities of organisms and their patterns of life, natural cycles, population changes, biogeography, and the like.

The definition of environment is not as clear. Environment, by some definitions, includes all natural systems in the world, yet other definitions say that environment is a representation of the various ecosystems. Most ecosystems, however, are overlapping, thus the confusion.

Often, scientists break the Earth down into regions with distinct types of climate, topographic features, water, soil, plants, and animals. Within these ecosystems, they study organisms living in groups (communities), and they call the most extensive communities biomes. Their ecological studies include the interaction of the chemical, physical, and biotic factors of the environment with the organisms in the region.

Topic: FOOD CHAINS

Grade Level: 1 – 3 **Activity Time:** 2 or 3 days

Materials Needed:

1. Pieces of cardboard or posterboard
2. Clothes hanger made of wire
3. Yarn, fishing line, or (small-gauge) string
4. Paints, crayons, or markers
5. Hole punch

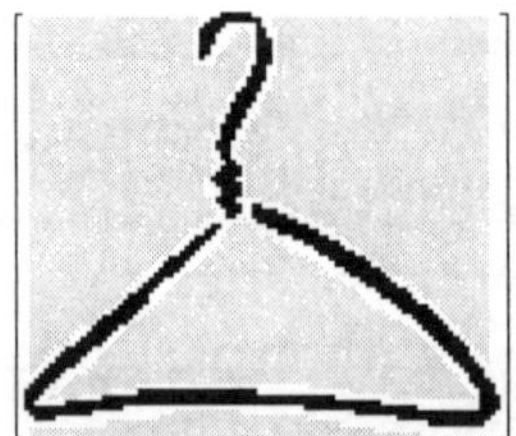

Objectives:

As a result of this activity, the learner will:

- explain how different animals eat different things in the food chain.
- explain what the terms carnivore, herbivore, and omnivore mean.
- construct a mobile that depicts a particular food chain (or web).

Introduction:

1. Ask your pupils to name some animals. List the names on the board.
2. Ask your pupils to name some things that these animals eat (e.g., rabbits eat carrots).
3. Ask your pupils to name some animals that might eat these animals. Introduce the words, *prey* and *predator*.
4. Show the pupils some cards (made of posterboard) that contain the names of various animals and plants. Ask the pupils to look at the cards and tell you what might eat what. Introduce the words, *carnivore*, *herbivore*, and *omnivore*.
5. Arrange the cards in the order that the pupils indicated (ex. carrots-rabbit-fox). Explain to your pupils that this is a *food chain*.
6. Tell your pupils that they are going to make an Eco Mobile using a particular food chain (of their choice or yours). Show them an example of a mobile and indicate to them how to assemble the mobile and balance the parts.

Major Instructional Sequence:

1. Organize your pupils into groups of two to four.
2. Provide each group with the materials (cardboard, posterboard, or thick construction paper) to make their animals/plants. Due to the age of the children and the potential problems with balancing a mobile, it may be helpful to have the outlines of the animals/plants already drawn (reproduced on a copy machine) on the material.

3. Ask your pupils to cut out their animal and plant outlines and to decorate them with the materials provided (paints, crayons, or markers).
4. Punch holes (with the hole punch) in the outlines so they will hang evenly. You will need to help with the placement of holes.
5. Instruct your pupils to take the string/yarn/fishing line and thread it through the holes. Help them balance the components on the clothes hangers.
6. Hang the mobiles from different parts of the ceiling. It is recommended that you enlist the aid of parents or older pupils to help you.

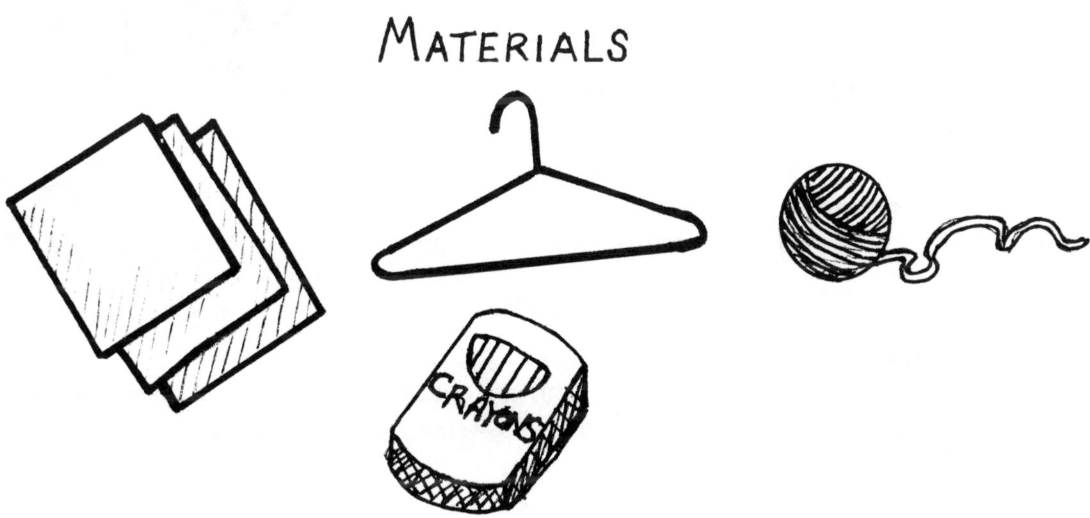

Closure or Evaluation:

1. Once the mobiles are hanging from the ceiling, gather your pupils together in a group and discuss what they have just created. Reemphasize terms such as *food chain, carnivore, herbivore,* and *omnivore.* Ask the pupils "why" they assembled the mobile in a particular manner (with one animal or plant underneath another, etc.). You could even ask them to think of other combinations.
2. Talk about the mobiles and how they had to be made in a particular manner (for balance). This is where you would introduce the concept *center of gravity.*

Note: You could utilize a clothes hanger and hang several different organisms at staggered levels, indicating a food web.

Topic: WASTE MANAGEMENT 1

Grade Level: 2 – 6 **Activity Time:** 1 – 2 days

Materials Needed:

1. Aluminum cans and 2-liter plastic bottles (soft drink)
2. Cloth and plastic diapers
3. Paper cups and plastic cups
4. Apple cores, potato peelings, etc. (in baggies)

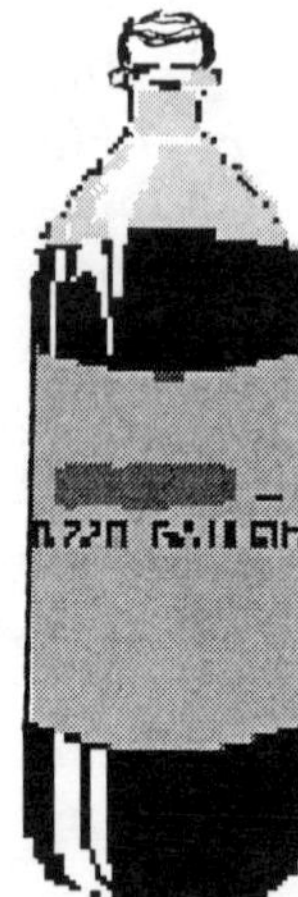

Objectives:

As a result of this activity, the learner will:

- compare the environmental advantages and disadvantages of using aluminum, cotton, paper and plastics.
- identify ways to help reduce landfill waste.

Introduction:

1. Ask your pupils what waste is. Point out to them that waste is all the discarded by-products of human consumption. There is *solid waste, liquid waste*, and *gaseous waste.*
2. Indicate to your pupils that you will be discussing solid waste today. Solid waste is generated from human activities, ranging from home and commercial establishments to industrial and mining operations. Disposing of solid waste has been an environmental nightmare for years. Americans alone are producing more than 150 million tons of garbage per year.
3. Ask your pupils how people can dispose of solid waste. The most likely choices are landfill disposal, incineration, recycling, and product replacement/redesign. *Landfill disposal* refers to burying the garbage in the ground. *Incineration* refers to burning selected materials to recover energy in the form of heat. This heat can be used to generate power for commercial/industrial agencies. *Recycling* refers to reusing the waste material. *Product replacement* refers to replacing an environmentally unsound material with one that is more "Earth-friendly." *Product redesign* refers to making the product more "Earth-friendly" before placing it in the economy.

Note: The degree of complexity with which you address this issue depends on the developmental level of your pupils.

4. Point out to pupils that burying the waste produces numerous "costs" which must be addressed: potential pollution and health problems; economic costs (because of lawsuits, etc.); and social costs (no one wants a landfill near their home). Try to get your pupils to see the value of alternatives to landfill disposal, particularly since fewer new landfills are being licensed and many of the old ones are likely to be closed in the next few years.
5. Introduce some new terms for the activity they will be doing. *Renewable resources* are materials that can be renewed or replenished (e.g., trees). *Nonrenewable resources* cannot be renewed or replenished (e.g., minerals, metals). *Organic materials* are compounds made of carbon (e.g., apple cores). *Biodegradable* refers to the conversion of one organic substance to another containing a smaller number of carbon atoms (e.g., the apple core breaks down into smaller organic components which will provide nutrients and energy for other life forms). *Nonbiodegradable* refers to the inability of the substance to be broken down into smaller numbers of organic molecules.
6. Ask your pupils if they think Native Americans and the early colonists had problems disposing of their waste. Ask the class why trash problems are different now than they were in prior centuries. If they need hints, steer the discussion toward the industrial age and its inherent problems (e.g., plastics, tires), compounded by a rapid increase in population. Discuss possible ways to utilize some of the methods the early Americans did when disposing of their waste (e.g., using more biodegradable products—some Native American tribes used corn husks for diapers); growing more food and buying more raw, unprocessed food (e.g., purchasing fresh peas from the farmers' market rather than canned peas from the grocery store).

Major Instructional Sequence:

1. Provide your pupils with an assortment of materials that might end up in a landfill.
2. Instruct each group (of pupils) to classify the materials based on the definitions discussed in class (see No. 5). Provide a worksheet (such as Table 1.1) for pupils.

3. Once each group has classified their materials, ask them to decide whether each by-product is acceptable for a landfill. Have them classify which materials could be buried in a landfill and which could be disposed of in another way.

Closure or Evaluation:

1. Ask your pupils (groups) to present their findings to the class. Encourage them to explain/clarify their answers.

2. Ask if there is an alternative to this product (or by-product)? What would it be? Could the packaging be redesigned to be more Earth-friendly? How?
3. Ask your pupils what conclusions they may have drawn from this activity.

Table 1.1
What Can We Do Instead?

Product

What type(s) of resources does it represent (e.g., renewable, nonrenewable, organic, biodegradable, nonbiodegradable)? Explain/defend your answer(s).

Is the product/by-product acceptable for landfill burial? Why or why not? Could it be disposed of in another way? How?

Is the product (or by-product) necessary? Why or why not?

Topic: ECOSYSTEMS 1

Grade Level: 2 – 6 **Activity Time:** 1 day

Materials Needed: (per group)

1. A collection of wildlife (and environmental) picture books and magazines
2. Paper and pencil

Objectives:

As a result of this activity, the learner will:

- create and write stories about animal pictures.
- interpret how animals relate to their surroundings.
- develop an increased interest in creative writing.

Note: A very important aspect of this activity is to write a story about an animal (or animals) and their relationship with their environment (their habitat).

Introduction:

1. Arrange the wildlife picture books and magazines on a large table.
2. Show your pupils a few examples of animal pictures.
3. Encourage pupils to discuss what they see in each picture. Be sure to emphasize the surroundings (environment) in which the animal(s) live. Tell pupils that we use the word *habitat* to describe an animal's surroundings; the atmosphere in which it lives.
4. Have your pupils describe the pictures in the form of a story. Let one pupil start the story and others can add details as the story progresses. Explain that the story they tell must address some ecological/environmental issue that is important for the animal(s).

Major Instructional Sequence:

1. Ask your pupils to browse through the books/magazines that have been previously placed on the table.
2. Instruct each pupil to select a particular picture and write a short story about the pictures (giving names to the animal(s), etc.).

Note: In small group or cooperative group formats, pupils stronger in verbal skills can help/assist the weaker pupils.

Closure or Evaluation:

1. Each pupil (or group) can read his or her story to the class while a pupil holds up the picture used as the inspiration for the story.
2. Pupils (or groups) may receive awards from the teacher, or from the class (by vote) for various categories (e.g., Most Creative Story).

3. Pupils can rework their stories so they can be displayed on the bulletin board (checking spelling, grammar and usage, and using their best penmanship).

Variation:

This activity may be modified for older pupils to include drawing pictures (illustrations) or cartoons, complete with captions or narratives.

Topic: WASTE MANAGEMENT 2

Grade Level: 3 – 6 **Activity Time:** 2 days

Materials Needed: (per group)

1. Samples of disposable materials from several fast-food restaurants.
2. Heavy duty garbage bag (13 gallon – 0.75 mil. recommended)
3. Paper sacks
4. Scissors and yardstick
5. Shovel
6. Materials for markers (wooden stakes about 2 inches wide and 12 inches long)
7. Tempera paint or magic markers (for decorating the stakes)
8. Water source and old towels

Objectives:

As a result of this activity, the learner will:

- classify disposable materials used in fast-food restaurants as either biodegradable or non-biodegradable.
- become aware of ways to deal with discarded products that cause waste disposal problems.

Introduction:

1. Discuss with your pupils the meaning of the words *biodegradable* and *non-biodegradable*. Encourage your pupils to think of examples of each.
2. Ask your pupils to bring in samples of disposable items from the fast-food restaurants they visit with their parents. They should bring in everything from unused condiment samples to plastic cups and straws. Instruct them to wash out any used materials (e.g., used cups, straws, plastic salad containers). It is best to obtain items in pairs (one for the garbage bag and one for outside the garbage bag).
3. Instruct your groups to decorate two of the wooden stakes provided. The top portion (top half) needs to be decorated so that the group can identify its own dig.

Major Instructional Sequence:

1. Divide your pupils into groups of three or four and have each group select a person to serve as *leader* and a person to serve as *recorder*.
2. Instruct the members of each group to separate their samples into two identical sets. Any materials not obtained in pairs must be cut in half, so there is an equal sample for both inside the bag and outside the bag.

3. Instruct the recorder of the group to record the items that will be used in the experiment.
4. Have the leader of each group obtain a garbage bag. The leader of the group is also responsible for making sure that the group places one half of their materials in the plastic garbage bag and one half of their materials in a marked paper sack.
5. Take your pupils to an area, either on campus or at another designated site, where they can bury the materials.
6. Have your pupils take turns digging two 1.5 ft. X 1.5 ft. holes approximately 2 feet deep. Some of the pupils' parents could accompany your class to the site and help with the digging.

Note: To use metric dimensions for digging, make the holes 0.5 m. X 0.5 m. and approximately 65 cm. deep.

7. Instruct your pupils to bury the garbage bag containing one-half of their materials in one hole, and the remaining material in the other hole (minus a garbage bag).
8. Instruct pupils to mark the sites with pre-decorated wooden stakes.
9. After 5 – 6 months has elapsed, escort your pupils back to the burial sites.
10. Instruct each group to use their shovels to dig up their buried material.
11. Instruct the groups to place each batch of materials into a new garbage bag. Make sure they don't mix the materials.
12. Have your pupils wash and dry the materials (as best they can) before analyzing the materials.

Closure or Evaluation:

1. Once the materials have been "cleaned," instruct your pupils to determine how much of the original material is still left intact (approximate percentage).
2. Ask your groups to record their estimates and present their findings to the class (complete with conclusions reached). You might want to construct a chart on a bulletin board, overhead sheet, posterboard, or the blackboard so each group can compare its results with those of the rest of the class.
3. Once every group has had a chance to present their findings, ask the class what conclusions they have reached based on the data recorded.
4. Ask your pupils to tell you which materials seem to be biodegradable and which materials seem to be non-biodegradable, based on the data.
5. Ask your pupils to identify materials that might be more of a waste disposal problem than others. Some important attributes to consider would include material size, material biodegradability, potential toxicity, and the like.

Variation:

1. This activity could be demonstrated with the class working together as a single group. Only two burial sites would be needed, making it easier to utilize the school grounds or other designated site.
2. This activity could also be structured in a more experimental style. Older pupils (groups) could practice the scientific method by establishing their own hypotheses, purposes, procedures, results, and conclusions. In short, this activity would be a good exercise in demonstrating to your pupils the scientific method (procedure) in experimentation.

Table 1.2
Sample Results

Materials Buried Per Site	% Degraded w/Bag	%Degraded w/o Bag
1/2 Salad Tray & Top	0-5	0-5
Barbecue Sauce & Top *	0-5	0-5
1/2 Hamburger Wrapper	70-75	100
2 Napkins	100	100
Bacon Bits *	0-5	0-5
Croutons *	0-5	0-5
Crackers *	0-5	0-5
1/2 McLean Deluxe Wrapper	70-75	90-95
Fork (Wrapped in Plastic)	0	0
9-Piece Chicken McNugget Box	25	50
Brown Bag (Recycled Paper)	100	100
2 Coke Cups (Medium)	10-20	20-25
2 Plastic Cup Tops	0	0
2 Straws (Plastic)	0	0
1/2 Child's Cardboard Hat	20-25	40-50
Biggie Fry Container	20-25	40-50

* Materials were ruptured by insects and/or weathering. All foods contained were eaten or lost. Percentage degraded based on plastic container, not food.

Sample Conclusions

1) Paper products definitely degrade faster than plastic materials.
2) Plastic materials should be used with more discretion due to the lack of degradation of the material.
3) Materials buried outside of plastic garbage bags tend to degrade slightly faster than the same materials buried inside of plastic garbage bags.
4) Fast-food restaurants should encourage consumers to eat within the building when possible. This might discourage the use of plastic salad trays, forks, spoons, cup tops and condiment containers, which do not degrade over a short period of time.
5) Fast-food restaurants should use paper straws instead of plastic straws, which do not readily degrade.

Topic: MEASURING THAT LEAK

Grade Level: 4 – 6 **Activity Time:** 1 – 2 days

Materials Needed:

1. One leaky faucet
2. One graduated cylinder (100 ml.)
3. One sample faucet (complete with internal parts: washers, etc.)

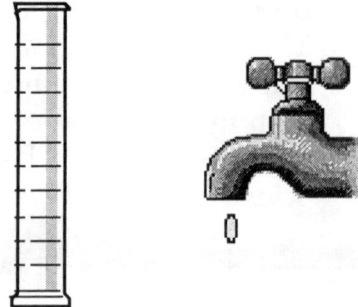

Objectives:

As a result of this activity, the learner will:

- predict how much water is lost from a leaky faucet over a given time period.
- compare the economic and ecological costs of having a faucet fixed versus letting the water continue to drip.

Introduction:

1. Ask your pupils, "How many of you have seen faucets dripping, either in your own home or somewhere else? How much water do you think was lost each day? Each week?" Your pupils will provide you with a variety of responses.
2. Ask your pupils if they can think of an alternative to letting the water continue to drip. The obvious answer would be to fix the faucet.
3. Pass the sample faucet around. This would be a good time to tell the class the most common problem with a leaky faucet, namely, the washer has deteriorated.
4. Show them a sample washer and point out how much it costs to replace. This amount will vary, but it should be around 20 – 40 cents.

Major Instructional Sequence:

1. Place the graduated cylinder under a leaky faucet and collect the water that drips out of the faucet. (If you prefer, you can have your pupils find any number of leaks around the school, *or* they can monitor a leak around their own houses as homework.)
2. Record the amount of water that drips into the graduated cylinder over a given time (e.g., 10 minutes, 30 minutes, 1 hour).
3. Ask your pupils how you can calculate the amount of water that was lost over a given amount of time (e.g., 1 hour, 24 hours, 1 week, 1 month).

Closure or Evaluation:

1. Record the data collected either from your classroom demonstration or from pupils' individual collections.
2. Calculate the actual amount of water lost over one hour, one day, one week, one month, and one year (see example below).
3. Have your pupils construct a graph that illustrates the water loss from different sources. It would be best if they could measure the water loss from all the faucets in the school, for example.
4. Ask them why we should repair leaks quickly (monetary costs, loss of fresh water, etc.).

Sample Calculations:

Calculation of actual amount of water lost over time:

If you collected 10 c.c. (ml.) of water over 30 minutes, then you would double that amount to get the volume collected over one hour.

10 ml. X 2 = 20 ml./hr.

If you collected 20 ml. over one hour, then you would multiply that number by 24 to obtain the volume collected over one day.

20 ml./hr. X 24 hr./day = 480 ml./day

If you collected 480 ml. over one day, then you would multiply that figure by 30 to obtain an approximate volume collected over one month.

480 ml./day X 30 days/month = 14,400 ml./month or 14.4 liters/month

If you collected 14.4 liters in a typical month, then you could calculate the water lost over one year (assuming the leak is constant) by multiplying the water lost per day (.48 liters) by 365.25 days.

0.48 liters/day X 365.25 days/year = 175.32 liters/year

30 min.	1 hour	1 day	1 month	1 year
10 ml.	20 ml.	480 ml.	14,400 ml.	175.32 liters
			or 14.4 liters	

Topic: STUDYING GARBAGE

Grade Level: 4 – 6 **Activity Time:** 2 or 3 days

Materials Needed:

1. One 30+ gallon garbage bag mixed with a variety of "sanitary" garbage (per group)
2. Freezer bags (in which to place banana peels, etc.)
3. Clipboards and pencils

Objectives:

As a result of this activity, the learner will:

- list some of the main sources of trash disposed by a "typical" family.
- make predictions about human society (people) based on its garbage.
- relate this activity to the work of archaeologists.

Introduction:

1. In advance of this activity, prepare the trash bags. Make sure you place a variety of trash items in each bag. Make each bag "unique" to a particular family, real or fictitious. Be sure to think about safety implications. Place potentially odorous or unsanitary items (such as a banana peel or an empty dog food can—minus the sharp lid) in a sealed freezer bag. Bottles should be washed to ensure sanitary conditions. This will eliminate most of the problem with bacterial growth and smell. Remove any labels that might provide a name or address (which would constitute an invasion of privacy).
2. Ask your pupils, "Where does trash come from?" "What does it consist of?" "How can we use it to obtain knowledge (information) about people?" "How could scientists (archaeologists) use garbage (things left behind by people) to discover clues about the lives of ancient people?" Hopefully, your pupils will provide you with a variety of responses.
3. Once you have conducted a discussion based on these questions, organize your pupils into groups of four. Indicate to your pupils that you are going to provide them with the opportunity to study some clues left behind by people. It is their job to observe the "artifacts" and to develop some inferences about the family that left the artifacts.

Major Instructional Sequence:

1. Place one sealed bag of trash in the middle of each group. Instruct pupils not to open the bags until you tell them.
2. When your pupils are "ready," instruct them to carefully remove the

items in the trash bag and place them in an organized pile. Ask each group to carefully record the items and discuss the possible implications of each item. Provide your pupils with a few sample questions to ask as they start investigating their "artifacts." Some sample questions might include: (1) Where might the family be located? Is there anything in the trash that could pinpoint their exact location? (2) What does the trash (artifacts) tell you about the people in the family? Are there items that indicate male and/or female adults in the family? Are there items that indicate that children might be in this family? (3) Is there any evidence of pets in this family? On what are you basing your answers? (4) What type(s) of diet(s) do the members of the family have? What evidence supports that conclusion?

Closure or Evaluation:

1. Once each group has finished the analysis of their trash and reached conclusions as to the lives of the owners, instruct your pupils to share their conclusions/ideas with the class. Make sure that they provide evidence to back up their conclusions/ideas. (One of the dangers with an activity such as this is that your pupils may make generalizations about a family without a sufficient amount of evidence on which to base their decision. Point out to your pupils that one box of Cheerios does not necessarily mean that the family is one in which children live. Adults do eat cereal!)
2. If you have specific information or knowledge about an actual family from whom you got trash, you might want to share certain information, such as the number of adults in the family, the number of children in the family, the ages and sexes of the children in the family, the basic dietary tendencies of the individuals in the family. This would provide your pupils specific information with which to compare their inferences for accuracy. Tell the class that they have an advantage over archaeologists, since they can obtain an actual description of the people they are studying. Archaeologists can only speculate on ancient cultures. They can never see how accurate they were in their inferences.

Note: This would be a good activity to introduce the concepts of facts, inferences, and fiction. A fact would be that a milk or orange juice container was found in the trash. An inference would be that milk or orange juice was probably part of the family's diet. An example of fiction would be that the family raised cows or tended an orange grove (there is simply not enough data to defend that claim).

Topic: ECOSYSTEMS 2

Grade Level: 4 – 6 **Activity Time:** 3 – 5 days

Materials Needed:

1. Various textbooks for pupil research (such as biology, ecology, environmental science, zoology)
2. Awards (optional)

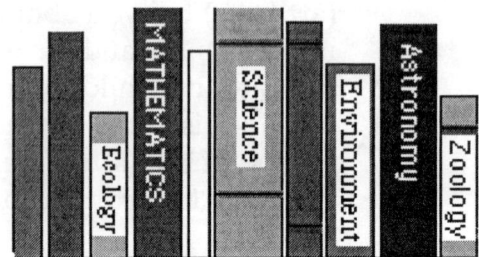

Objectives:

As a result of this activity, the learner will:

- create a "new animal" on Earth based on research of existing (or previously existing) animals, predator-prey relationships, and ecosystems.
- analyze and evaluate how a "new animal" or "space alien" would affect the ecosystem of Earth.

Introduction:

1. Organize your pupils into small, cooperative groups of four per group.
2. Instruct them to use their combined research and thinking capabilities to investigate each of the basic concepts (see Figure 1.1 at end of this activity).

Major Instructional Sequence:

1. Instruct your pupils (groups) to research and answer each of the questions for each basic concept. In addition to these basic concepts, your pupils could delve into other, more specific characteristics, such as basic ambient temperature, type of reproduction, basic locomotion characteristics, specific digestion capabilities, and potential value to humanity (particularly of an ecological nature).
2. Once each group has researched its "new creation," named it, come to a group consensus of its characteristics and attributes, and drawn a picture of the creature, reconvene the class for group presentations.
3. Instruct each group to present its findings (complete with picture) to the class. Each group should answer questions generated from the class, including a defense of their presentation.
4. In phase II, pupils (groups) could conduct research on the various planets and moons in our solar system. Using this data, pupils could synthesize a being from another world (space alien). Remind pupils that the conditions on the particular location (planet, moon) must be investigated thoroughly to ensure that the group's "alien" is congruent with the environment to which it will be subjected. Once such factors as temperature, gravitational pull, weather (or lack of weather),

and terrain are identified, the group can concentrate on "designing" its alien in an adaptive manner. Using our own solar system provides data for reconstructing the approximate ecological habitats on each planet or moon.

5. Some additional questions that might be addressed (if you decide to pursue the "space alien" route) would be:
   a) What types of adaptive equipment would this organism need to survive in its present habitat? (This would include, e.g., adaptations to atmospheric conditions or temperature ranges).
   b) How would the presence of this alien interfere with the carrying capacity of the habitat? With the food web?
   c) Which ecological habitat on Earth would be more conducive for your alien? Why?
   d) Would the respiratory activities of your alien interfere with any of the cycles of nature? (water cycle, nitrogen cycle, photosynthetic cycle, etc.)
   e) Would the chemical constituency of your alien interfere with normal ecological activities on Earth? Would the decomposing forces on Earth be able to break down this alien upon its death?

Closure or Evaluation:

1. Pupil groups may receive awards from the teacher or the class (vote) for various categories (e.g., Most Creative Animal, Most Creative Animal Defense Mechanism, Most Creative Animal Adaptation). The most important aspect of this activity is the need not only to be creative, but to defend that "creativity" with a reasonable, scientific defense. Logical thought should be more important than aesthetic value.

Variation:

If additional specificity is the intent, an activity such as Design-a-Fish (or Design-a-Bird) may be of more immediate use in the classroom. Pupils can explore the various adaptations of fish, such as mouth structure, fin structure, tail structure, coloration, predation tools, and habitat. Pupils can then create (and draw) their own new fish species based on the research of preexisting ones. Once again, emphasis should be placed on accuracy of detail and defense of presentation, rather than just purely aesthetic value.

Note: These activities allow teachers to incorporate science process skills into the science classroom, providing pupils with the opportunity to find and solve problems based on "real-life" simulations. Pupils can demonstrate proficiency in collecting, analyzing, classifying, and interpreting data; recognizing causal relationships in ecological systems; and making and defending valid arguments (or decisions) to problems or questions. In addition, the seeds can be sown for some "enlightened" classroom discussions resulting from group presentations.

Figure 1.1
Ecological Inquiry: Design-an-Animal

1. **Habitat** — Where will the animal live? Why do you want "your animal" to live in this environment? What are the advantages and disadvantages of living in this environment? (Note: habitat may include both local and global information.) Could this new animal potentially disrupt the habitat in which you placed it? How?

2. **Color** — What color(s) is/are important for your animal? Why? What advantages does coloration have for your animal? Does your animal blend in with the environment (habitat) that you listed earlier? Does its color provide any natural advantages/disadvantages towards predator/prey relationships? Why or why not?

3. **Size/Shape** — What is the size of the animal? What is its general shape? Why did you select that general size and shape? What are the advantages and disadvantages of the size and shape you chose?

4. **Protective Features** — Does your animal possess any particular protective features that may be utilized for defense? What are they? (This might include information from previous concepts). Does your animal possess any particular defensive weapons? If so, what are they? What would be the advantage of such defensive weapons?

5. **Food Sources** — What types of food will your animal seek for nutritive purposes? (Classify the organism as carnivore, herbivore, or omnivore.) Why did you choose these types of food? What advantages/disadvantages will these food sources have for your animal's continued well-being? Where is this animal located on the food chain (or food web)? How does this animal affect the carrying capacity of the habitat in which it is living? Construct a modified food chain (or food web) to illustrate the new animal's niche.

6. **Food Seeking Skills** — What particular set of skills will your animal possess so as to be able to obtain the foods you listed in No. 5? Why are these skills important to your animal?

7. **Classification** — What current group of organisms would be most closely related to this organism? Why? Are there particular advantages for that classification?

Topic: ECOLOGICAL EXPLORATION

Grade Level: 4 – 6 **Activity Time:** 1 week

Materials Needed:

1. Research books containing information about various rivers of the world (e.g., Amazon, MacKenzie, Mississippi, Rhine)
2. Magazines containing pictures of various types of animals, plants, food, clothing, and supplies
3. Various pieces of materials (e.g., boards, styrofoam) that can be used to make boats or ships in class
4. One poster-size display board and markers for each group
5. Scissors, glue sticks, and various colors and types of paint (spray paint works well for painting the overall boat/ship)
6. Newspapers for painting

Objectives:

As a result of this activity, the learner will:

- explain where a river is located and the type of terrain that surrounds it.
- explain what types of clothing, food, and general supplies would be needed when making a trip up/down this river.
- identify various types of fauna and flora that populate the shore or live in this river.
- create a model of a boat/ship that would be able to navigate this river.

Introduction:

1. Review for your pupils the proper procedures for researching topics and writing papers (including bibliographies if necessary).
2. Ask your pupils to name some rivers of the world. Have a pupil compile a list on the board. Provide them with additional names, which you can find in any encyclopedia.
3. Ask where each of these rivers are located in the world. If you have a map of the world (or particular continents), ask some of your pupils to point out the location of each river on the map.
4. Ask your pupils if they can tell you what types of animals or plants one might find in or near this river. Have some sample pictures of animals and plants to show your pupils. Then ask them at which river they might be found.

Major Instructional Sequence:

1. Arrange your pupils into groups of two or three.
2. Instruct each group to select a river they would like to investigate. They may choose from the list provided by the class or from a supplemental list you provide.

3. Each group will draw a map of the river, complete with geographic points (e.g., cities, towns, boundaries of states or countries, and tributaries). This map must be drawn on a poster or display board.

Note: Display boards are expensive but much better for displaying the group's work. Inquire into PTA funding to purchase the boards.

4. After they have researched their river thoroughly, tell the groups to find and cut out pictures that depict the animal life, plant life and overall habitat of the area through which the river runs. Once they have cut out the pictures, ask them to glue some of them on the poster (display) board to one side of the map.
5. Instruct each group to research what types of clothes, food, and special supplies it would need if it were making a trip from one end of their river to the other. The types and amounts will depend on the length of the river and the time it would take to travel the river from one end to the other.
6. Once the groups have researched the items listed in No. 5 above, ask them to find and cut out some pictures that illustrate the items they discovered in their research. These pictures will be glued on the other side of the map.
7. Finally, instruct your pupils (groups) to research the type of boat or ship that they would need to travel on this river from end to end. Make sure they understand that they may need to carry this boat overland at points and travel over rapids, depending on the terrain. Once they have completed their research, ask them to construct a facsimile of the boat/ship using materials you have provided them or materials from home. Tell the pupils to paint or decorate the boat/ship as realistically as possible.

Closure or Evaluation:

1. Ask each group to present its finished products to the class. Make sure the pupils defend their rationale for including various pictures on the display board. Make sure they defend their boat design as well.
2. Encourage your pupils to ask questions about the projects presented.
3. Groups may receive awards from the teacher or the class (vote) for various categories (e.g., Most Creative Display, Most Creative Sailing Vessel, Best Looking Display). The most important aspect of this activity is the need not only to be creative but to defend that "creativity" with a reasonable, scientific (and rational) defense. Logical thought should be more important than aesthetic value.

Topic: ECOLOGICAL ORIENTEERING: READING THE COMPASS

Grade Level: 5 – 6 **Activity Time:** 2 days

Materials Needed:

1. One Compass (Central Scientific) per group of 2 – 3 pupils
2. Ecological questions, animal/plant pictures and models
3. Clipboard, pencil

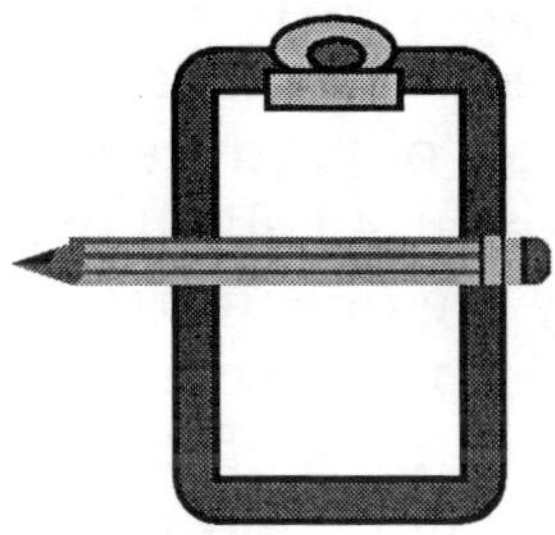

Objectives:

As a result of this activity, the learner will:

- navigate his or her way through a course using a compass.
- construct his or her own orienteering course using a map and compass.
- identify and collect samples of specific specimens discussed in class.

Note: This activity is to be conducted outside in a park with a woodland setting if possible. If pupils will be presenting specimens, consider having them go out with collecting jars (clean baby food jars work well). If they are going to take pictures, have inexpensive disposable cameras available (cameras and film could be paid for by contributions or grants).

Introduction:

1. Divide your pupils into groups of two or three.
2. Instruct your pupils how to use a compass. Teach them how to find north. Show them how to move the degree setting on the dial around the compass. Instruct them on finding the appropriate direction for each degree setting (pointer on compass). Ask your pupils to point in the direction of each setting you provide them (e.g., 30 degrees, 110 degrees, 175 degrees).
3. When you are satisfied that they have mastered the compass, ask your pupils to find the 40-degree mark, walk 35 paces in that direction, and stop. Ask them to find the 160-degree mark and walk 35 paces in that direction. Finally, ask them to find the 280-degree mark and walk 35 paces in that direction. Check their locations. If they correctly used the compass, they should be very close to their original starting point. Hint: remind them that a pace will be defined as one regular step.
4. Provide your pupils with a second practice run to ensure that all groups have mastered the use of the compass.

Major Instructional Sequence:

1. Provide the groups with a new course that eventually returns to its starting point. Assign each group of pupils a different starting point somewhere within the course (e.g., if group 3 starts at point 3, it should travel in the direction of point 4; if group 7 is the last group, it will begin at point 7 and proceed to point 1).
2. Provide each group with a list of specimens to gather at each point in the course. As each group arrives at a particular point or area, ask them to collect specific specimens that correspond with that particular area. They could find examples of producers, consumers, decomposers, almost anything you have talked about in class that is present in the environment they are orienteering. These specimens can be collected (physically picked up), drawn on sketch sheets, or simply photographed. If you have previously investigated the flora and fauna prior to their orienteering, ask them to find specific types of plants, trees, and wildlife. It might be best to mark particular trees or plants to help them in the identification process. You could ask the pupils to dig into the soil, look under rocks or in rotting logs to find and identify living things (such as earthworms, beetles, spiders). You could even leave molds of animal prints on the trail for them to find and attempt to identify. If a particular species of bird inhabits the particular territory your pupils are orienteering, alert them to what the bird looks like and what types of sounds it makes. This could provide a valuable opportunity to turn the orienteering into a birdwatching experience as well.

Note: Make sure your pupils return the area to its former state to the greatest degree possible. Your job is to facilitate. Make sure they are orienteering into the right areas and finding what you want them to find.

3. When all the groups have completed the course, ask them to assemble in one large group outdoors (or back in the classroom).

Closure or Evaluation:

1. Ask your pupils (in groups) to present what they found at various checkpoints.
2. Ask them what they found when they examined the rotting logs, rocks, and/or soil. What were the physical conditions of the trees? Did they look healthy? Were any tree roots exposed? What might have caused this? Were the lighting conditions (for the trees) the same? Were the smaller trees able to get enough sunlight? Moisture? Use questions like these to generate information from your pupils (it would probably be best to provide them with these questions before they go out and investigate). Generate discussion by asking them why these conditions existed.

Variation:

Pupils (in groups) could be asked to construct their own orienteering course, complete with a map and directions. Each group could then run the class through its course. This would let you know if they have truly mastered orienteering. Pupils could even provide their own ecological questions for the class (as a review).

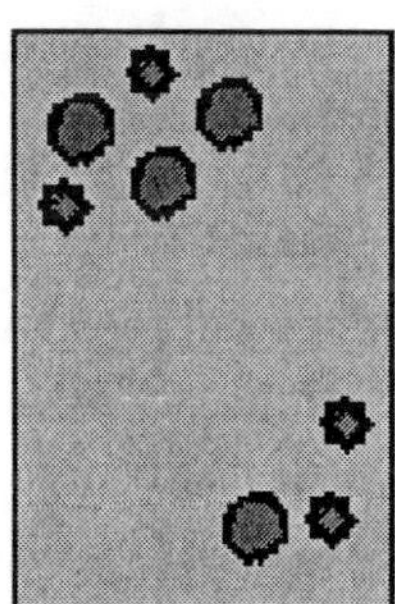

Topic: MAKING ENVIROSAFE CLEANERS

Grade Level: 5 – 6 **Activity Time:** 2 or 3 days

Materials Needed:

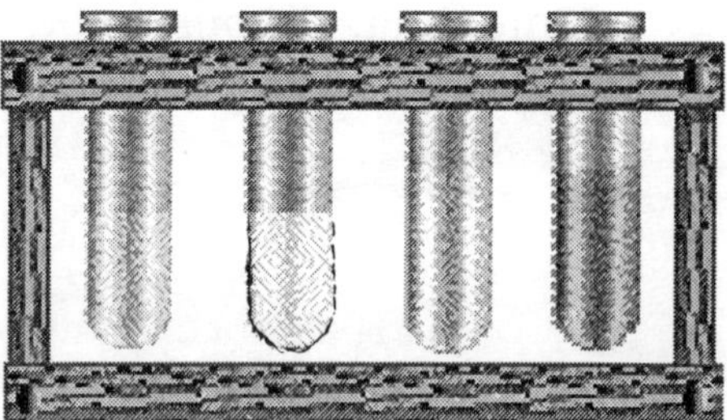

1. Vegetable oil (olive oil works well)
2. Borax
3. Clear vinegar
4. Lemon juice
5. Cornstarch
6. Baking soda
7. Salt
8. Cloths, spray bottle, sponges, buckets, cotton balls, etc.
9. Remnants of carpet and/or cloth
10. Remnants of materials used in making floors, sinks, wood cabinets

Objectives:

As a result of this activity, the learner will:

- explain why envirosafe cleaners should be used instead of conventional cleaners (from the store).
- compare and contrast envirosafe and manufactured cleaners for cleaning power and economic efficiency.

Introduction:

1. Introduce the concept of envirosafe cleaners. Start by refreshing your pupils' minds regarding the types of materials that can be found in "traditional" (manufactured) cleaners and the potential hazards they represent to the environment. Chemicals from these cleaners can cause global environmental problems, such as ozone depletion and non-point source water pollution. Environmental pollutants can also cause a variety of health problems. For example, people tend to associate a certain smell (such as the scent of pine) with cleanliness and believe that "if a little is good, more must be better." The average person may not realize that the "natural" scent of pine found in some household products may, in reality, be chemically reproduced, and that even small amounts of certain chemicals or combinations of chemicals may cause harm to humans (e.g., asphyxiation, cancer).

   Once you have discussed the problems of conventional/traditional cleaners, introduce the concept of envirosafe cleaners. All of the ingredients listed above, such as baking soda, borax, lemon juice, olive oil, and clear vinegar, are natural substances which have been shown to be harmless to human health and the environment.

2. Introduce the concept of economy. Economy consists of weighing the cost of purchasing a conventional/traditional cleaner versus the cost of making an equal amount of envirosafe cleaner. Illustrate the point with one example, the cost of the traditional window cleaner vs. the cost of making the envirosafe window cleaner (with clear vinegar and water).

Teacher's Illustration:

A typical window cleaner might cost $1.98 for 32 oz. (approximately six cents per ounce). You can illustrate this by dividing the $1.98 by 32. A 16-oz. bottle of clear vinegar might cost $0.48. If you mix 1/4 cup or approximately 2 oz. to 30 oz. of water (the envirocleaner), you have a window cleaner that basically does the same job for less. You can calculate for the children the cost of the vinegar used ($0.06) by dividing the forty-eight cents by 16 (the number of ounces) and multiplying by two, since you used 2 oz. of vinegar in your cleaner. Obviously, there is a big difference between $1.98 and $0.06! If a pupil decides that you should factor in the cost of the spray bottle, then factor in another $1.48 (the average cost of three different brands of 32-oz. spray bottles. If your pupils inform you that the difference between $1.98 and $1.54 is not significant, then ask them to look at the long-term effect. The 16 oz. of vinegar can be used to make 8 bottles of envirosafe glass cleaner. Eight times six cents, with the $1.48 for the bottle figured in, produces a total cost of $1.96 for 8 bottles. If you were to buy 8 bottles of the leading glass cleaner, you would pay $15.84 ($1.98 X 8). Point out that this means they would pay $13.88 more for 8 bottles of cleaner!

Major Instructional Sequence:

1. Place pupils in groups (3 – 4) and provide them with the ingredients and directions for making some/all of the envirocleaners.
2. Once the pupils have made their envirocleaners, instruct them to construct an experiment that will test the cleaning capabilities of the envirocleaner with the cleaning capabilities of the conventional/traditional. You may need to provide them with tables, wood, etc., in addition to the items already in your classroom (such as glass windows).
3. Ask your pupils to compare the cost of a conventional/traditional cleaner with the cost of their envirosafe cleaner using the teacher illustration above as an example.

Directions for Envirocleaners:

1. Carpet cleaner: Sprinkle baking soda on the carpet. Wait 15 minutes and vacuum. (Cornstarch can also be used.)
2. Spot remover (carpet, cloth): Rub with damp cloth sprinkled with borax. Let it dry and brush/vacuum off (a sponge can also be used).
3. Counter/cabinet cleaner: Mix 1/2 cup of borax in one gallon of water.

4. Floor cleaner: Add 1/2 cup of vinegar with one gallon of warm water.
5. Room odors: Place cotton balls in vanilla extract. Remove the cotton balls and place them on a saucer, pie pan, or small dish.
6. Window cleaner: Add 1/4 cup of vinegar to one quart of water (place in a spray bottle). Add a bit of salt and it can be an all-purpose cleaner.
7. Furniture polish: Mix olive oil (vegetable oil) with lemon juice.
8. Silver cleaner (variation for older pupils): Place 8 tablespoons of baking soda in 1 gallon of water. Stir and dissolve the baking soda into the water. Place some of the solution into a large aluminum pan. Place aluminum foil into the solution (make sure it is completely covered by the liquid). Heat the solution slowly with a hot plate (do not boil). While the solution is hot, place the tarnished silver into the pan (use tongs and gloves to prevent burns when dropping the silver into the pan). Make sure the silver is touching the aluminum in the bottom of the pan and is completely submerged in the solution. When the silver appears clean (in a few minutes), remove it from the solution using the tongs and wash the silver in running water (tap water is fine). *Note: This particular activity is not listed in the Materials Needed section. Teacher discretion is advised because of the hot water necessary for the activity.*

Closure or Evaluation:

1. Ask your pupils to present their data regarding the perceived efficiency of the cleaners and their economic efficiency (cost to consumer).
2. Record the data from each group on the board (or overhead) and guide the pupils in a discussion of their findings. If a group felt that one product was particularly better than another, allow them to defend their finding. The other groups should be allowed input/ questions to verify or challenge a group's findings. Remind them it's okay to disagree, as long as you are not disagreeable.
3. Relate the experiments back to your initial presentation of the dangers of environmental pollutants to the general health of animals and plants, as well as the global environmental problems that can occur. Ask them if this influences their viewpoint as to which cleaner they would use and why. Which has the greater cost, long term as well as short term?

Topic: COMPOST KITCHEN WASTE

Grade Level: K – 6 **Activity Time:** 2 – 4 months

Materials Needed (per group):

1. Worm bin (a wooden or plastic box with a lid and air holes)
2. Kitchen waste from home
3. 8 – 10 red worms (available in bait shops)
4. Newsprint
5. Soil
6. Small pan of water

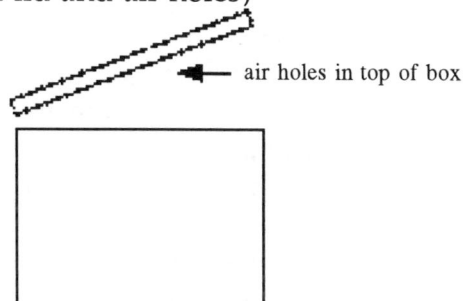

Objectives:

As a result of this activity, the learner will:

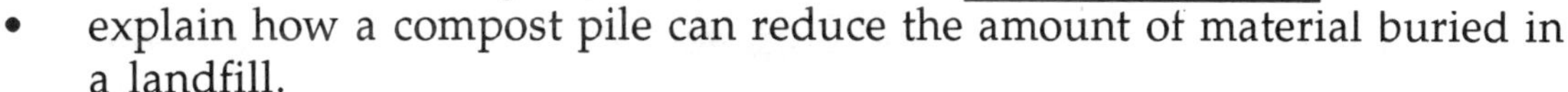

- explain how a compost pile can reduce the amount of material buried in a landfill.
- explain how the compost material can be used in flower gardens.

Introduction:

1. Discuss with the class that a landfill is a place where a community disposes of its trash by burying it.
2. Tell the class that approximately one-tenth of the trash in a landfill comes from kitchens. Explain how landfills are gradually filling up.
3. Ask your pupils how they could reduce the amount of material being buried in landfills. Focus on kitchen waste.
4. Introduce the concept of *compost* to the class. (Compost is a mixture of decaying organic matter, as from food scraps, leaves, and manure, used to improve soil structure and provide nutrients.) Discuss the variety of kitchen wastes which can be placed in a compost pile.
5. Explain to your pupils that they will be making a worm-bin compost pile. Ask them to bring kitchen scraps from home (see the list below).

Materials for the Compost Pile:

1. Any fruit or vegetable parts.
2. Eggshells and coffee grounds.
3. Just about anything organic (derived from living organisms), except for the following: fatty foods, such as meat scraps, oil, grease, bones (unless ground), butter, cheese, fish scraps, mayonnaise, milk, peanut butter, salad dressing, sour cream, vegetable oil, or yogurt.
4. Some materials, like bread, could be composted, but would be better broken into pieces and fed to the birds.

Major Instructional Sequence:

1. Divide pupils into groups of 4 – 7.

2. Have the groups fill their worm bins one-third full with soil.
3. Show the groups how to tear the newsprint into small pieces, moisten, and mix into the soil. (This provides a bedding for the worms.) Circulate, monitor, and assist as needed as the groups tear, moisten, and mix two or three pages of newsprint into the soil of their worm bins.
4. Have the groups place the red worms into their bins.
5. Instruct the groups to mix about one quart of kitchen scraps into their worm bins (compost piles). Tell them to make sure the kitchen scraps are buried. Circulate and check to make sure they are burying the proper items.
6. Find a suitable area around the school to place the bins. They may be stored next to a building. Make sure that the bin holes will allow for water drainage to protect the worms.
7. Make sure that the compost bins are somewhat secure from animals in the vicinity. Raccoons and dogs, for example, could dig into the bin searching for food. Make pupils aware that fats and proteins in the scraps (such as meat) will attract unwanted visitors, such as fire ants.

Closure or Evaluation:

1. Ask your pupils to check the bins periodically to determine what is happening to the kitchen waste.
2. Discuss with the class how composting can help landfills and the environment.
3. Explain to the class that the *humus* (decayed organic matter) created in the compost pile is suitable for use on house plants. In fact, pupils could transpose the worm bins into flower gardens within a few months, if you did not wish to continue the composting experiment.

Variation:

An alternative to the wooden/plastic bin idea would be to build flower beds (without the flowers) and place the items listed in the beds.

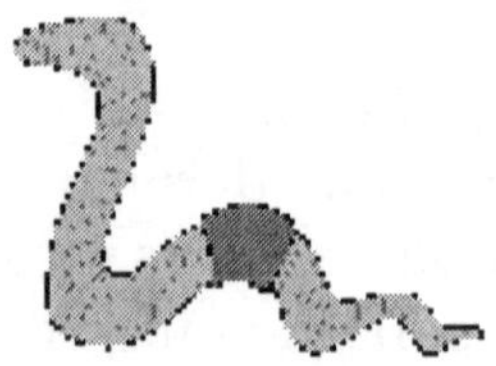

CHAPTER TWO
Habitats

A habitat is the area in nature where an animal lives. It is characterized by the surroundings of the area, determined chiefly by the vegetation. Oceans, rivers, and forests are examples of the more obvious habitats, but unusual habitats exist, too, such as caves. Some of the larger habitats and some of the animals that live in them include:

Deserts (hot, dry regions): camels, bobcats, coyotes, kangaroos, mice, gila monsters, scorpions, rattlesnakes.
Tropical Forests (warm, humid climate): orangutans, gibbons, leopards, tamandua anteaters, tapirs, iguanas, parrots, tarantulas.
Grasslands (flat, open lands): African elephants, kangaroos, Indian rhinoceroses, giraffes, zebras, prairie dogs, ostriches.
Mountains (highlands): yaks, snow leopards, vicunas, bighorn sheep, chinchillas, pikas, eagles, mountain goats.
Polar Regions (cold climate): polar bears, musk oxen, caribous, ermines, arctic foxes, walruses, penguins, Siberian huskies.
Oceans (sea water): whales, dolphins, seals, manatees, octopuses, stingrays, coral, starfish, lobsters, many kinds of fish.

Habitat degradation occurs when there is damage or partial destruction of a habitat. The damage or destruction of a habitat by physical means can be caused by either natural or human activity. The degradation of a barrier island habitat by a hurricane is an example of a natural means; the degradation of wetland habitat by highway construction is an example of human activity.

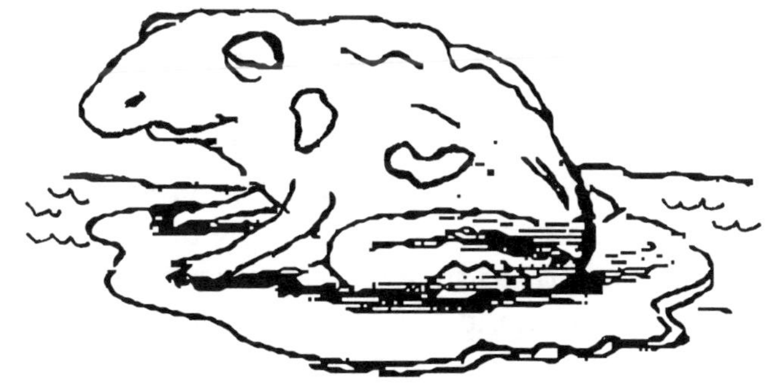

Topic: CAMOUFLAGE-COUNTERSHADING: COLORATION AND SURVIVAL

Grade Level: 3 – 6 **Activity Time:** 2 or 3 days

Materials Needed:

1. Four boxes of elbow macaroni (per 30 pupils)
2. Brushes and tempera paints (brown, green, and red; try to obtain hues that are similar to those commonly found in nature rather than bright, neon colors, e.g., the green of the grass, the brown of fallen dried leaves)
3. Newspaper, paper towels, and cups of water
4. Tape measure and string for measuring off a 20′ x 20′ area
5. A stop watch, note pad, and pencil for each group recorder

Objectives:

As a result of this activity, the learner will:

- explain how color makes a difference in the survival of animals in the wild.
- relate this activity to the concepts of camouflage and countershading.

Introduction:

1. Divide your pupils into groups of three.
2. Assign one of the pupils in each group the role of recorder.
3. Demonstrate how to paint the elbow macaroni with the tempera paint. Instruct the pupils prior to painting that they should paint on the newspaper, using it as a drop cloth.
4. Show your class samples of previously painted macaroni.
5. Have your pupils count out 200 pieces of macaroni.
6. Have them paint 50 pieces brown, 50 pieces green, and 50 pieces red (50 pieces will remain unpainted).
7. Assist the class in cleaning the brushes with water and paper towels.
8. Allow the painted macaroni to remain undisturbed overnight on the newspaper.

Major Instructional Sequence:

1. Prior to the time of the activity, have your group recorders mark off 20′ x 20′ areas in the grass outside and distribute 100 pieces of macaroni (25 of each color) within the group's area. (Make sure the other members of the group are not in the vicinity while this is being done.)
2. Have your group recorders use their stopwatches and tally the number of macaroni pieces picked up by each member of the group in one minute . Instruct the groups to make sure that each member of the group not currently being used as a test subject is secluded from the test site to avoid contaminating the results.

3. Duplicate the experiment again using a differently colored area, such as the patches of green and brown around trees as the test site (or use areas with colorful flowers or shrubs).
4. When all the test subjects have had their turn, return to the classroom and ask each group to report their individual data for the two experiments (record each group's data on the board).

Closure or Evaluation:

1. Ask your pupils if they see any trends in the data (e.g., more of certain colors collected than others).
2. Relate the data to the concepts of *camouflage* and *countershading*. Use pictures to illustrate these concepts. Examples might include:
    a. *Birds*: Show pictures of male and female birds of the same species (e.g., cardinal, killdeer). Ask the pupils to hypothesize why male birds are much more colorful than female birds (female birds that nest on the ground tend to be camouflaged with a dull brownish color, sometimes speckled, which helps them blend in with their surroundings). Birds that nest in trees tend to be darker on top and lighter on the bottom. This type of countershading scheme helps protect them from predators above and below.
    b. *Insects*: Show pictures of insects such as the praying mantis, walking stick, or the swallowtail caterpillar. Ask the class how their appearance can protect them from predators. The praying mantis uses its leafy twig appearance for both predation (prey comes close because it doesn't recognize the praying mantis until it is too late) and protection (birds cannot distinguish the praying mantis easily from leafy tree branches). The swallowtail caterpillar resembles a bird dropping. Ask pupils how that might be helpful in protecting the organism (birds do not eat their own droppings).
    c. *Fish*: Show pictures of fish, such as the flounder, which illustrate the idea of countershading (the outer top surface resembles the surrounding seabed and the fish can half bury itself to increase the effect). Ask pupils how this would make the fish hard to see.
    d. *Reptiles*: Show pupils pictures of various types of lizards, such as the chameleon, which can change its color to fit almost any background.

Note: The lesson sequence provided is based on an inductive (discovery) model. The instructional sequence can be modified to fit a deductive approach by simply introducing the topics of camouflage and countershading first before proceeding into more of an experimental design, complete with hypothesis, using the coloration and survival activity.

Topic: WHAT'S IN "DIRT?"

Grade Level: K – 2 **Activity Time:** 1 – 2 days

Materials Needed: (per group)

1. Gummy worms, raisins, cupcake sprinkles (red), rock candy
2. Crushed graham cracker crumbs
3. Chocolate chip cookies
4. Aluminum pie pans
5. Plastic baggies
6. Hand lenses (magnifying glasses)

Objectives:

As a result of this activity, the learner will:

- observe and describe various components in soil.
- explain (and describe) where soil comes from.

Introduction:

1. Explain to your pupils how dirt actually comes from rocks that break up (weathering effect). The small grains of the rock become what we know as dirt, or soil.
2. Ask your pupils to place 1 – 2 chocolate chip cookies in a baggie. (Do this in groups to conserve costs.)
3. Instruct your pupils (groups) to crush the cookies into smaller pieces.
4. Ask your pupils to observe the pieces. If they need to, they could pour the pieces onto a napkin or paper towel to observe the pieces better.
5. Instruct them to use the hand lenses to observe the "dirt" and "rocks" better. Encourage them to record their observations.
6. Ask your pupils (or groups) to present their findings to the class.
7. Explain to them that soil and sand come from the weathering of rocks. Wind, water and ice cause large rocks to become smaller. The material lost breaks up into smaller pieces (particles) of soil and sand.

Major Instructional Sequence:

1. Divide your pupils into groups of three or four.
2. Instruct each group to obtain a pie pan, crushed graham cracker crumbs, 1 – 2 gummy worms, 3 – 4 raisins, 5 – 10 red cupcake sprinkles, and several pieces of rock candy.
3. Ask your pupils to place their "dirt" (the crushed graham cracker crumbs) into the pie pan.
4. Instruct your pupils to arrange their gummy worms (worms), raisins (bugs, beetles, etc.), cupcake sprinkles (ants), and rock candy in ways

they think would be similar to that of "real" soil or parts of the soil. You might cut long strips of chocolate (from solid chocolate candy bars) to use as tree branches. You could even cut pieces of Fruit Rollups or Fruit-by-the-Foot to use as leaves.

Closure or Evaluation:

1. Ask your pupils to go outside and look at the soil in various points around the school. You need to scout out the areas beforehand and place markers where the pupils can find them.
2. Instruct your pupils to observe the areas carefully, using hand lenses to view the dirt. Ask pupils to record their observations.
3. After pupils have returned to class, encourage discussion about their observations.
4. Ask your pupils to "fix" any discrepancies they might have in their "soil" samples (e.g., more or less of certain items in their samples to more accurately resemble their observations of real soil). Ask your pupils to brainstorm about what additional things might be found in soil.

Topic: LIFE CYCLE CARDS

Grade Level: 3 – 6 **Activity Time:** 1 – 3 days

Materials Needed:

1. Pictures and reference books describing different life cycles of animals (e.g., frogs, butterflies)
2. Note cards (3 x 5 or 4 x 6)
3. Crayons, colored pencils or markers
4. Glue and scissors

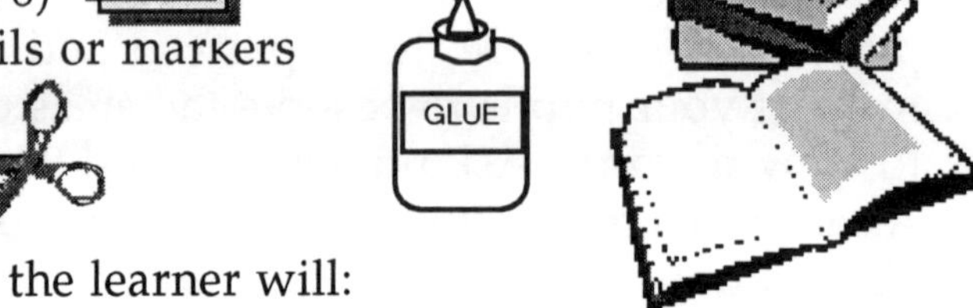

Objectives:

As a result of this activity, the learner will:

- describe the life cycle of various animals.
- explain why animals look different in various stages of their life cycle.

Introduction:

1. Have your pupils bring in pictures representing different stages in their lives. (As a prior assignment, younger children could bring in several pictures of a parent at various ages.)
2. Ask them to compare their pictures and indicate what changes have occurred to date. They should indicate hair color and length, height or body length, weight, etc.
3. Ask them to describe how they will look later as an adult. This is where the availability of pictures of one or more parents would help younger pupils understand what you're asking.
4. Discuss what types of changes will occur. You could even have pupils try to match the pictures of adults with some of their baby pictures.
5. Discuss the life cycles of various animals with which they would be familiar (e.g., dogs, cats).

Major Instructional Sequence:

1. Assemble the materials for the activity in a central location (e.g., table).
2. Have your pupils form groups of three to five.
3. Instruct two pupils from each group to obtain the materials needed for the activity.
4. Inform the groups that they are going to cut out and paste different developmental stages of some common animals (frogs, butterflies, etc.) on individual note cards. Instruct your pupils to label each note card for future reference.
5. Once they have made their note cards, ask each group to assemble the note cards in chronological order of appearance (youngest stage to oldest stage).

Note: It is possible to use frog eggs or tadpoles to follow the development of the life cycle process (or larvae and pupae for the butterfly). Pupils could sketch different phases of the life cycle from direct observation.

Closure or Evaluation:

1. Examine the placement of the note cards for each group (particularly for accuracy).
2. Ask your pupils to describe the life cycles they found.
3. Ask them to explain why animals look different in various stages of their life cycles. Discuss the concept of *metamorphosis* with pupils. Encourage discussion about why we say that frogs and butterlies "metamorphose," as opposed to dogs and cats.
4. Have your pupils create a new animal and describe the life cycle of that animal, complete with drawings (optional). They can even make note-card sketches to illustrate the life cycle.

Variation:

For older children, you could show illustrations of the life cycles of alien creatures from movies, such as *Alien*. You could even purchase some of the toys on the market (such as *Predator)* to illustrate similarities and differences in the creature.

Topic: HABITAT: WHERE DO THEY LIVE?

Grade Level: K – 6 **Activity Time:** 2 days

Materials Needed:

1. Pictures of various ecological habitats (e.g., rain forest, deciduous forest, swamp)
2. Pictures of various animals and plants (from a variety of habitats)
3. Long rolls of "butcher paper"
4. Tempera paints or permanent markers

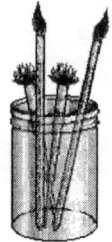

Objectives:

As a result of this activity, the learner will:

- classify animals and plants to a specific habitat.
- classify animals and plants to a specific location within a habitat.
- construct a habitat complete with the animals and plants that inhabit the region.

Introduction:

1. Assemble the pictures and other materials on a flat surface (e.g., table).
2. Discuss with your pupils what a habitat is and some of the different types (marine aquatic, fresh water aquatic, rain forest, deciduous forest, desert, etc.). For younger children, simplify the names (ocean, swamp, forest, jungle, etc.).
3. Ask your pupils to find pictures of various habitats discussed in class.
4. Ask them also to find pictures of various plants and animals that would inhabit the particular habitats mentioned in class. You might want to mention only the types of habitats indigenous to your area of the country.
5. Have your pupils share the pictures they found. Encourage them to explain which type of habitat(s) they found and how they arrived at their conclusions. Ask them to share the pictures of the plants and animals. Ask your pupils to classify the habitat(s) in which they might belong.

Major Instructional Sequence:

1. Divide your pupils into groups of three or four.
2. Assign each group the task of creating a habitat. You can either assign them a particular habitat or let them choose.
3. Instruct each group to work together drawing/painting the various components of their habitat on butcher paper (e.g., sand and cacti for deserts; shrubs, ferns, palms, and huge trees for a rain forest).
4. Once the habitat is created (and has dried), instruct your pupils to draw/paint (on separate pieces of paper) animals that might inhabit the area and cut out and glue them on their habitats. A rain forest, for example, might include a jaguar, a boa constrictor, an armadillo, tree

frogs, leaf cutter ants, termites, spider monkeys, a sloth, parrots and macaws drawn/painted on the scene. Encourage your pupils to research which animals would live in a particular region, what size they would be, and what color they would be.

Closure or Evaluation:

1. Exhibit the finished products on the walls. You could display some or all of the habitats on the walls outside your classroom for others to view.
2. Once the habitats have been created and exhibited, encourage your pupils to explain why they chose to draw/paint the particular plants and animals.
3. Encourage your pupils to name additional plants and animals that might inhabit the region(s).
4. Ask your pupils if they can identify any food chains or webs in the habitats.
5. Depending on the age of the pupils, ask them what types of specific products humans obtain from each habitat (e.g., lumber, medicine, food sources).

Topic: THE NATURE WALK: LOOKING FOR ANIMALS

Grade Level: 4 – 6 **Activity Time:** 1 – 2 days

Materials Needed:

1. Pictures (drawings, photographs, etc.) of various animals
2. Area for nature walk that has animal life or signs of animal life (e.g., the local forest preserve)
3. Adult volunteers

Objectives:

As a result of this activity, the learner will:

- observe and explain differences in the appearance and behavior of various animals.
- explain how animals adapt to their environments.
- develop observational skills necessary for animal watching.

Introduction:

1. Ask your pupils what types of things they see when they go outside. They will probably brainstorm a number of different things. Focus your questioning toward animals.
2. Pass your animal pictures around. Ask your pupils to tell some of the differences between the animals. Be sure to point out that insects are animals too!
3. Focus on pictures that portray different features of the animals, such as feet, claws, paws, bills, jaw size, body size and orientation.
4. Ask your pupils what kinds of things each animal would eat. How would they defend themselves? How would they find and capture prey? You could introduce several terms here: *prey, predator, herbivore, carnivore, omnivore,* and the like.
5. Tell the class they will be going on a nature walk. Ask your pupils to tell you what types of animals might be found in the area they will be visiting. Ask them if the time of the season makes any difference in what they might see. The nature walk can be around your school, neighborhood, park, or out in the country. Make sure you explain to your pupils what they are to look for (birds, insects, etc.).

Major Instructional Sequence:

1. Assist the adult volunteers in separating the class into small groups which can be spaced apart from one another and work independently (each group should have one or more adult volunteers).
2. Assign one of the pupils in each group the role of recorder. This individual must record every animal the group sees during its excursion.

3. Instruct your groups to record more than simply the name of the animals they see (bird, insect, etc.). Ask them to record the color of the animal, the habitat (where it was found), and any particular characteristics they may have seen. Have them look for signs of animals, such as tracks or droppings.

Note: A naturalist from a local society or university might be helpful to you and the children during your nature walk. They can identify animals not only by sight, but by sound and the tracks they leave. They also know where to find the animals and information about their particular adaptations.

Closure or Evaluation:

1. Ask your pupils to explain what they found (recorded) during their nature walk.
2. Ask the pupils to describe any peculiar (particular) animal characteristics and behaviors they discovered during their walk. This might include the flight pattern or sound of a bird, the tracks of a snake or deer, the difference in coloration patterns of male and female birds of the same species, for example.
3. Pupils could write (in a diary or log) about their nature walk. They could also write a letter or note to a pen-pal or a parent indicating what they observed on their walk.

Variation:

Depending on your locale, you might want to consider adapting this activity solely to bird watching. Birds will most likely dominate most habitats, and they lend themselves quite nicely to observation and discussion. You can have your pupils describe the bills or beaks, the overall size, the flight characteristics, the foot pattern or structure, the songs, the colors, and distinctive patterns of movement. There should be a fairly wide variety of birds available, even on campus.

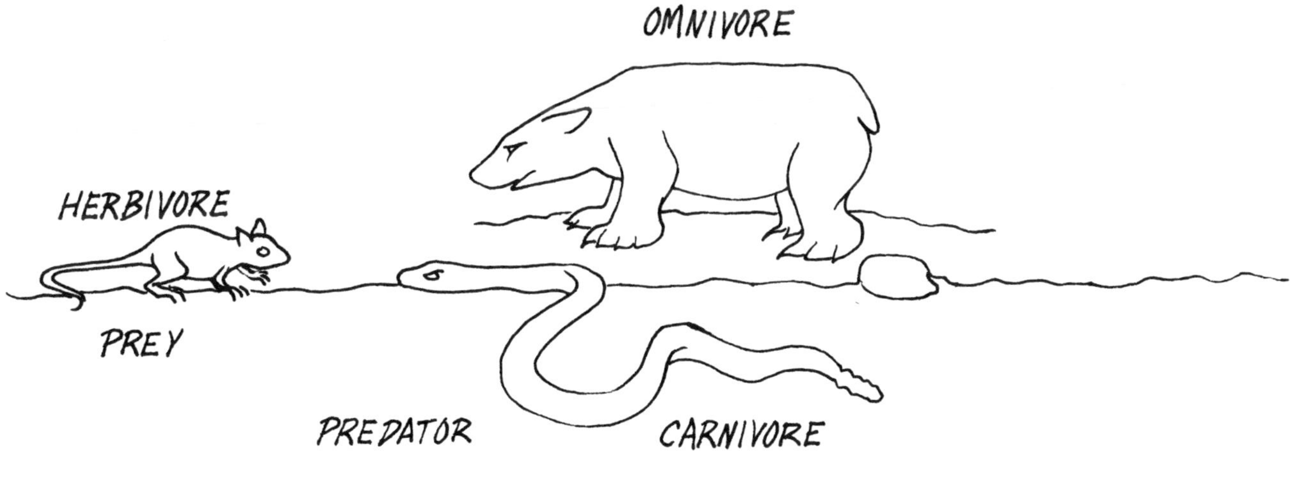

CHAPTER THREE

Animals

Different types of animals are so plentiful on the Earth that scientists devised a way to categorize them into groups. A scientist named Carolus Linnaeus, who lived in the 1700s, devised a system for classifying both animals and plants, and his system of classification is still used today. All of the animals on Earth are said to be in the animal kingdom. The animal kingdom is separated into two large groups. Animals that have backbones are called vertebrates. Animals without backbones are called invertebrates. The classification system divides these large groups into smaller groups called *phyla.* The phyla, then, are divided into even smaller groups called *classes.* When the animals in each group have bodies that are similar in certain ways, they are classified together. Some examples are:

VERTEBRATES: (animals with backbones)
FISH: Swordfish, tuna, salmon, trout, halibut; AMPHIBIANS: Frogs, toads, mud puppies; REPTILES: Turtles, alligators, crocodiles, lizards; BIRDS: Sparrows, owls, turkeys, hawks; MAMMALS: Kangaroos, opossums, dogs, cats, bears, seals, rats, squirrels, rabbits, chipmunks, porcupines, horses, pigs, cows, deer, bats, whales, dolphins, monkeys, apes, humans

INVERTEBRATES: (animals without backbones)
PROTOZOA: The simplest one-celled form of animals; COELENTERATES: Jellyfish, sea anemones, coral, hydra; MOLLUSKS: Clams, snails, squid, oysters; ANNELIDS: Earthworms; ARTHROPODS: *Crustaceans* — Lobsters, crayfish, Centipedes, Millipedes; *Arachnids* — Spiders, scorpions; *Insects* — Butterflies, grasshoppers, bees, termites, cockroaches; ECHINODERMS: Starfish, sea urchins, sea cucumbers

Topic: ANIMAL INSULATION

Grade Level: 3 – 5 **Activity Time:** 1 or 2 days

Materials Needed:

For Activity 1 each group will need:

1. Two Erlenmeyer flasks with one-hole stoppers
2. Two laboratory-grade thermometers (0°-230° F/-20°-110° C)
3. One bag of cotton balls and glue (cheesecloth or ace bandages may be substituted here)
4. Pitcher of warm water
5. One fan (optional)
6. Timer

For Activity 2 each group (or the teacher) will need:

7. Two disposable vinyl gloves
8. Pitcher of water and pitcher of ice
9. String (to tie off the fingers on one glove)
10. Ice bath and warm-water bath (plastic container with ice water or warm water)
11. Two thermometers (see above)
12. Timer

Objectives:

As a result of this activity, the learner will:

- explain the significance of fur and feathers for insulation purposes.
- explain why whales don't have arms and legs (limbs).
- graph changes in the rate of heat loss over time.

Introduction:

1. Ask your pupils to define the word *insulation.* Establish that insulation is any substance that reduces/prevents the passage of heat, electricity and sound into or out of a material. Focus on the passage of heat.
2. Ask your pupils to tell you what types of insulating structures might be used by an animal to prevent the loss of heat. Focus on skin, feathers, fur, and fat concentration in warm-blooded animals. Differentiate between warm-blooded (*homeothermic*) or constant body temperature, and cold-blooded (*poikilothermic*) or variable body temperature, usually slightly higher than the temperature of the surrounding environment.
3. Ask your pupils how each body structure might be significant for insulation purposes. Certain types of feathers and fur can actually trap a layer of warmed air (warmed by the body) next to the body.
4. Ask the class if they think appendages, such as arms, legs, and fins make a difference in preventing heat loss by a body.

5. Indicate to the class that you are going to engage in two activities to determine the influence of fur and appendages on the rate of temperature change.

Major Instructional Sequence:
Activity 1

1. Separate the pupils into groups of 3 or 4.
2. Instruct the groups to glue cotton balls on one of the flasks. If you do not want to work with glue (due to the mess), an alternative would be to wrap the flask with cheesecloth or 1 – 2 ace bandages.
3. Ask your pupils to place their flasks (insulated and noninsulated) in the designated area. Have them place their thermometers through the holes in the rubber stoppers. *Note: You may want to do this yourself, prior to class, because of the possibility of the thermometer breaking and cutting their hands. Glycerine works well for lubricating the thermometer so it slides more easily into the hole in the rubber stopper.*
4. Fill the flasks with warm water.
5. Ask your pupils to record the changes in temperature that occur as the water cools (2-minute intervals). (Fans work well to speed up the process.)
6. Have each group record data on the board or on an overhead sheet. Allow each group to see how close or accurate their results were, compared to the others.

Activity 2

1. Activity 2 should be done as a teacher-led demonstration. First fill a vinyl glove with a specific volume of warm water. Tie the glove off with a thermometer in it.
2. Fill your second vinyl glove, this one with the fingers tied off, with an equal amount of warm water. Tie the glove off with a thermometer in it. Make sure the temperature of the water is similar to that in the first glove.
3. Now place the two gloves in an ice bath and monitor the rate of change in both gloves over a specified time (2-minute intervals). Have your pupils help you observe and record data on a chart. As a further extension, you could take the same gloves and place them in a hot-water bath first, then the cold-water bath, recording the rate of temperature change over time for both experiments.

Closure or Evaluation:

1. Ask your pupils to present the data they collected for each activity.
2. If there were discrepancies, ask them how these discrepancies might have occurred. Remind them to brainstorm about general variables that could have influenced the outcome. It is paramount that your pupils not try to place the blame on anyone or any particular group.

3. Allow your pupils to graph the rate of heat loss over time. They should see that heat loss (temperature change) occurs more slowly with the fur-covered flask and the fingerless glove.
4. Allow your pupils to draw conclusions as to the significance of fur and limbs in heat loss.
5. Have your pupils graph the rate of temperature change over time for both activities.

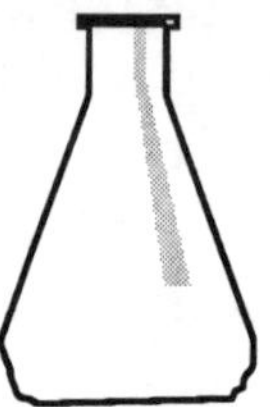

ERLENMEYER FLASKS

Note: Many lab supplies, chemicals, and electronic kits are available from Santa Barbara Science, P. O. Box 41960, Santa Barbara CA 93140-1960. Their web site is located at http://www.west.net/~science/. Send e-mail to: science@west.net.

NOTICE TEMP. OF FINGERLESS GLOVE
NOTICE TEMP. OF UNTIED GLOVE

Topic: DESIGN YOUR OWN ANIMAL

Grade Level: 4 – 6 **Activity Time:** 2 or 3 days

Materials Needed (per group):

1. Reference books and pictures of animals
2. Posterboard and crayons (paints optional)
3. Paper and pencil

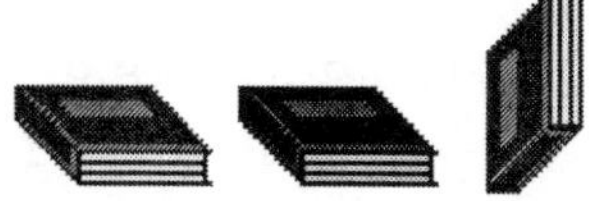

Objectives:

As a result of this activity, the learner will:

- create a "new animal" on Earth based on the research of existing (or previously existing) animals.
- relate predator/prey relationships and ecosystems (habitats) to his or her animal design.
- demonstrate proficiency in collecting, analyzing, classifying and interpreting data.
- recognize causal relationships in ecological systems.
- make and defend valid arguments (or decisions) to problems or questions.

Introduction:

1. Ask your pupils to name a few animals. Record their responses.
2. Discuss with your pupils how each animal lives. This would include feeding behavior, habitats, coloration, size/shape, protective features, and classification.
3. Ask them to name some animals that are extinct.
4. Ask them to explain why these animals don't exist anymore.
5. Compare their responses with the brainstorming done in No. 2 (above).

Major Instructional Sequence:

1. Organize your pupils into groups of three or four.
2. Provide each group with study sheets and ask them to research several existing (or previously existing) animals and create a "new animal" on Earth. Tell them that they will have to use their combined research and thinking capabilities to investigate the basic concepts outlined in the study sheet. (See questions for study sheets below.)
3. Have the pupils in each group work together cooperatively to create their "new animal." This will include a picture of the animal.
4. Circulate among the groups, check for understanding, and provide assistance as needed. Raise provocative questions as you circulate, like, "Could your new animal disrupt the habitat in which it is being placed?"

Closure or Evaluation:

1. Once the group has researched its "new creation," named it, and come to a group consensus of its characteristics and attributes, the group can present its findings, complete with a picture, to the class. Each group should answer questions from the class about its animal.
2. Groups could receive honors from the teacher, or the class, for various categories (e.g., Most Creative Animal, Best Animal Defense Mechanism). When honoring groups, the emphasis should be on scientific and logical thought.

Pupil Study-Sheet Questions

1. Habitat — Where will the animal live?
2. Color — What color(s) is/are important for your animal? Why?
3. Size/Shape — Describe the animal's size and shape.
4. Protective Features — Does your animal possess any particular protective features that may be utilized for defense? Describe.
5. Food Sources — What types of food will your animal seek for nutritive purposes? Is this animal a carnivore, herbivore or omnivore?
6. Food Seeking Skills — What particular set of skills will your animal possess to obtain the foods listed in No. 5 above?
7. Classification — What current group of organisms would be most closely related to this organism? Why?

Note: Each of these questions should be on a separate sheet. This would provide each group with sufficient space to answer each section.

Topic: MAKE AN ANIMAL BOOK

Grade Level: K – 6 **Activity Time:** 2 or 3 days

Materials Needed:

1. Various drawings or pictures of animals
2. Drawing paper, construction paper, posterboard
3. Scissors, paste, crayons, markers and paints
4. Collection of books and encyclopedias with information and pictures of various animals (particularly in their habitat)

Objectives:

As a result of this activity, the learner will:

- work in cooperative groups to create an illustrated book on a particular animal (or animals).
- develop an interest in a particular animal (or animals).
- research various reference and resource books for information about a particular animal (or animals).

Introduction:

1. Show your pupils some examples of various types of animals.
2. Ask them what types of habitats (environments) they might live in and what they might eat.
3. Allow the pupils to browse through some reference/resource books about animals.

Note: The advantage of allowing pupils to choose the animal(s) is to create a more intrinsically motivating environment for pupil research. Pupils have the opportunity to choose anything between a bumble bee and a dinosaur.

Major Instructional Sequence:

1. Divide your pupils into groups of three to four.
2. Explain to each group that they will create an illustrated book describing the life of a particular animal or animals using the pictures they create and the research they conduct. A short written description (may be a caption) should accompany each picture. Ask older pupils to write a story about the animal(s).
3. Point out to them that they will need to thoroughly look at pictures of habitats (environments) as well.

Closure or Evaluation:

1. Have each group present their book (story) to the class and share the pictures and descriptions written about their animal(s).
2. Place the animal books in an exhibit which may include other artwork.

Topic: MAKE AN ANT

Grade Level: K – 3   **Activity Time:** 1 day

Materials Needed:
1. Playdoh™ or modeling clay (any color)
2. Pipe cleaners (black) – cut to 5 cm. lengths (approximately 2 inches)
3. Straight pins
4. Paper plates or cardboard squares (optional)

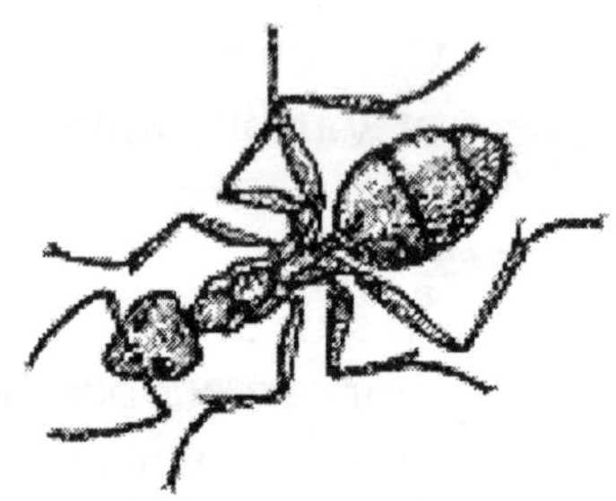

Objectives:

As a result of this activity, the learner will:
- produce a model of an ant.
- describe some characteristics of ants.

Introduction:
1. Show your pupils some examples of ants (pictures or models).
2. Discuss with your pupils some of the different groups of insects that are similar in structure to the ant (e.g., termites).
3. Ask your pupils to describe some characteristics of ants. This may include physical attributes as well as other characteristics (e.g., ants are attracted to sugar, food).
4. Show your pupils a sample model of an ant. Indicate to them that they will construct their own ants. Introduce the terms, *head, thorax, abdomen, legs,* and *antennae*. Point out what you used for each part.

Major Instructional Sequence:
1. Have each pupil obtain the materials they need from the supply table. The pupils can construct their models on paper plates or pieces of cardboard so that they can be handled more easily.
2. Demonstrate to your pupils how to separate the Playdoh™ into three pieces (three different sizes — the smallest for the head, the next largest for the thorax, the largest for the abdomen).
3. Once they have constructed the bodies, instruct your pupils to take the six pieces of pipe cleaner and attach three on either side of the thorax. Remind them the thorax is the middle piece. They can bend the legs in one or two places to simulate more realistic-looking legs.
4. Once the legs are in place, ask each pupil to place two straight pins in the front part of the head (they should form a V shape). Make sure they understand that the sharp points of the pins are dangerous and should be placed carefully into the Playdoh™. Only the flat end of the pin should be sticking out of the ant.

Note: You may want to find a substitute for the straight pins. Pieces of pencil lead (graphite for mechanical pencils) could be used as a substitute.

Closure or Evaluation:

1. Let your pupils display their ants to the class.
2. Exhibit your pupils' work in an area of the class or in an exhibition area for the school.

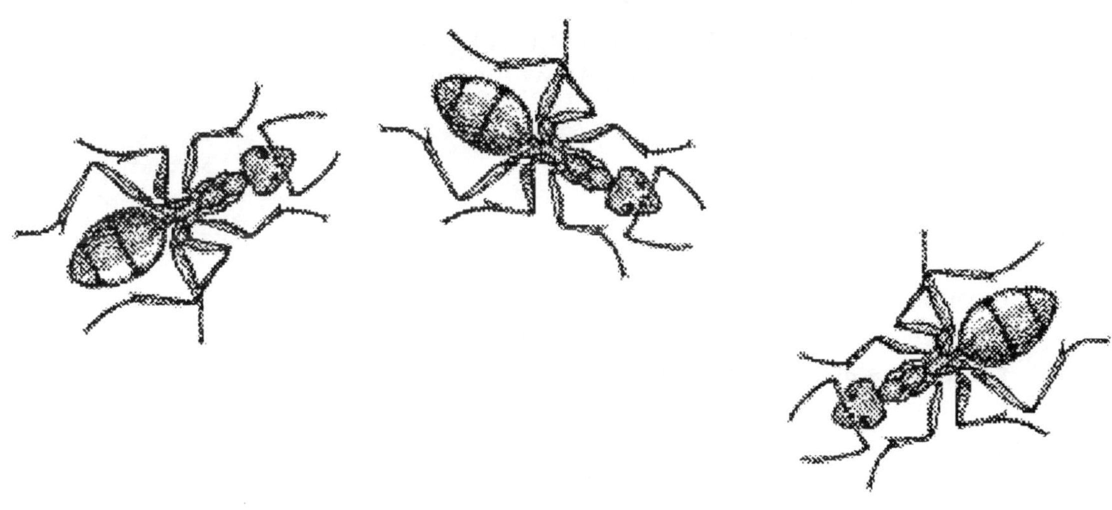

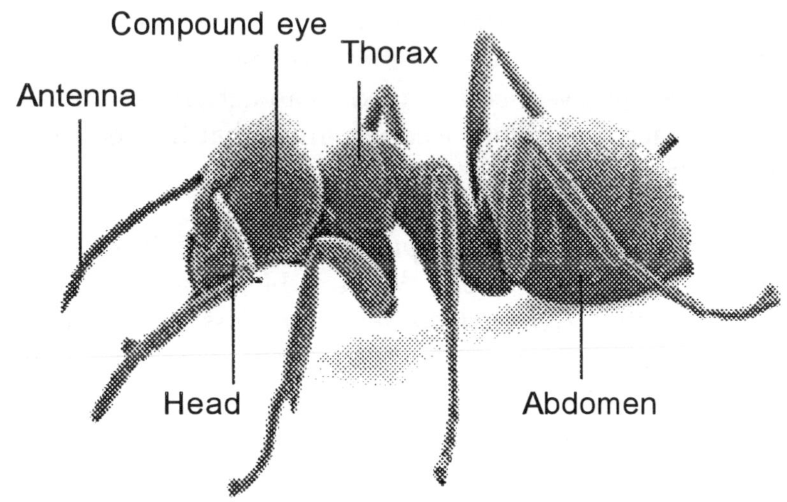

Topic: WHICH COLORS DO INSECTS PREFER?

Grade Level: K – 4 **Activity Time:** 1 – 3 days

Materials Needed:

1. Various colors of posterboard or construction paper
   Note: You can purchase posterboard in an 11″ x 14″ size (Mead™)
2. Tempera paints (brown, green, and red) and brushes — optional
3. Newspaper, paper towels, and cups of water — optional
4. Small medicine cups and sugar water (optional)
5. Clipboard and pencil
6. Tape measure

Objectives:

As a result of this activity, the learner will:

- explain how color makes a difference in attracting insects.
- explain how insects may be attracted by smell (optional).
- relate this activity to insect behavior outdoors.

Introduction:

1. Ask your pupils what types of things they see when they go outside. They will probably brainstorm a number of different things. Focus your questioning toward insects.
2. Ask your pupils to identify ways in which insects are beneficial to them and ways in which insects are a nuisance.
3. Ask your pupils what attracts insects. They will probably brainstorm numerous possibilities. Guide them toward color.
4. Point out that they will be engaged in an activity to determine if insects are truly attracted to color. Keep in mind that the season of the year is important here!

Note: If you decide that you want your pupils to paint pictures of flowers on the posterboard sheets (you may want to cut the 11 x 14 pieces in half), then you will need to use tempera paints. Demonstrate for your class the proper procedures for painting and cleaning up. It is advisable not to have more than two colors on the posterboard. More than two colors might cause confusion about which colors attract the insects.

Major Instructional Sequence:

1. Divide your pupils into groups of three or four.
2. Assign two of the pupils in the group the roles of lead experimenter and recorder.

3. Have your lead experimenters and recorders mark off 30′ x 30′ areas in the grass outside and distribute the various colors of posterboard or construction paper. They may need to place small pebbles to keep the materials from blowing away from the group's area. Make sure that the pupils put as much distance between the colors as possible. Also, make sure that there is a distance of at least fifty feet between group boundaries.
4. Instruct the members of the group to help the recorder tally the number of times an insect hovers over or lands on or within a few inches of a color. Ask them to keep a record of how many times different types of insects (fly, bee, etc.) come to each color.
5. Point out to your pupils that they need to collect data for a specified time period (e.g., 20 minutes, 30 minutes).

Closure or Evaluation:

1. Ask your pupils if they saw any trends in the data (e.g., more of certain insects than others, particular colors that seemed to attract more insects).
2. Ask them to relate the data to the concept of color.
3. Ask some pupils to compare insect behavior they have observed in the past to the pattern exhibited in this activity.
4. Use pictures of insects or other types of animals to illustrate (or reinforce) these concepts.

Variation:

Place a squirt of cologne on a sheet of clear plastic and repeat the experiment to determine if insects are attracted to smell. The procedure is essentially the same, with groups marking off their areas and recording the number of times an insect hovers over or lands on or within a few inches of the material.

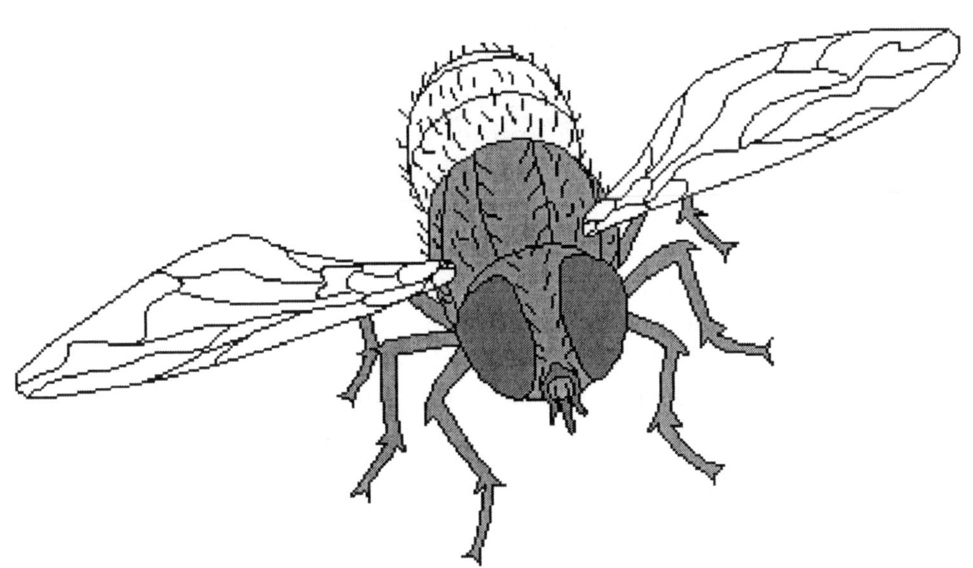

Topic: SONGBIRDS

Grade Level: K – 6 **Activity Time:** 1 – 5 days

Materials Needed:

1. Field guides of birds in the region (Audubon Society or Peterson)
2. Tape recorder
3. Binoculars (one pair per group)
4. Notebook for recording data

Objectives:

As a result of this activity, the learner will:

- associate a particular bird vocalization (or song) with the proper bird.
- describe the characteristics of various birds in the region.
- identify birds in the region by sight.
- produce a personal field guide of birds in the region (optional).

Introduction:

1. Show your pupils some examples of the birds of their region. For maximum effect, let them listen to various songs that each bird produces. (You might enlist the services of a professional bird watcher for obtaining sample bird vocalizations.)
2. If you play sample bird vocalizations (songs) for the pupils, have them write down a description of what they heard. For example, a crow produces a "caw-caw-caw" sound and a killdeer produces a "kill-deeah" sound. These sound descriptions can be found in the field guides for each bird.
3. Pass out the field guides and guide the pupils through the proper usage of the books. If you do not possess a sufficient number of field guides, you may wish to obtain permission from the author/book company to duplicate a few sample pages for instruction purposes. You may want to write a mini grant proposal for the purposes of obtaining a sufficient number of field guides (PTA, banks, etc. are willing to spend money on relevant teaching materials).

Major Instructional Sequence:

1. Organize your pupils into small groups. One can be responsible for physically describing the bird (using binoculars). Another can be responsible for writing down the descriptions into the group's notebook. A third can be responsible for looking up the bird in the field guide. The entire group can be responsible for describing the bird's vocalization.

2. Take your class into a quiet area where they can find birds. If there is an area around or near the school that is wooded, you could organize a class or school effort to place bird feeders in the region to attract birds.
3. Have the pupils remain quiet for 15 – 20 minutes and record data for any birds that are in the area.
4. If time is available, move your pupils to another area and repeat the steps in No. 3 above.

Closure or Evaluation:

1. Let each group work on producing a "bird guide" of the area. They will need to supplement their observations with the information in the field guides. The finished products may be distributed to other classes or schools for use in field studies.
2. Exhibit your pupils' work in an area of the class or in an exhibition area of the school. If you obtained money from the PTA, local bank, etc. for this activity, you might wish to present the group with a compilation of the pupils' work.

Topic: MAKE A BUG

Grade Level: K – 6 **Activity Time:** 2 – 5 days

Materials Needed:

1. Balloons (round and elongated) and X-Acto knife

2. Strips of newsprint paper measuring about 10″ x 12″
3. Liquid starch
4. Tempera paints (various colors) and brushes
5. Newspaper, paper towels, and cups of water
6. Various pieces of materials for wings, legs, antennae, etc.

Objectives:

As a result of this activity, the learner will:

- produce a model of an insect.
- paint and decorate an insect according to its natural coloration.
- research and present information about a particular insect.

Introduction:

1. Show your pupils some examples of insects (pictures or models).
2. Discuss with your pupils some of the different groups of insects (phylum, class, family). The age and developmental level of your pupils should dictate the level of detail in your discussion.
3. Indicate to your pupils that they are going to research and make a model of a particular insect. Provide them with a list of insects that have rounded or elongated shapes, since most balloons are either round or elongated. Again, the age and developmental level of your pupils should dictate how much detail you will require in their research.

Major Instructional Sequence:

1. Have your pupils inflate their balloons. (Smaller children may need help with this.) The shape of the balloon should be determined by the shape of the insect they researched.
2. Assemble the paper strips and containers of liquid starch at group work areas.
3. Demonstrate for your pupils how to dip paper strips in starch and place in layers on the balloon.
4. After the balloons have been fully covered, allow them to dry overnight.
5. Assemble the tempera paints at work areas.
6. Demonstrate to your class how to paint an insect model with the tempera paint.

7. Ask your pupils to paint (decorate their insects) according to their research. Tell them to wait for the paint to dry before adding wings, legs, etc.
8. Demonstrate to your class how to clean the brushes with water and paper towels.

Note: For very long insects you could use long balloons that can be twisted to make distinct sections. This would allow the pupil to have the head, thorax, and abdomen all connected.

Closure or Evaluation:

1. Let your pupils display and explain their insects for the class. Make sure they explain why they placed various components (number of legs, antennae, etc.) on the model.
2. Awards (certificates, etc.) could be given for various categories.
3. Hang the insects by strings from the ceiling, or place them in particular areas of the room so pupils can view and examine them. If the school has designated a particular area for pupil displays, allow some or all of the models to be seen by the entire school.

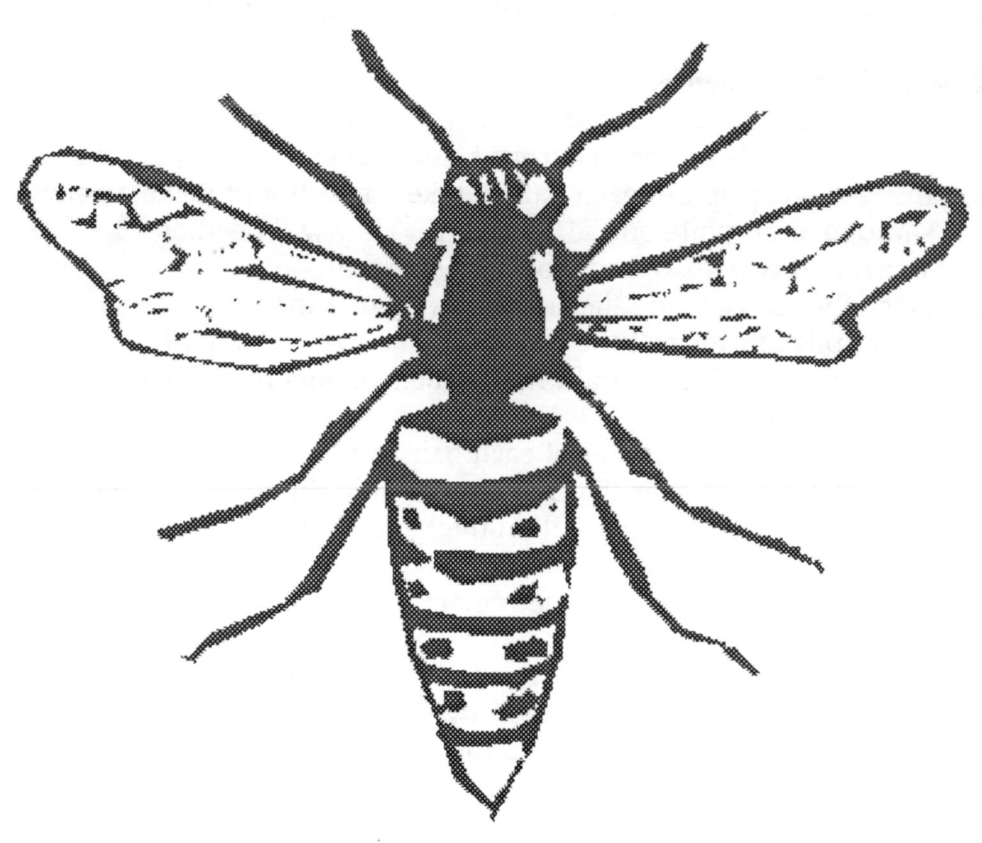

Topic: COMPARING FINGERPRINTS

Grade Level: K – 6 **Activity Time:** 1 – 2 days

Materials Needed:

1. Notecards (3 x 5 and 4 x 6)
2. Transparent tape (Scotch brand Magic™ tape works well)

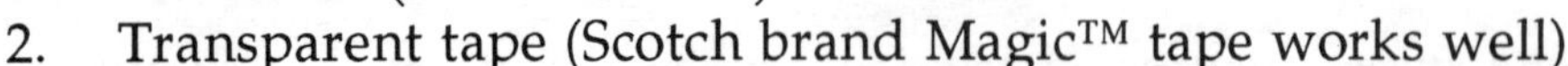

3. Pencils
4. Baby wipes

Objectives:

As a result of this activity, the learner will:

- compare and contrast fingerprints.
- describe some characteristics of their fingerprints.
- compare their fingerprints to those of other relatives (optional).

Introduction:

1. Show your pupils some examples of fingerprints, complete with a description of some of the basic patterns: arches, loops and whorls.
2. Discuss with your pupils how fingerprints can be used for identification and law enforcement purposes.
3. Discuss how relatives can have similar fingerprint patterns.

Major Instructional Sequence:

1. Divide your class into pairs. One pupil in each pair will help the other pupil make his or her fingerprint card. Then they can trade roles.
2. Instruct one pupil in each pair to take a pencil and make a heavy smudge of graphite on the 3 x 5 card. They will need one 3 x 5 card for the smear and two 4 x 6 cards for the fingerprints.
3. Once they have made the smudges (about 2 inches by 2 inches), instruct the pupils to rub the little fingers on their right hands repeatedly across the smudges. They should notice their fingers becoming covered with a graphite film.
4. Have the second member of each pair tear off a one-inch piece of tape and place it carefully over the first pupil's little finger. Tell them to carefully remove the tape and place it on their prepared 4 x 6 cards. Make sure they carefully label the cards.
5. Repeat the procedure for the remaining four fingers, then start on the left hand.
6. Once the first of each pair's hands have been printed, instruct the pupils to clean their hands thoroughly with the baby wipes and repeat the procedure for the second pupil.

Closure or Evaluation:

1. Instruct your pupils to study their fingerprints and determine which basic patterns (arch, loop or whorl) are present for each print.
2. Review how fingerprints (and even footprints) can be used for identification purposes.
3. Exhibit your pupils' work in an area of the class or in an exhibition area for the school.

Note: Your pupils could use this procedure to fingerprint their siblings and/or other relatives. This would be very useful in determining hereditary connections.

CHAPTER FOUR
Plants

A plant is any of various photosynthetic, eukaryotic, multicellular organisms of the kingdom *Plantae* which characteristically produce embryos that contain chloroplasts. Plants have cellulose cell walls and lack the power of locomotion. Plants which have no permanent woody stem are called herbaceous. The science which studies plants is called botany and plant-studying scientists are called botanists.

Most scientists say that plants were the first living things on Earth, appearing about three billion years ago. The first plants grew in or near water and were called algae. Land plants appeared on Earth about 300 – 400 million years ago, long before animals. All plants have three important characteristics in common: they create their own food from air, sunlight, and water; they are rooted in one place and don't move around; and their cells contain cellulose, a substance that keeps plants rigid and upright. Plants grow everywhere on Earth except in most of Antarctica and near the North Pole.

Topic: PHOTOTROPISM: HOW DOES LIGHT AFFECT PLANT GROWTH?

Grade Level: K – 6 **Activity Time:** Several weeks

Materials Needed:

1. Fast-growing plants (vine producers work best)
2. Large shoeboxes (adult or athletic shoe size)
3. Flower pot (complete with soil) for each plant
4. Scissors
5. Aluminum foil

Objectives:

As a result of this activity, the learner will:

- explain how plants grow towards light (phototropism).
- make predictions about plant growth.
- relate this activity to how plants (indoors and outdoors) orient themselves to sunlight.

Introduction:

1. Ask your pupils if there are any factors which influence growth. Possible answers will be air, oxygen, water, soil, sunlight, temperature, etc.
2. Explain to your pupils that they are going to do an activity (experiment) over a period of a week or two to illustrate a particular phenomenon called *phototropism,* the orientation of plants toward sources of light — particularly sunlight.

Major Instructional Sequence:

1. Organize your pupils into groups of four to six, depending on the number of plants and shoeboxes you have.
2. Have each group cut a hole (circular or otherwise) approximately 5 to 7 centimeters in diameter. The actual size of the hole is dependent on the size of the shoebox.
3. Place some aluminum foil inside the box to keep the box from getting wet. Instruct your pupils to place the plant in the middle of the shoebox, submerged below the lid. Make sure the plant is well watered.
4. Have each group place their shoebox near a source of light. Make sure that the hole is pointed towards the light source. Have each group label its box for identification purposes.
5. Ask your pupils (groups) to observe and record their observations of the plant's growth every two days. They can water the plant while they are making their observations.

Closure or Evaluation:

1. Ask each group to present their findings to the class.
2. Ask why the plants grew toward the light.
3. Depending on their age and developmental level, ask some additional questions:
   a) What would happen if you changed the orientation of the box periodically?
   b) What would happen if there were several different holes in the box?
   c) What would happen if you changed the orientation of the pot within the box periodically?

Note: Not only could you ask these questions but ask the pupils to actually devise and perform the activities (experiments).

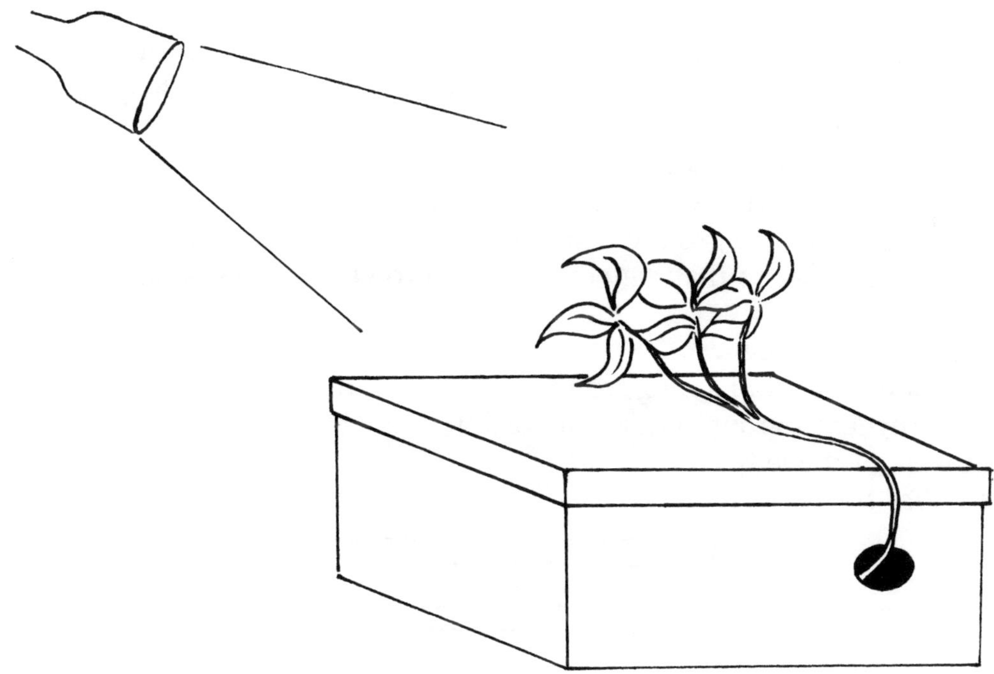

Topic: HOW DOES GRAVITY AFFECT SEED GROWTH?

Grade Level: 2 – 5 **Activity Time:** 8 days

Materials Needed (per group):

1. One clean (clear) jelly jar
2. Several paper towels and tape
3. Plant seeds (radish, bean, etc.)
4. Source of water

Objectives:

As a result of this activity, the learner will:

- relate the growth of the plant's roots/shoots to the influence of gravity.
- relate this activity to how seeds develop and grow in soil without the influence of sunlight.

Introduction:

1. Ask your pupils to tell you what happens when a seed grows.
2. Ask them if they have to place the seed in the ground in a special way (e.g., with a certain side pointing up).
3. Inform them that they are going to conduct an experiment with seed growth to determine if it really matters which way the seed is positioned in the ground. Remind them that you will be using a clear (jelly) jar so that they can see the growth as it takes place.

Major Instructional Sequence:

1. Divide your pupils into groups of two or three.
2. Instruct each group to place a portion of a wet paper towel around the inside of the jelly jar.

Note: Wet the paper towel so that it adheres to the glass portion of the jar.

3. Have each group place several seeds (radish, bean, etc.) at different points between the glass and the paper towel. Make sure your pupils place the seeds in various positions (up, down, sideways).
4. Ask each group to place their jars in a dark place (e.g., a closet).
5. Instruct your groups to take out their jars and observe the seed growth once a day (at a designated time). Make sure they record their observations on the data sheet (see Figure 4.1).

Closure or Evaluation:

1. Ask each group to present their observations to the class.
2. Remind them that the darkness (closet) was essential to eliminate the light variable from consideration. Since seeds grow in a moist, dark environment, it was necessary to duplicate that environment as closely as possible.

Figure 4.1

How Does Gravity Affect Seed Growth?
Data Sheet

Day 1 Observations:

Day 2 Observations:

Day 3 Observations:

Day 4 Observations:

Day 5 Observations:

Day 6 Observations:

Day 7 Observations:

Day 8 Observations:

Conclusions:

Topic: EVAPORATION: WHERE DO RAISINS COME FROM?

Grade Level: K – 6

Activity Time: 2 – 4 days

Materials Needed: (per group)

1. Grapes
2. Aluminum pie pan or waxed paper plate
3. Balance scale (for weighing)
4. Source of water

Objectives:

As a result of this activity, the learner will:

- describe how raisins are made from grapes.
- calculate how much water is lost from the grapes.

Introduction:

1. Ask your pupils where raisins come from. You may have to provide hints for them (depending on their developmental stage).
2. Once they have established that raisins come from grapes, ask them to speculate what might have happened to the grapes in order for them to become raisins. (Loss of water is key here.) Ask them what type of energy would be needed to remove water from (dehydrate) a grape (heat).
3. Distribute the aluminum pie pans (or waxed paper plates) and grapes. Ask them to devise an experiment to make raisins from grapes. Depending on their age group, you might let them construct their own experiment. Make sure they understand that heat (oven or sunlight) is imperative in dehydrating the grapes.

Major Instructional Sequence:

1. Divide your pupils into groups of three or four.
2. Instruct each group to place several grapes on the plate.
3. Have each group place their plates in areas where heat can get to the grapes (e.g., sunlight, heaters, ovens). Each group could carefully cut the skin of each grape (in one or two places) to speed up the process.
4. Have your pupils observe the grapes/raisins each day for three or four days. Ask them to record their data.

Closure or Evaluation:

1. Ask each group to present their finds (observations) to the class.
2. Ask your pupils to compare the physical characteristics of the grapes and raisins.
3. Ask a pupil to summarize (review) what the class observed.

Variation:

Older pupils are capable of actually weighing the grapes before and after the experiment. Make sure they wash and dry the grapes before weighing. The difference in weight before and after placing them near a heat source is essentially lost water (dehydration). Another adaptation to this activity would involve comparing the loss in weight of two plates of grapes. One plate is placed in the sunlight, while the other plate is placed in an oven or near a heater. The pupils could then hypothesize which grapes will lose water more quickly, and test their hypothesis (See Figure 4.2).

Note: It is possible that the grapes will grow mold. If that happens, explain mold as the growth of various fungi that often cause disintegration of organic matter.

An additional variation: Ask the class to design an experiment involving plums and prunes (using the format described above).

Figure 4.2

Measuring Water Loss in Grapes

Mass of grapes (Plate A) ____________________

Mass of raisins (Plate A) ____________________

Total mass of water lost (Plate A) ____________________

Percentage of mass lost (Plate A) * ____________________

* (Divide the total mass of water lost by the original mass of grapes.)

Mass of grapes (Plate B) ____________________

Mass of raisins (Plate B) ____________________

Total mass of water lost (Plate B) ____________________

Percentage of mass lost (Plate B)* ____________________

*(Divide the total mass of water lost by the original mass of grapes.)

Which plate had the greatest loss of water? Why?

Compare the physical characteristics of the raisins on both plates. Do they look the same? Why or why not?

Topic: GERMINATION: GROWING SEEDS

Grade Level: K – 2 **Activity Time:** 1 – 2 weeks

Materials Needed:

1. One packet of seeds (such as radish, bean, marigold) per group
2. Five small paper cups (bathroom variety) per group
3. Potting soil and cotton balls
4. Permanent markers for labeling, and rulers
5. Watering can
6. One spoon (for planting) per group

Objectives:

As a result of this activity, the learner will:

- list which factors are most important for seed growth.
- measure and compare the rate of growth of seeds with varied conditions.
- create a bar graph to illustrate the rate of growth of the seeds.

Introduction:

1. Ask your class what things (factors) are needed to help seeds (plants) grow. Write them on the board. You may need to help them list the more important ones: air (oxygen), soil, water, sunlight, and warm temperature.
2. Indicate to your pupils that they will investigate which of these factors are the most important.

Major Instructional Sequence:

1. Divide your pupils into groups of two or three.
2. Give each group five paper cups, a packet of seeds and a spoon.
3. Place a container (beaker) containing potting soil in each group area.
4. Instruct the leader of the group to label each cup (cup 1, cup 2, etc.) and scoop potting soil into cups 1 – 4. Have another member of the group place 5 – 6 cotton balls into cup 5.
5. Ask your pupils (groups) to "plant" four or five of their seeds in each cup. Instruct them to place them approximately one inch below the soil level (or per instructions on the seed packet) for the first four cups, and in the middle of the cotton balls in the fifth cup.
6. Instruct the groups to place their cups in the following environments:
   a) Cup 1 – sprinkle with water (lightly) each day and place in a sunny area of the classroom.
   b) Cup 2 – sprinkle with water (lightly) each day and place in a dark area of the classroom (such as a closet).
   c) Cup 3 – do not add water. Keep in a sunny area of the classroom.

d) Cup 4 – sprinkle with water (lightly) each day and place in a cool area of the classroom (e.g., near the air conditioner).

e) Cup 5 – sprinkle the cotton balls with water (lightly) and place in a sunny area of the classroom.

Circulate among the groups, checking for understanding, and providing assistance as needed.

Note: You could add other possible variations, such as another cup similar to number five, but placed in a dark area.

7. Instruct your pupils to check on their seed growth once every day, recording their observations.

Closure or Evaluation:

1. Ask your pupils to present their findings to the class. Write down their data on the board (see Figure 4.3).
2. Ask your pupils what factor/condition each cup was testing. They should tell you that cup 1 was testing water, soil, light and warm temperature; cup 2 was testing water and soil with no light; cup 3 was testing light, soil and warm temperature only (no water); cup 4 was testing water and soil with a cool temperature; cup 5 was testing water, light, and warm temperature only (no soil).
3. Ask your pupils if they have come to any conclusions concerning what things (factors) are needed for seed growth. Which seeds seemed to grow faster/better?

Figure 4.3

Seed Growth
Data Sheet
Cup 1

Day	Number of Seeds Sprouting	Height of Stems	Color of Stems/Leaves
1			
2			
3			
4			
5			
6			
7			
8			

What did you learn from the results you obtained with this cup?

Topic: WHY ARE FLAT LEAVES THAT SHAPE?

Grade Level: K – 6 **Activity Time:** 1 – 3 days

Materials Needed (per group):

1. Different types of flat leaves
2. Scissors
3. Scotch tape
4. Flexible drinking straws
5. 12″ aquarium (plastic) air tubing
6. Modeling clay
7. Polyethylene wash bottle (125 or 250 ml.)
8. Aluminum roasting pan

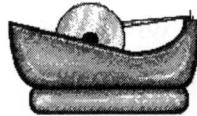

Objectives:

As a result of this activity, the learner will:

- describe which shapes tend to drain water more easily.
- explain why leaves tend to be found in particular shapes.

Introduction:

1. Ask your pupils to describe some of the types (shapes) of leaves they have seen. Show younger children some samples of leaves immediately, and ask them to describe the types of shapes they see.
2. Ask them to speculate why leaves might be in a particular shape. The main idea here is for draining water efficiently.
3. Ask your pupils if all types of shapes would work as well. Have them describe which shapes may not be conducive for draining (e.g., square, rectangle, round). Pupils could also draw some of the shapes.
4. Depending on the age (and developmental level) of your pupils, you could even ask them to design an experiment to test their hypotheses regarding their designs (leaf shapes).

Major Instructional Sequence:

1. Arrange your class into groups of three to four pupils.
2. Distribute various-shaped leaves to each group.
3. Instruct one pupil in each group to cut a straw two inches (approximately 5 cm.) from the flexible portion of the straw.
4. Have another pupil attach a twelve-inch piece of plastic (aquarium) tubing to one end of the straw. Have them seal the connection with modeling clay.
5. Instruct each group to attach the unconnected portion of the flexible straw to one of the leaf shapes. Scotch tape works fine here.
6. Have one pupil from each group place the nozzle of the wash bottle into the tubing and squeeze (slow trickle). Remind them to hold

the apparatus over the roasting pan (catch pan). Ask your pupils to observe and record how the leaf handles the water flow. Instruct them to look for whether the water seems to collect on the leaf, drain easily away from the leaf, or whether the leaf seems to give way and collapse.

6. Ask each group to repeat steps 4 and 5 with the other leaves. Make sure they use some of the leaves they believed would not be as efficient at draining water.

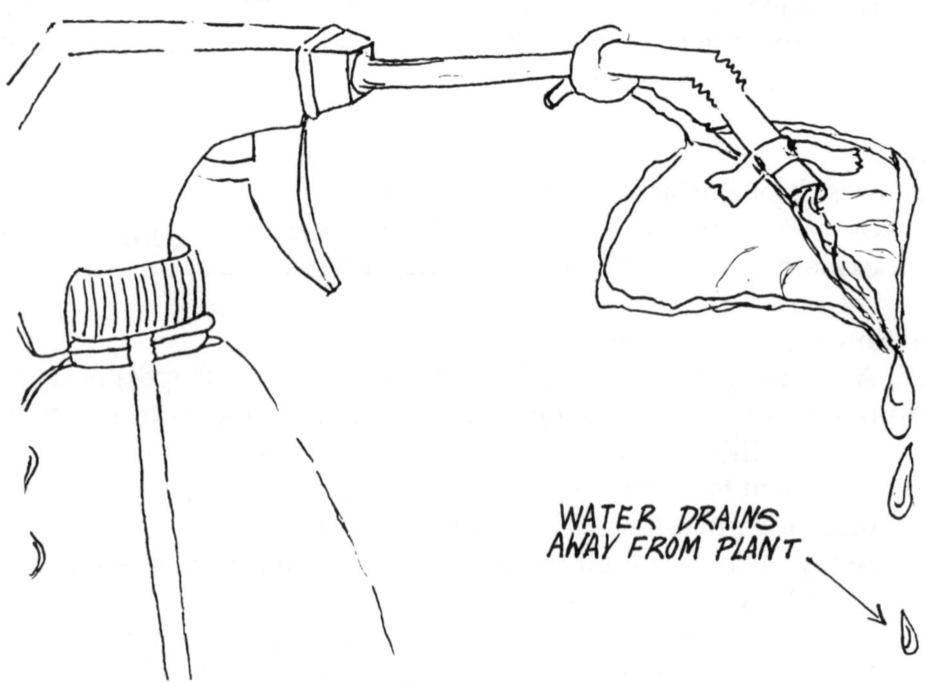
WATER DRAINS
AWAY FROM PLANT

Closure or Evaluation:

1. Ask each group to report their findings from the activity. Direct the pupils into a discussion concerning why some shapes worked better than others.
2. Ask a few pupils to describe the shapes that worked best in the activity.
3. Ask some other pupils to explain why leaves might be in certain basic shapes (review). Discuss other reasons, such as capacity to receive maximum sunlight, and the like.

Note: The polyethylene wash bottles may be purchased from any scientific supply house (approximately fifty cents each).

Topic: CREATING A LEAF COLLECTION

Grade Level: K – 6 **Activity Time:** Several weeks

Materials Needed:

1. Several sheets of construction paper (white works best)
2. Several samples of leaves
3. Heavy books
4. Old newspapers
5. Picture frames of various sizes
6. Photo albums with resealable plastic page overlays
7. Books and other resources on trees and leaves

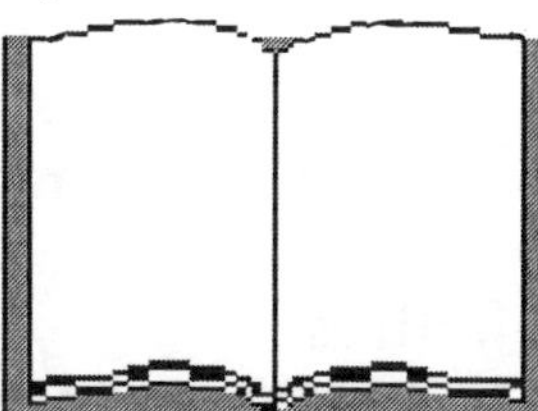

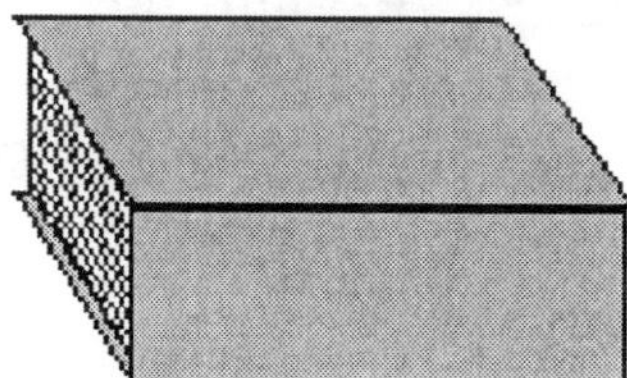

Objectives:

As a result of this activity, the learner will:

- identify various leaves in the community.
- make a leaf collection.

Introduction:

1. Take your pupils on a short tour of the school campus.
2. Instruct your pupils to collect leaves from various trees in the area. Caution them only to take one leaf from each tree.

Major Instructional Sequence:

1. Once you return to the classroom, ask your pupils to identify the leaves using resources in the classroom. A parent or other resource person who is familiar with tree leaves would be helpful here.
2. Place several sheets of newspaper down on a table. *Make sure that the area can remain undisturbed for at least two weeks.*
3. Place the best specimens between two pieces of construction paper.
4. Place several heavy books on top of the construction paper.
5. After approximately two weeks, remove the books and uncover the leaf specimens.

Closure or Evaluation:

1. Pupils can create leaf displays using the picture frames and photo albums (complete with identification).
2. Place the picture frames and photo albums in a centrally located area as a display for the entire school.

Note: The leaf collections can be utilized to teach plant classification.

Topic: ASEXUAL REPRODUCTION IN PLANTS

Grade Level: 2 – 6 **Activity Time:** Several weeks

Materials Needed:

1. Baking potatoes and sweet potatoes
2. Plastic drink cups
3. Toothpicks
4. Large planters, potting soil and water

Objectives:

As a result of this activity, the learner will:

- explain how new plants can develop without sexual reproduction.
- grow new plants from cuttings taken from an old plant.
- relate this activity to how plants can reproduce both sexually and asexually.

Introduction:

1. Introduce the concepts of *sexual* and *asexual* reproduction. Be sure to identify the various types of asexual reproduction.
2. Discuss some of the advantages of asexual reproduction (e.g., growing identical plants faster and producing seedless fruit).

Major Instructional Sequence: Activity 1

1. Place several baking potatoes in a closet or other closed area for about two weeks.
2. Have your pupils observe the potatoes every 2 – 3 days.
3. Separate the eyes (swollen stems) from the potatoes and plant them in the large planters. The planters should be at least 8 – 10 inches high and packed with potting soil.
4. Add water periodically to the planters and observe the plants once a week.

Major Instructional Sequence: Activity 2

1. Place four toothpicks into the center of a sweet potato (approximately ninety degrees apart).
2. Place the potato into a clear plastic drinking cup filled with 20 ml. of water.
3. Support the potato with the toothpicks. Half of the potato should be sticking out of the cup.
4. Observe the potato over the next 2 – 3 weeks.

Closure or Evaluation:

1. Ask your pupils to describe what happened to the baking potato stems (eyes) that you planted.
2. Ask them to describe what happened to the sweet potato that was left in the cup.
3. Review with your pupils the differences between sexual and asexual reproduction. Explain how seedless fruit is obtained through vegetative propagation.

Topic: FLOWER DISSECTION

Grade Level: 2 – 6 **Activity Time:** 1 – 2 days

Materials Needed (per group):

1. A variety of flowers (These can be donated by local florists or brought from home.)
2. A model of a flower (either two- or three-dimensional)
3. Reference books with pictures of flowers (cross-section)
4. Posterboard (cut to 11″ x 7″) and glue sticks
5. Permanent markers (fine point)

Objectives:

As a result of this activity, the learner will:

- list the parts of a flower and their functions.
- explain how plants pollinate.
- create a display of the parts of the flower.

Introduction:

1. Using a model of a flower, review with your pupils the parts of the flower and the purpose of each. There are wonderful plastic models available from many of the biological supply companies. The giant dicot flower model by Denoyer-Geppert costs approximately $380. It is great for teaching the reproductive functions of flowers, angiosperm pollination and fertilization. A less costly alternative would be to make your own model of a flower (two-dimensional) using posterboard. Although not as dynamic looking, it gets the job done.

Major Instructional Sequence:

1. Arrange your pupils into small groups of three or four.
2. Instruct one member of each group to obtain one or two samples of flowers from the front table.
3. Ask the pupils to identify the parts while the flower is still intact. Instruct them to look at the pictures provided in the reference books.
4. Once they are familiar with the parts, instruct each group to dissect the parts and glue them onto the small posterboard provided.
5. Ask them to label the parts properly.
6. Circulate among the groups, checking for understanding, and providing assistance when needed.

Closure or Evaluation:

1. Ask each group to share its display with the class. Place the displays in a central location for parents or the rest of the school to view them.

Note: Spraying the flower parts with lacquer will help preserve them for longer viewing.

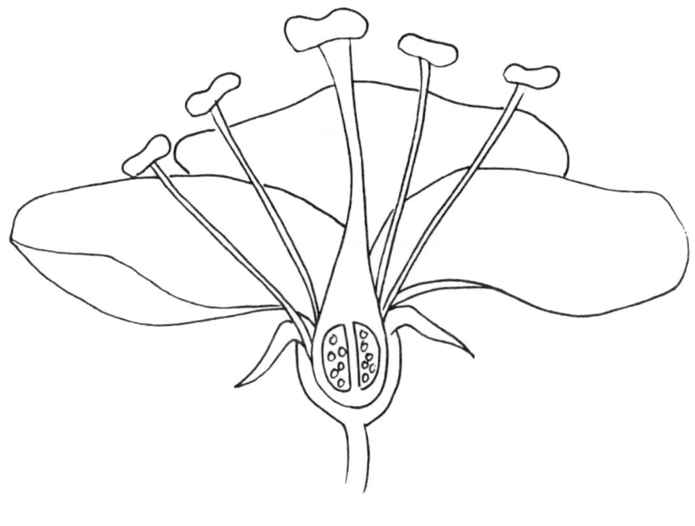

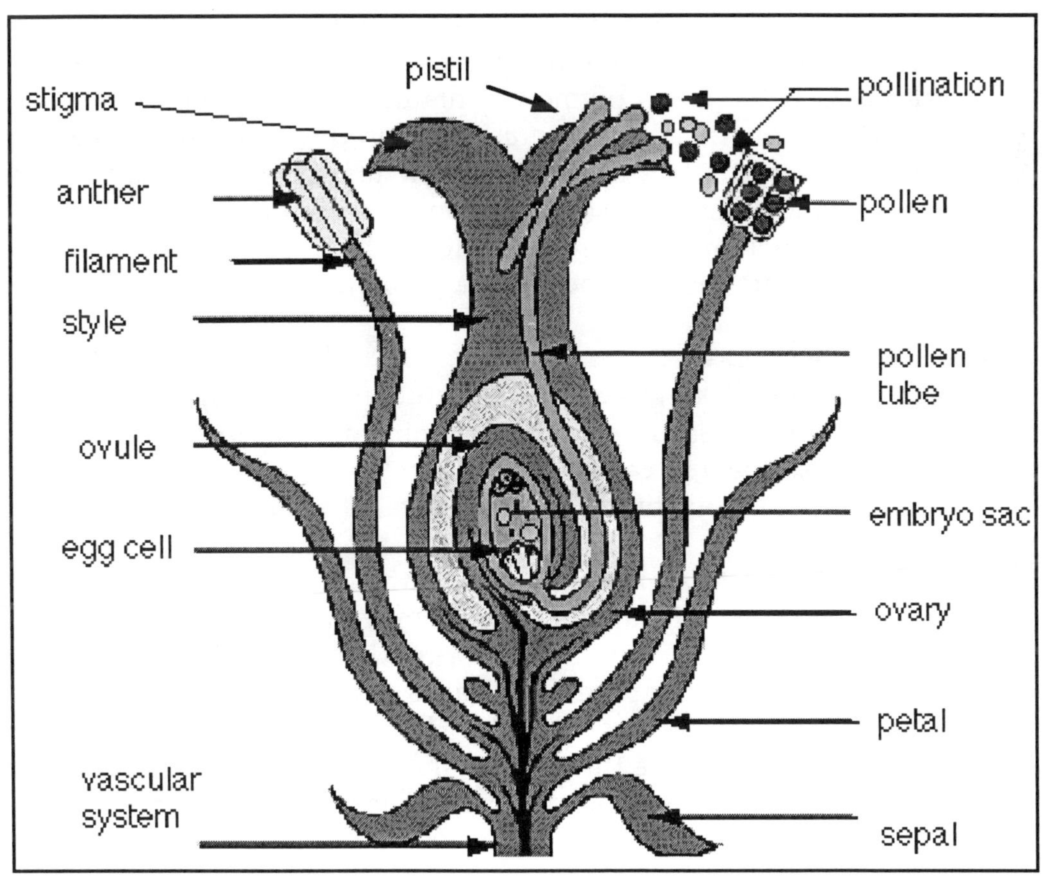

Topic: CHLOROPHYLL EXTRACTION

Grade Level: 4 – 6 **Activity Time:** 1 – 2 days

Materials Needed (per group):

1. Several fresh, green leaves (different types)
2. Rubbing alcohol
3. Beakers (minimum of 100 ml.)
4. Graduated cylinders (minimum of 25 ml.)
5. Utensil to remove leaf from alcohol bath (i.e., fork or tongs)

Objectives:

As a result of this activity, the learner will:

- demonstrate that the pigment, chlorophyll, is present in fresh leaves.
- explain how chlorophyll plays a role in the production of sugars and starches.

Introduction:

1. Review the process of photosynthesis with your pupils. Point out how sunlight (energy), water and carbon dioxide (products of respiration), chlorophyll and nutrients from the soil are important in the manufacture of sugar and starches within the plant. Remind your pupils that chlorophyll is the green pigment contained within plants.
2. Review what the sugars and starches are used for. These sources of food are utilized by the plant to construct new plant material and produce energy for the plant. Excess food is stored within the plant.
3. Tell your pupils that they are going to be involved in an activity which will demonstrate the presence of the pigment chlorophyll.

Major Instructional Sequence:

1. Assign your pupils to groups of 2 – 4 students.
2. Instruct them to measure 50 ml. of rubbing alcohol in the graduated cylinder. Ask them to carefully pour the liquid into a clean beaker.
3. Demonstrate for your pupils how to place a (fresh) green leaf into the beaker.
4. Allow the leaves to sit in the alcohol baths for a minimum of four hours.
5. Demonstrate for your pupils how to remove the leaf from the alcohol bath using the utensil provided.
6. Ask your pupils to compare their leaves to some sample leaves that have not been placed in the alcohol bath. Have them record their observations.
7. Instruct them to observe the color of the alcohol in the beaker. Provide the class with a fresh sample of rubbing alcohol to compare the color difference. Ask them to record their observations.

Note: The alcohol solution containing the chlorophyll pigment could be utilized in a chromatography activity (see Magic Marker Chromatography in Chemical Properties section). The pigment will separate just like the permanent marker in that activity (although with less dramatic results).

Closure or Evaluation:

1. Ask your pupils to share their observations. Point out how the observations coincide with your review of photosynthesis (see Introduction).
2. Ask some of your pupils to explain what chlorophyll is and what part it plays in the process of photosynthesis (production of sugar and starches).

Variation:

An easy variation of this activity involves taping pieces of construction paper over a portion of several fresh green leaves growing on a plant. Leave the construction paper on the leaf areas for approximately three to four days. Remove the construction paper and observe the areas previously covered. The covered portions of the leaves should be much paler compared to the uncovered portions. This demonstrates the importance of sunlight to the process of photosynthesis.

Topic: MAKING A TERRARIUM

Grade Level: K-6 **Activity Time:** 2 days

Materials Needed:

1. Glass or plastic aquarium
2. Small pebbles, sand, potting soil, peat moss, vermiculite, aquarium charcoal, water (spray bottle recommended)
3. Piece of rotting log (with insects) & mosses
4. Ladies' hose
5. Measuring cup, ruler & scissors
6. Plastic sherbet containers (1 qt./946 ml.)
7. Garden trowel or large spoon
8. Plastic wrap (Glad Cling Wrap™, etc.)

Objectives:

As a result of this activity, the learner will:

- construct a terrarium that resembles an ecosystem.
- list some components necessary for an ecosystem to work, such as drainage system, insects, plant(s), soil, sunlight and water.
- explain how the water cycle occurs in a closed system.

Introduction:

1. Discuss with your pupils what things a woodlands area needs to survive. *Sunlight, oxygen, carbon dioxide, water, and food (nutrients).*
2. Discuss with your pupils how the water cycle works. *The water cycle, also called the hydrologic cycle, is the cycle of evaporation and condensation that controls the distribution of water on Earth. As water evaporates from lakes, streams, rivers, etc. (bodies of water), it rises as water vapor, condenses, precipitates, and returns to those bodies of water in a cycle.*
3. Discuss with your pupils how photosynthesis and respiration work between plants and their environment. *Photosynthesis is the process in green plants and certain other organisms by which carbohydrates are developed from carbon dioxide and water using light as an energy source. Photosynthesis releases oxygen as a byproduct. Respiration is the process by which a plant exchanges gases with its environment. Carbon dioxide and water vapor from respiration are needed to make glucose and oxygen in photosynthesis.*

Major Instructional Sequence:

1. Rinse the pebbles and charcoal with water.
2. Cover the bottom of the terrarium with a layer of pebbles approximately one inch deep.

3. Cover the pebbles with a thin layer (1 cm.) of charcoal (aquarium charcoal will do nicely).
4. Cover this "drainage system" with some cut-up nylons (women's hose). Make sure the nylon pieces cover the entire drainage system. This will help prevent the soil and plant roots from getting into the drainage system.
5. Cover the drainage system with a three-inch layer of the "soil mixture." This mixture consists of five parts potting soil, two parts peat moss, one part vermiculite, one part aquarium charcoal, and one part sand.
6. Place three or four small plants into holes made in the soil mixture. Make sure that you place about 10 ml. of water in each hole prior to planting.
7. Add a piece of rotting log, complete with the insects living in the log, to the system. Add mosses, earthworms, snails, and the like, that your pupils can find or bring from the woods.
8. Spray the system with water and seal the top with the plastic wrap.
9. Place the terrarium in a place that receives sunlight (but not direct sunlight).

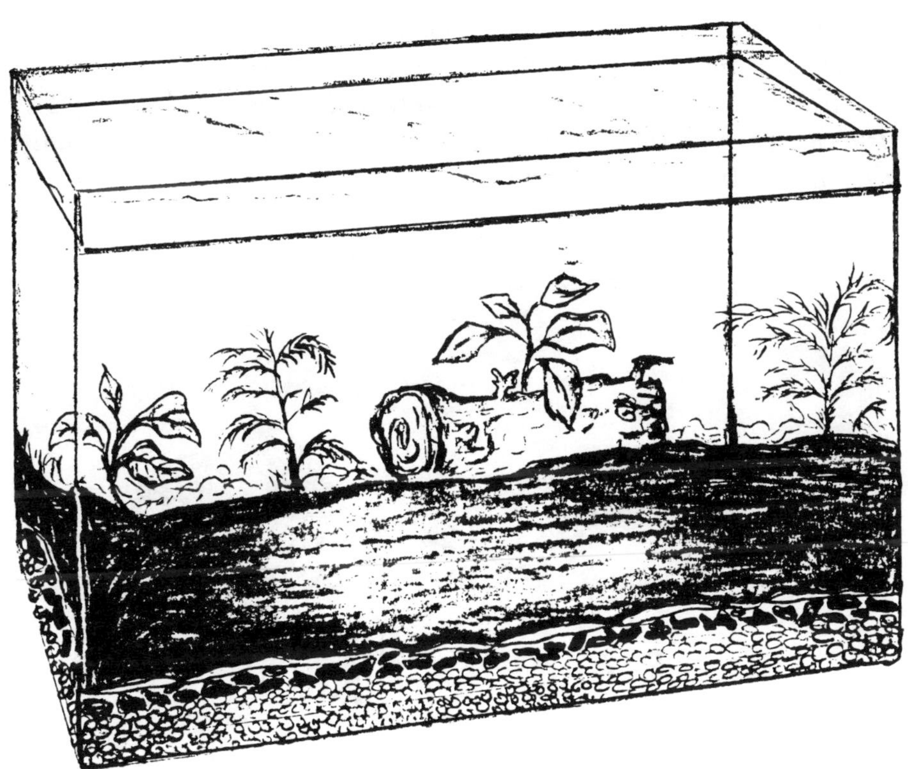

Closure or Evaluation:

1. Ask your pupils if they see anything unusual (i.e., water droplets on the plastic wrap). *Note: if you don't see water droplets, then remove the wrap and add some water to the system. If the system appears too wet, remove the wrap and let it dry for a few hours before reapplying the wrap.*
2. Have pupils describe how the water cycle works in this closed system. *The roots pull the water from the soil. This water passes through the plant's stems into the leaves, where it evaporates into the air (water vapor) due to the heating of the system. The water vapor condenses on the plastic wrap due to its being cooled by outside air. This results in a "rain" of droplets back down to the plants and soil.*
3. Ask your pupils how the plants survive in this closed system. *The respiration of the plants and animals in the system provides the system with the needed carbon dioxide and water vapor for photo-synthesis to continue. The decaying log contains sufficient insects, fungi, mosses, lichens and bacteria to provide new organic material to the system. The plants release oxygen into the system through photosynthesis.*

Note: The age and developmental stage of the learner is important in this activity. The discussion of the water cycle and photosynthesis would be better suited for fourth graders and above. In addition, experiments featuring the new closed ecosystem which includes variations of water, salt, light, and changes in the soil constituency can be performed in grades 4-6. However, K-3 pupils will still enjoy creating this interesting environment and can certainly learn about the "needs" of plants.

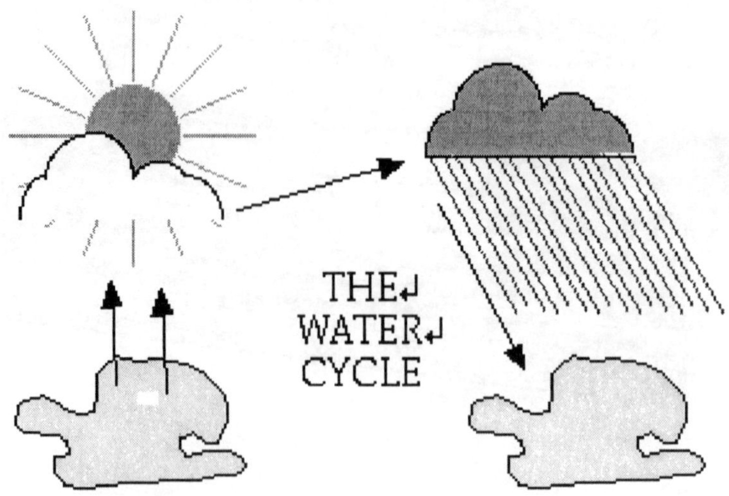

CHAPTER FIVE
Dynamic Changes in the Earth

The Earth is the third planet from the sun. Other bodies in the solar system possess oceans (although probably not of water) and/or an atmosphere, but Earth is the only planet known to be inhabited by carbon-based life forms. A globe is a tiny model of the Earth. Geologists study the composition, structure, processes, and history of the Earth. The interior of the Earth is inaccessible, but geologists have discerned its many layers, primarily through studying earthquakes and seismic waves (earthquake vibrations). Additionally, geologists study magnetic, thermal, and gravitational characteristics to investigate the Earth's interior. Geologists call the solid outer portion of the Earth its crust. The thickness of the crust varies widely, ranging between 3 and 7 miles thick beneath the oceans and between 12 and 40 miles thick beneath the continents. The Earth's mantle lies beneath the crust and is about 1,802 miles thick. The upper mantle is solid and is composed of iron and magnesium silicates, as typified by the mineral olivine. The lower part of the mantle, also solid but more dense than the upper mantle, likely consists of a mixture of oxides like magnesium, silicon, and iron. The Earth's core is composed of an inner, solid core at the center of the Earth which is about 800 miles thick and an outer, molten-liquid core (just outside the inner core) which is about 1,400 miles thick.

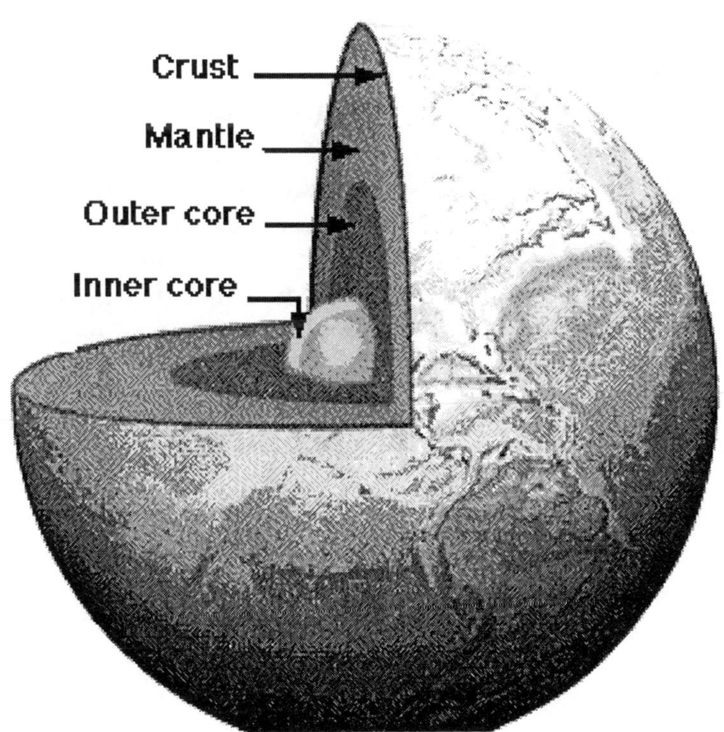

Topic: UNDERSTANDING EROSION

Grade Level: K – 6 **Activity Time:** 1 day

Materials Needed (per group):

1. Plywood boards (2′ x 4′ x 5/8″) and bricks
2. Grass sod (2′ x 4′)
3. Soil and water
4. Watering bucket (for plants)

Objectives:

As a result of this activity, the learner will:

- describe how rainfall (water) can erode bare soil more quickly than it can soil containing a root system.

Introduction:

1. Explain to your pupils how in certain areas erosion is a tremendous problem. You will need to explain that the smallest particles of earth are known as sediment and that soil is a collection of various sediments, together with organic matter (decayed animal and plant material). Sediment comes in different sizes, ranging from tiny clay silt and sand to boulders.
2. Explain to your pupils that water is one of the primary ways that sediments are shifted (rearranged) in their orientation. Water reshapes the Earth on a daily basis.

Major Instructional Sequence:

1. Divide the class into small groups (3 – 4 pupils). Take them outside for the activity.
2. Ask two pupils in each group to obtain the materials necessary for the activity from a central point already set up by you.
3. Instruct each group to place a handful of soil on the plywood board.
4. Angle the board by placing one end on a few bricks and the opposite end on the ground. (Do not stack the bricks on top of each other!)
5. Instruct the pupils to slowly pour water from the watering bucket onto the soil. Ask your pupils to observe and record their data.
6. Instruct your pupils to scrape the soil off into a small pile (for recycling purposes).
7. Ask them to place the grass sod on the board and duplicate the first experiment. Have them observe and record their data.

Closure or Evaluation:

1. Ask some of your groups to present their findings to the class. They should have noticed that the soil started washing away immediately, while the soil held by the roots of the sod resisted the flow of water.
2. Ask them why this happened. (The roots in the grass slows the rush of water through the soil underneath. The blades of grass on top also prevent the water from pounding the soil.)
3. Ask your pupils to speculate on why trees, plants and grass are important to soil conservation. Discuss the effects of deforestation. Tell the class about the "dust bowl" that occurred in the United States in the 1930s. Discuss how modern, environmentally-conscious farmers and landscapers can minimize the effects of erosion.

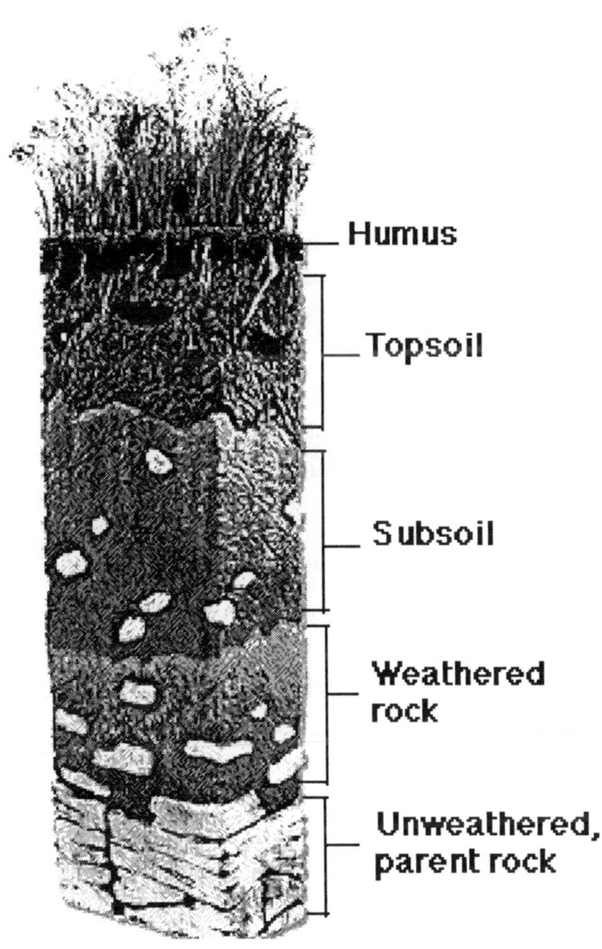

Topic: CORE SAMPLING IN THE CLASSROOM

Grade Level: 1 – 5 **Activity Time:** 1 day

Materials Needed (per group):

1. Three or four different colors of Playdoh™
2. Drinking straws
3. Small, sharp scissors (manicure scissors work well)

Objectives:

As a result of this activity, the learner will:

- explain how core samples from the Earth contain distinct layers.

Introduction:

1. Explain to your pupils how the Earth is composed of different layers of soil and how scientists penetrate the Earth with metal pipes (coring devices) to analyze the soil. Scientists can understand such puzzles as the origin and composition of the Earth by studying rock (soil) formations. Geologists utilize a technique called *core sampling* to study hidden formations. By analyzing core samples, scientists can construct a picture of prior geological events that occurred in each layer. By comparing the analyses of core samples from numerous sites, geologists can obtain a clearer picture of geological events in a region.

Major Instructional Sequence:

1. Divide your pupils into groups of two or three.
2. Ask them to flatten several pieces of Playdoh™ into thin sheets and stack them on top of each other (approximately one inch thick). They should see something that resembles the different layers of a sandwich.
3. Ask your pupils (each group) to cut a two-inch piece from the straw. *Note: Cut the straw for younger pupils.*
4. Demonstrate how to push the straw into the Playdoh™.
5. Ask pupils to hold a finger over the protruding end of the straw and pull the straw out from the Playdoh™. They should notice some Playdoh™ stuck in the bottom of the straws.
6. Have your pupils cut the straws carefully away from the Playdoh™ by inserting the manicure scissors and carefully cutting upward until they are past the Playdoh™. *Note: Cut the straw for younger pupils.* Then instruct them to carefully remove the Playdoh™ by pulling the straw apart and pulling the Playdoh™ out. An alternate way to remove the Playdoh™ is to blow into the straw, pushing the Playdoh™ out the other end. *Caution: If utilizing this method, make sure whoever blows into the straw is the one who placed their finger on the top of the straw.*

Closure or Evaluation:

1. Ask your pupils to review what they found in their core samples.
2. Ask them how this compares to the information you gave them at the beginning of the lesson.

Variation:

Use a real sandwich (e.g., peanut butter and jelly or, for more layers, use a thinly-layered club sandwich). Not only can pupils see the core, they can eat it as well!

Topic: EDIBLE ROCKS

Grade Level: 2 – 6 **Activity Time:** 1 – 2 days

Materials Needed (per group):

1. Samples of rocks (e.g., granite, an igneous rock; limestone, a sedimentary rock; gneiss, a metamorphic rock)
2. Several large pieces of "rocky road" fudge
3. Butter knives
4. Hand lenses (magnifying glasses)

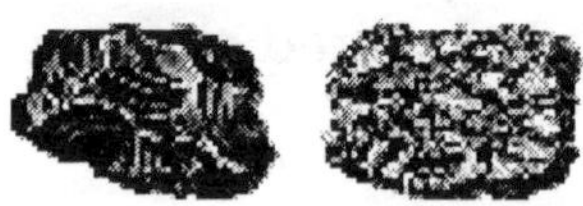

Objectives:

As a result of this activity, the learner will:

- observe and describe various properties in rocks (e.g., color and composition).
- explain (and describe) what conglomerates are.

Introduction:

1. Explain to your pupils how the Earth is composed of different types of rocks (*igneous*, *metamorphic*, and *sedimentary*). Show your pupils some samples of these types of rocks. Encourage them to look through the hand lenses to investigate differences between rocks (e.g., grain size, color).
2. Ask your pupils to list the properties they observed for the three types of rocks on the board. Discuss their similarities and differences.
3. Point out to your pupils that some rocks are actually a mixed variety of several different types of rocks, called *conglomerates*. These rocks are generally sedimentary rocks that contain several types of rocks "cemented" together. Show your pupils examples of these rocks. Encourage them to investigate differences and similarities between the rocks.

Major Instructional Sequence:

1. Divide your pupils into groups of three or four.
2. Instruct each group to obtain a sample of your "fudge rock" (rocky road fudge).
3. Ask your pupils to cut through the sample at various points, loosening the various "rocks" held in the "conglomerate."
4. Encourage your pupils to record their observations.

Closure or Evaluation:

1. Ask your pupils to review what they found out about igneous, metamorphic and sedimentary rocks. Allow them to eat their "conglomerates."

2. Ask them how the conglomerate rocks compared to the three types of rocks they observed.
3. Ask your pupils what they observed about the "rocky road fudge" rocks. Ask them to compare the "fudge rocks" to actual conglomerates. Point out that each different component of the fudge represents a different type of mineral (or rock). Rocks are combinations of minerals. Conglomerates are combinations of rocks.

Variation:

Make the fudge from scratch. Pupils could insert raisins, various types of nuts, and marshmallows into the fudge to represent the various components of the conglomerate.

Topic: FOSSIL FUN

Grade Level: 2 – 5 **Activity Time:** 1 – 2 days

Materials Needed (per group):

1. One plastic or wooden dinosaur skeleton kit (such as those manufactured by Safari LTD. Mailing Address: P.O. Box 630685, Miami, Florida 33163. Toll Free Phone: 1-800-615-3111. Homepage: http://www.safariltd.com/ E-Mail: sales@safariltd.com)
2. Plastic container filled with sand (or dirt and gravel)
3. Reference books w/pictures of dinosaurs

Objectives:

As a result of this activity, the learner will:

- observe and describe how fossils may be found in the environment.
- explain (and describe) how fossils may be rebuilt into full specimens.

Introduction:

1. Explain that dinosaurs came from different geologic regions (or habitats). Show pictures of some of the recreated dinosaur skeletons and/or artist renditions of them.
2. Explain how the bones became preserved in the rock.
3. Discuss with your pupils whether organisms other than dinosaurs can be found in the Earth.

Major Instructional Sequence:

1. Divide your pupils into groups of three or four.
2. Instruct each group to sift through the material in their container and find any "bones" that may be present.
3. Ask your pupils to hypothesize (suggest, propose, theorize, speculate) to what type of organism the bones might have belonged (and see if they can identify the type of bone it is — leg bone, backbone, etc.). Encourage them to look in the reference books to find answers that support their hypotheses.
4. Instruct them to put the dinosaurs bones together to form a complete specimen. Depending on the age of your children, it might be wise to provide them with the directions for their particular dinosaur (supplied in the kit).
5. Circulate among the groups, checking for understanding, and providing assistance as needed.

Closure or Evaluation:

1. Ask your pupils to present their assembled dinosaur to the class (complete with any facts they might have discovered through their readings).
2. Review with your pupils the process of how dinosaurs may have ended up in the Earth and how their skeletons are reconstructed by archeologists.

Topic: MAKING A CRYSTAL GARDEN

Grade Level: 3 – 6 **Activity Time:** 1 – 2 weeks

Materials Needed (per group):

1. Shallow cake pan (aluminum) or pie pan
2. Three charcoal briquettes
3. Laundry bluing agent
4. Household ammonia
5. Food coloring (optional)
6. Salt
7. Water
8. Hand lens (magnifying glass)

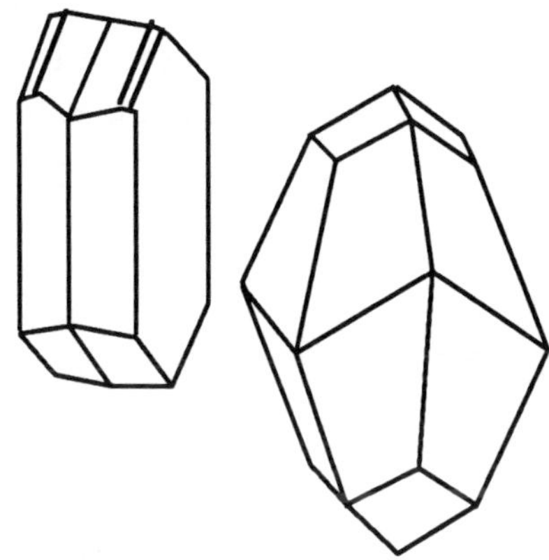

Objectives:

As a result of this activity, the learner will:

- make a crystal garden.
- examine the shape and color of the various crystals.
- relate the crystal garden to rocks formed by the process of crystallization.

Introduction:

1. Review with your pupils the different ways in which rocks are formed. Point out that some of them are crystalline in nature.
2. Ask your pupils to indicate some potential uses of crystals (jewelry, electronics, timepieces, etc.).

Major Instructional Sequence:

1. Divide the class into small groups (3 – 4 pupils).
2. Supply each group with the materials listed above.
3. Instruct each group to place its charcoal in the pan. Instead of simply placing two or three pieces of charcoal in the pan, consider breaking the charcoal up into smaller pieces with a hammer. This would provide more surface area.
4. Ask a pupil to pour salt over the charcoal (covering the top of each piece).
5. Have the group mix 3 – 4 tablespoons of household ammonia with 1/4 cup of bluing agent and 1/3 cup of water.
6. Instruct one pupil in the group to pour the mixture over the briquettes (slowly) until they are saturated (wet, soaked).
7. Have a pupil carefully squeeze a few drops of food coloring over each of the pieces (optional).
8. Instruct the groups to place their pans in a designated area where they can remain undisturbed for 1 – 2 weeks.

Closure or Evaluation:

1. Ask your pupils to observe their crystals carefully every two to three days. A magnifying glass will dramatically enhance their observations.
2. Have each group report on the progress of their crystals.
3. Review with your pupils how rock (mineral) crystals are formed by the process of crystallization.
4. Place the best crystals in a special location for the rest of the school to see.

Topic: STALACTITES AND STALAGMITES

Grade Level: 2 – 6 **Activity Time:** 1 week

Materials Needed (per group):

1. Two clear plastic drinking cups (or baby food jars)
2. Epsom salts
3. Cotton twine (string)
4. Washers
5. Wax paper
6. Scissors
7. Spoon (or stirrer)
8. Hot water source

Objectives:

As a result of this activity, the learner will:

- describe how stalactites and stalagmites are formed.
- make small stalactite and stalagmite (crystals).

Introduction:

1. Tell your pupils how stalactites and stalagmites are formed in caves. Explain that surface water seeps through porous limestone rock formations, carrying dissolved minerals onto the ceiling of the cave. The mineral-laden water seeps through cracks in the ceiling. Part of the slowly-dripping water evaporates while clinging to the ceiling. The mineral deposit it leaves forms the *stalactite.* Some of the water drips down to the floor of the cave where it evaporates, leaving behind a mineral deposit (of calcium carbonate) that builds up over time. This is the *stalagmite.* The calcium is supplied by the limestone, while the carbonate portion is formed in the reaction with carbonic acid (surface water reacting with the carbon dioxide in the atmosphere).

Major Instructional Sequence:

1. Divide the class into small groups (3 – 4 pupils).
2. Instruct each group to obtain two cups and a piece of wax paper (approximately four inches, or 10 cm. long). Cut the pieces prior to class, or have the pupils cut the pieces.
3. Cut the cotton twine (string) into pieces approximately 10 inches (25.4 cm.) long. Designate one pupil from each group to obtain one piece of string for their group. Have them tie a washer to each end of the string.
4. Mix the Epsom salts in some hot water and stir until the Epsom salts will no longer dissolve (supersaturated, thick, gooey, solution).
5. Pour the salt solution into the cups of each group. The layer of liquid should be approximately one inch (2.5 cm.) from the top.

6. Instruct each group to place each end of the string in the two cups. Make sure they soak the string in the salt solution first.
7. Have your pupils separate the cups so that there is a slight bend in the middle of the string between the cups. Have them place the wax paper directly under the middle bend. Make sure the cups are placed in an area where they can remain undisturbed.
8. Instruct your pupils to leave the cups undisturbed for 3 – 4 days. Increase the number of days if the stalactites and stalagmites are not forming quickly enough.

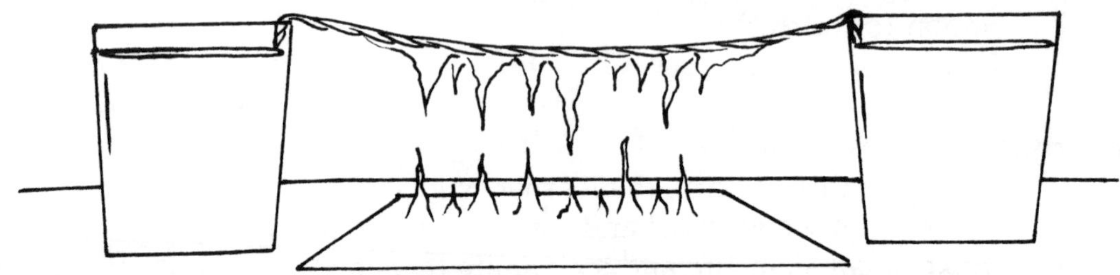

Closure or Evaluation:

1. Have your pupils observe the progress of the stalactite/stalagmite formations each day.
2. Ask them to describe what they have observed.
3. Review the process of formation. Make sure you point out that the cave formations would form much more slowly because the salt solution is less concentrated and the drip is extremely slow.

Note: If you could visit and film (with a camcorder) a nearby cavern where formations are present, it would greatly enhance the pupils' knowledge of stalactites and stalagmites.

Topic: THE EFFECT OF ACID ON LIMESTONE

Grade Level: 2 – 6 **Activity Time:** 1 – 2 days

Materials Needed (per group):

1. Chalk
2. Vinegar (clear)
3. Clear plastic cup (10 oz.)
4. Small pieces of rock (other than limestone)

Objectives:

As a result of this activity, the learner will:

- conduct an experiment to show the effects of an acid on limestone.
- describe how acid rain affects limestone.

Introduction:

1. Review the reasons why rainwater is acidic in many portions of the United States and of the rest of the world.
2. Point out to your pupils that limestone is one of the most plentiful types of rocks used in buildings and some statues.
3. Indicate that acids can react with limestone causing a deterioration or weakness in the structure. Explain that not all types of rock are affected as easily as limestone. Also tell pupils that chalk is limestone and vinegar is acidic.

Major Instructional Sequence:

1. Divide the class into small groups (3 – 4 pupils).
2. Instruct each group to pour approximately 4 – 5 oz. of clear vinegar into its plastic cup.
3. Ask one pupil from each group to break the piece of chalk in half and place one piece in the vinegar.
4. Allow the acid to react with the chalk and observe at 15 – 30 minute intervals. Let your pupils compare their cups to the cups of earlier classes (if applicable). This allows them to see the reaction accelerated over time. The alternative is to observe the chalk the next day.

Closure or Evaluation:

1. Ask some of your groups to present their findings to the class. They should have noticed that the chalk has deteriorated dramatically over time. There should have been an increase in bubbles around the chalk. This is carbon dioxide gas, a by-product of the reaction.
2. Review how acid rain can be damaging to buildings over time.

CHAPTER SIX
Space

Nine planets, including Earth, travel around the sun. These planets, together with the sun, form the solar system. The sun is a star, just like the other stars we see at night, but we are much closer to the sun. Our sun, astronomers have found, is hotter, bigger, brighter, and more massive than most other stars. The sun's diameter is 864,000 miles (Earth's is 7,926 miles) and has a gravitational pull 28 times greater than Earth. The planets orbit the sun in elliptical, oval-shaped paths called revolutions. Each planet travels in its own orbit. The Earth takes one year, 365 1/4 days, to revolve around the sun, a distance of nearly 600 million miles, and travels at a speed of 66,000 miles per hour. Planets that are farther from the sun take longer and planets that are closer to the sun take less time. Each planet also spins, or rotates, on an imaginary axis as it revolves around the sun. The Earth rotates once each day (actually, 23 hours, 56 minutes, 4.1 seconds). Some planets have one or more moons that orbit the planet in much the same way that the planets orbit the sun. The Earth has one moon that is about 238,900 miles from the Earth. The moon is the only body in the solar system to which people have traveled. The moon is 2,160 miles in diameter. It takes the moon the same amount of time to rotate on its axis (27 days, 7 hours, 43 minutes) as it does to orbit the Earth. For this reason, only one side of the moon faces the Earth.

Besides the planets and their moons, there are thousands of other objects in the solar system. These include comets, asteroids, and satellites. Comets are fast-moving chunks of ice, dust, and rock that form long tails of gas. Asteroids are solid chunks of rock or metal that orbit the sun, and they range in size from a grain of sand to the size of a minor planet. Satellites are objects that orbit a planet. Moons are natural satellites. Some satellites are launched by humans for scientific investigations.

Topic: PHASES OF THE MOON

Grade Level: 2 – 5 **Activity Time:** 1 Day

Materials Needed: (per group)

1. Beach ball and tennis ball
2. Light source (e.g., a flashlight)
3. Pictures or photographs of the moon in different phases

Objectives:

As a result of this activity, the learner will:

- illustrate how the moon may be seen in different phases.
- explain why the different phases of the moon occur.

Introduction:

1. Ask your pupils if they know why the moon appears to change its shape during its cyclical pattern (every 29.5 days). The most common misconception is that the Earth casts a shadow on the moon. The Earth only casts its shadow on the moon during a lunar eclipse.
2. Tell your pupils that the amount of the moon that is illuminated by the sun is constant. We simply cannot see the entire portion because of the angle of the moon in its orbit around the Earth.
3. Indicate to your pupils that they are going to see a demonstration which illustrates this point. Make sure they compare the pictures of the various phases of the moon with the demonstration as it occurs.

Major Instructional Sequence:

1. Instruct one pupil to sit in a chair and hold the beach ball above his or her head. (This represents the Earth.)
2. Instruct another pupil to hold the light source (which represents the sun) on the same level as the beach ball and shine the light beam toward the beach ball (Earth).
3. Hold the tennis ball at different positions in an elliptical orbit. Make sure that you move the ball at an angle. (This represents the moon.)
4. Ask your pupils to watch the position of the moon (tennis ball) relative to the sun (light source).
5. Arrange your class into small groups of three or four.
6. Assign each group a portion of the classroom for their activity.
7. Instruct each group to perform the activity as you demonstrated, stopping to view the shadow on the tennis ball at various points. Ask them to record their findings. They may need to make rough sketches to illustrate what they actually saw.

Closure or Evaluation:

1. Ask the pupils to present their findings to the class.
2. Indicate to the pupils that half of the moon is always illuminated and half of the moon is always dark. Point out that the phase they see is actually dependent on the position of the moon relative to their viewing point on Earth.

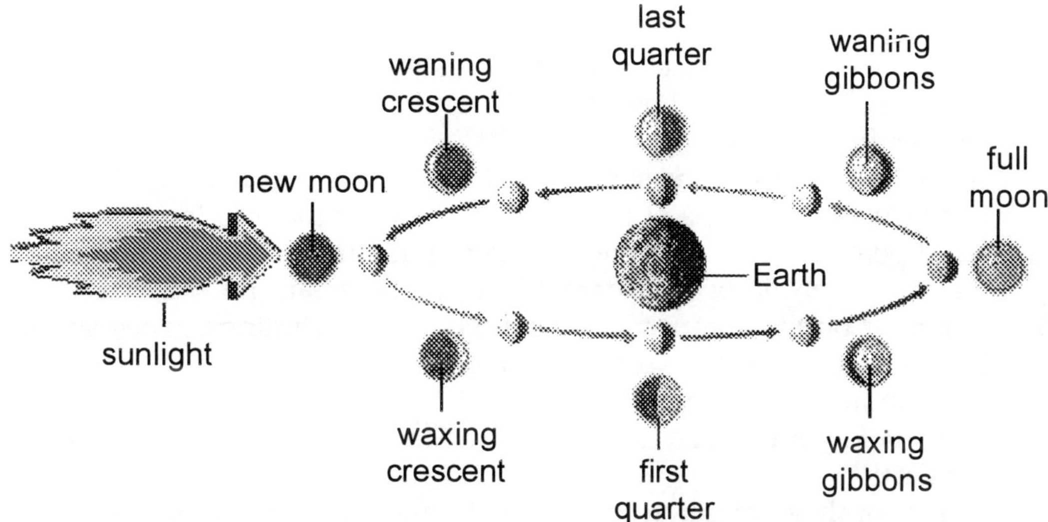

Topic: NORTH STAR MODEL

Grade Level: 3 – 6 **Activity Time:** 1 – 2 days

Materials Needed (per group):

1. Piece of posterboard
2. Scissors
3. Thumbtack or tiny nail (picture-framing variety)
4. Pencil and string

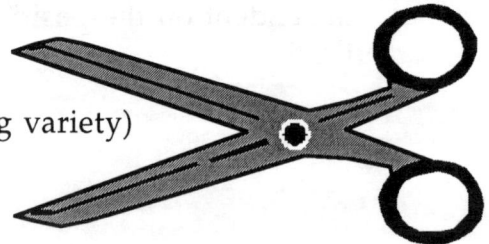

Objectives:

As a result of this activity, the learner will:

- demonstrate how the North Star appears to remain stationary while the stars surrounding it in the night sky seem to move.

Introduction:

1. Using an overhead sheet or the board, show your pupils where they may find the North Star. Show them the Little Dipper and Big Dipper formations.
2. Ask them to look at the sky at regular intervals that night and record the approximate positions of the dippers. Instruct them to look from the same point each time so they can determine if there is any movement in the stars. The aid of their parents may be necessary for this activity.
3. Ask your pupils to report (the next day) on the findings. They should have noticed that the North Star seemed to remain stationary while the surrounding stars seemed to move.
4. Indicate to your pupils that the North Star is almost over the axis of the Earth.
5. Tell them they are going to construct a model or simulation to illustrate what they saw the night before.

Major Instructional Sequence:

1. Separate pupils into groups of 4 – 5 per group.
2. Before class, tie a piece of string to the pencils so that each group can make a circle with a diameter of approximately seven inches on the posterboard.
3. Instruct the groups to cut out their circles.
4. Assist each group in filling in the approximate positions of the stars with a pencil dot on the circle piece. Make the North Star the center of the nighttime sky. (You can obtain copies of the night sky for each month from *Science and Children* and *Science Scope*.)
5. Once each group is satisfied with their positioning of the stars, and you have verified the positions, have the groups proceed to punch out the pencil dots with a thumbtack (or tiny nail).

6. Have each pupil in the group take turns putting a pencil lead into the underside of the North Star point and rotating the circle while holding the star chart above their heads. They need to hold the circles into the light so as to amplify the star points. A slow rotation will produce the needed effect. You could place a chart on the overhead and produce a similar effect.

Closure or Evaluation:

1. Ask your pupils to explain what they observed.
2. You could use some of the rides at a carnival or fair to illustrate the same point (e.g., the ferris wheel).

Topic: MAKING A MOON LOG

Grade Level: K – 6 **Activity Time:** 1 month

Materials Needed:

1. Lineless notebook (or sketch pad) and pencil

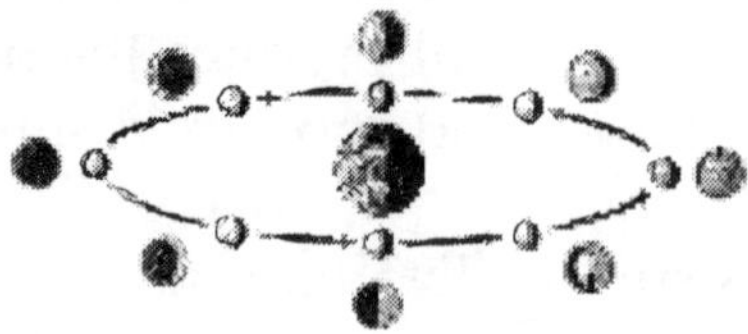

Objectives:

As a result of this activity, the learner will:

- maintain a log (diary) of changes in the moon's movement and shape.
- describe the four basic phases of the moon.
- sketch the apparent changes in shape of the moon.
- relate the moon's apparent movement through the sky to the turning of the Earth (optional).

Introduction:

1. Discuss various myths about the moon that have developed over time.
2. Review with your pupils how the moon orbits the Earth.
3. Ask your pupils to comment on the various shapes of the moon that they have noticed in the past. Ask them why these shapes may be occurring.
4. Point out some of the names of these shapes, such as full moon, new moon, and crescent moon. Draw pictures on the overhead or board so your pupils will understand these shapes.
5. Review with your class the procedure for maintaining a log.

Major Instructional Sequence:

1. Instruct your pupils to keep a log of the moon's activity over the next thirty days.
2. Point out to them that they should go outside with their parents and find the moon once an hour from dusk until bedtime. Each time they find the moon, they should write down in their log its approximate location in the sky (based on north, south, east, and west) and what it looks like.
3. Ask them to draw pictures of the moon, indicating both apparent shape and location in relation to still objects. If they draw the picture with a house, tree, or some other permanent object in the view they will gain a better perspective of the moon's apparent movement through the sky (not to mention the change in shape).

Closure or Evaluation:

1. Ask some of your pupils to share their data with the class. Have one pupil record the data on the board (or overhead).
2. Display each pupil's work in a central location for the class or school to see.

Topic: MAKING A SUNDIAL

Grade Level: K – 6 **Activity Time:** 1 – 5 days

Materials Needed (per group):

1. Tinkertoys™ (rods & connector spools)
2. Posterboard (11″ x 14″)
3. Chalk
4. Permanent marker
5. Scotch™ tape
6. Watch or clock

Objectives:

As a result of this activity, the learner will:

- sketch the position of a sundial-rod's shadow each hour during the school day.
- relate the sun's apparent movement in the sky to time.
- investigate the accuracy of the sundial over time.

Introduction:

1. Discuss with your pupils how the sun's position in the sky changes during the day. Point out to them that the sun starts out low in the eastern horizon during dawn and eventually dips down below the western horizon at dusk.
2. Review with your class how it is the Earth's rotation that makes the sun appear to move across the sky.

Major Instructional Sequence:

1. Organize pupils into groups of three or four and assign each group a number for identification.
2. Show the groups how to put the Tinkertoys™ rod (needs to be 25 cm. or longer) into the connector spool.
3. Demonstrate how to tape the rod and connector spool assembly onto the middle of the posterboard to create a sundial.
4. Instruct each group to assemble their rods and connector spools and tape them onto their posterboards.
5. Take the groups outside and have each group select an area on a concrete surface (such as a sidewalk) and trace their posterboard with the chalk.
6. Instruct each group to identify (mark with chalk) their area with their assigned number. This allows each group to reposition the sundial if it is accidently moved or reposition the sundial on another day to test its accuracy. This is particularly important to determine the accuracy of the sundial.
7. Ask each group to mark the shadow position of the rod on the posterboard

for each hour. It is probably best that you indicate the time using only one timepiece to keep the sundials uniform. After they mark the positions of the rod's shadow on the posterboard, ask the members of the group to chart the position of the sun in the sky (direction) on a piece of paper.

Closure or Evaluation:

1. Ask your pupils to discuss their findings with the class. Have the groups compare their sundial marks and examine the position of the sun at various times.
2. Review again that it is the Earth's rotation that makes the sun appear to move in the sky. (Easily demonstrated with a globe.)
3. Take your groups outside on several different days to test the accuracy of their sundials. Discuss their findings.
4. Display each group's work in a central location for the class or school to see.

Topic: PLANETARY SCALE

Grade Level: 2 – 5 **Activity Time:** 2 – 5 days

Materials Needed (per group):

1. Yellow posterboard
2. Scissors, pencils, rulers, 3 x 5 cards and string
3. Reference books and pictures of the planets and our moon

Objectives:

As a result of this activity, the learner will:

- research a planet in our solar system.
- demonstrate skill in measurement.
- observe and describe how the planets relate to each other in diameter.
- demonstrate the relative distances of the planets from the sun.
- explain why it is difficult to draw the solar system to scale (optional).
- explain (and describe) how the relative distances of the planets relate to space exploration (optional).

Introduction:

1. Assemble the books and pictures on a large table. Review with the class the order of the solar system from the sun to Pluto using some of the pictures and books available along with the overhead or chalkboard.
2. Organize your pupils into groups of three or four.
3. Assign each group a celestial object in our solar system (a planet or the sun) to research. Instruct the groups to use the reference books and pictures to obtain their information.
4. Have each group share their research with the class.

Major Instructional Sequence:

1. Instruct each group to make a representation of their celestial object (except the sun) on a 3 x 5 card. See Table 6.1 for the relative planetary diameter.
2. Have the group representing the sun cut a length of string approximately 28 – 30 cm. and tie a sharpened pencil to one end.
3. Show the groups how to use the pencil and string as a compass to draw a circle 50 cm. in diameter on the piece of yellow posterboard.
4. Have them cut out the yellow circle (sun) with scissors.
5. Instruct your pupils to compare the relative sizes of the planets to the sun. Point out that the outermost planets are much larger in size (with the exception of Pluto) than the innermost planets, particularly the *jovian* or Jupiter-like planets. These are also called *gas giants*.
6. To simulate the relative distances of the planets to the sun, take your groups outside. Instruct the group that constructed the sun to stand near

the edge of the school building.

7. Instruct each group to mark off a distance in paces (see Table 6.1) that corresponds to their particular planet. Start with Mercury, then Venus, etc. Your pupils will discover that they probably won't get past Earth or Mars before they run out of space!

Closure or Evaluation:

1. Discuss with your pupils how they might walk off the distance of each planet in our solar system if they used tiny paces.
2. Investigate with your pupils how they could downsize the distances provided. If possible, have the pupils create a new model with smaller distances taken into account.

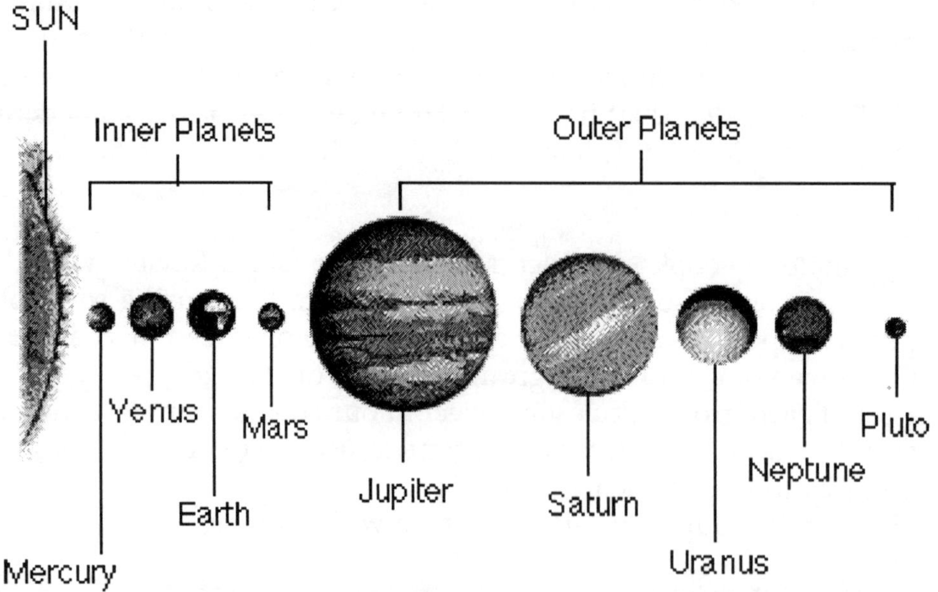

Table 6.1
Planetary Diameter and Relative Distance From the Sun

Celestial Object	Diameter	Distance From Sun
Sun	50 cm.	----
Mercury	1.7 mm.	60 steps
Venus	4.3 mm.	115 steps
Earth	4.5 mm.	160 steps
Mars	2.5 mm.	240 steps
Jupiter	5.1 cm.	830 steps
Saturn	4.3 cm.	1,525 steps
Uranus	1.8 cm.	3,075 steps
Neptune	1.8 cm.	4,800 steps
Pluto	0.8 mm.	6,325 steps

Topic: THE MOVEMENT OF THE EARTH

Grade Level: 3 – 6 **Activity Time:** 1 day

Materials Needed (per group):

1. One raw egg and one hard-boiled egg
2. Felt-tip marking pen
3. A paper towel
4. One globe (for the entire class)

Objectives:

As a result of this activity, the learner will:

- explain how the composition of the Earth affects its rotation.

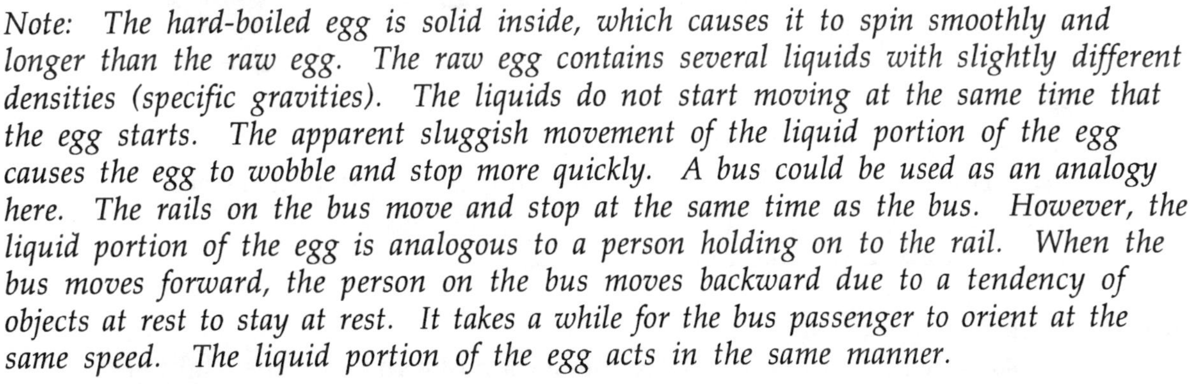

Note: The hard-boiled egg is solid inside, which causes it to spin smoothly and longer than the raw egg. The raw egg contains several liquids with slightly different densities (specific gravities). The liquids do not start moving at the same time that the egg starts. The apparent sluggish movement of the liquid portion of the egg causes the egg to wobble and stop more quickly. A bus could be used as an analogy here. The rails on the bus move and stop at the same time as the bus. However, the liquid portion of the egg is analogous to a person holding on to the rail. When the bus moves forward, the person on the bus moves backward due to a tendency of objects at rest to stay at rest. It takes a while for the bus passenger to orient at the same speed. The liquid portion of the egg acts in the same manner.

Introduction:

1. Use the globe to demonstrate how the Earth rotates on its axis.
2. Point out that the Earth wobbles a bit in its rotation.
3. Tell pupils that the composition inside the Earth plays a role in its wobble.

Major Instructional Sequence:

1. Divide pupils into groups of three.
2. Provide each group with a raw egg and have them mark it "R."
3. Provide each group with a hard-boiled egg and have them mark it "B."
4. Assist each group in finding a space on the floor on which to lay out their paper towel flat.
5. Instruct the groups to spin each egg separately on the paper towel and observe what happens.

Closure or Evaluation:

1. Have groups report what they observed with the spinning of the two eggs.
2. Discuss with the class why the raw egg wobbled and stopped more quickly, and the hard-boiled egg spun more smoothly and for a longer time.
3. Demonstrate with the globe how much of the Earth is water. Explain that much of the Earth's inside is molten liquid. Like the raw egg, this causes the Earth to wobble slightly as it rotates (one wobble every 50,000 years).

Topic: THE APPARENT MOVEMENT OF STARS

Grade Level: 3 – 6 **Activity Time:** 1 – 4 days

Materials Needed (per group):

1. Black butcher paper (or black posterboard as a substitute)
2. Three Styrofoam™ balls (different sizes)
3. White, yellow, silver and gold tempera paint
4. Thread
5. Scotch™ tape
6. Ruler and black permanent marker
7. Felt tip marking pen
8. Paint brushes of various sizes
9. Old newspapers

Objectives:

As a result of this activity, the learner will:

- determine how the distance of a star affects its apparent motion, or parallax.
- collect data and make inferences from the data.

Introduction:

1. Discuss with your pupils how the stars move through the night sky.
2. Inform your pupils that they are going to participate in an activity to demonstrate the apparent movement of stars.

Major Instructional Sequence:

1. Lay out all of the materials on a supply table.
2. Separate your pupils into groups of three or four.
3. Assist the groups in laying several newspaper pages overlapped on the floor to serve as the group's work area.
4. Ask two pupils from each group to obtain black butcher paper, paint, one of each size Styrofoam™ ball, and several thin paint brushes from the supply table.
5. Instruct the groups to paint dots and blotches on the black paper to represent stars.
6. As each group finishes painting its stars, assist them in taping the black butcher paper to the wall horizontally at a height roughly equal to the pupils' line of sight.
7. Demonstrate how to paint one of the Styrofoam™ balls.
8. Instruct the groups to paint their largest ball yellow, the next largest ball silver, and the smallest ball gold.
9. Once the balls have dried, have your pupils attach one end of a piece of thread to each of the balls with tape.

10. Assist each group in taping the other end of the thread to the ceiling so the balls are hanging at eye level in front of the stars on the black butcher paper. Instruct the groups to hang the yellow ball approximately three meters from the stars and the silver and gold balls approximately 75 cm. and 150 cm., respectively, from the stars.
11. Once all the star systems are constructed, assist each group in marking its sun with four spots. Place one spot on the side nearest the stars; then, moving counterclockwise, a second spot at 90 degrees, a third spot at 180 degrees, and a fourth spot at 270 degrees.
12. Direct pupils in the groups to take turns walking around the sun in a counterclockwise direction, keeping their eyes on the stars. Explain that when at the spot closest to the stars, the view of the stars represents winter on their part of the Earth. Then, moving in a counterclockwise direction, the 90 degree spot represents the view in spring, the 180 degree spot represents the view in summer, and the 270 degree spot represents the view in fall. As pupils walk around the sun, tell them to pay close attention to the positions of the silver and gold stars as seen from each interval (winter, spring, summer, fall).
13. Have the pupils repeat the movement around the sun with the ruler in their hand. Have them measure the approximate gap between the silver and gold stars at each interval. To measure, they should hold the ruler about three inches in front of their eyes positioned to measure the gap between the two stars. Have one pupil in each group record the data from each group member.
14. Instruct each group to determine the mean (average) distance for each season (e.g., sum for winter of all group members divided by the number of group members).

Closure or Evaluation:

1. Ask your groups to share what their conclusions were concerning the apparent movement of the two stars.
2. Review how astronomers use such information to help determine the relative alignment of stars to each other. Have pupils pick one star and measure the gap between the star and the balls. (They should find that the star closest to them has the biggest shift.) This is how astronomers measure star distances.

CHAPTER SEVEN
Water Investigations

Water is a compound made up of hydrogen and oxygen. Usually, we think of water as a liquid, but, depending on its temperature, it can also be a solid or a gas. At low temperatures, below freezing (32 degrees Fahrenheit or 0 degrees Celsius), water is a solid called ice. At warmer temperatures, it is a liquid. Water boils at very high temperatures (212 degrees Fahrenheit or 100 degrees Celsius or higher) and becomes a gas, which is called steam. Water also evaporates and becomes a gas, which is called water vapor. Wet clothes drying in the sun is an example of evaporation. When water vapor is chilled, it condenses into a liquid. Water droplets forming on the outside of a cold glass on a humid day is an example of condensation. When water vapor in the air comes in contact with an extremely cold glass window in very cold weather, the water vapor immediately turns to ice.

The water cycle (hydrologic cycle) is the continuous interchange of water in the oceans, the atmosphere, and on land. This interchange affects the balance of water geographically and physically around the world.

More than seventy percent of the Earth is covered by oceans, streams, rivers, seas, and lakes. Water serves as a rich resource for animals and plants and must be constantly protected from pollutants.

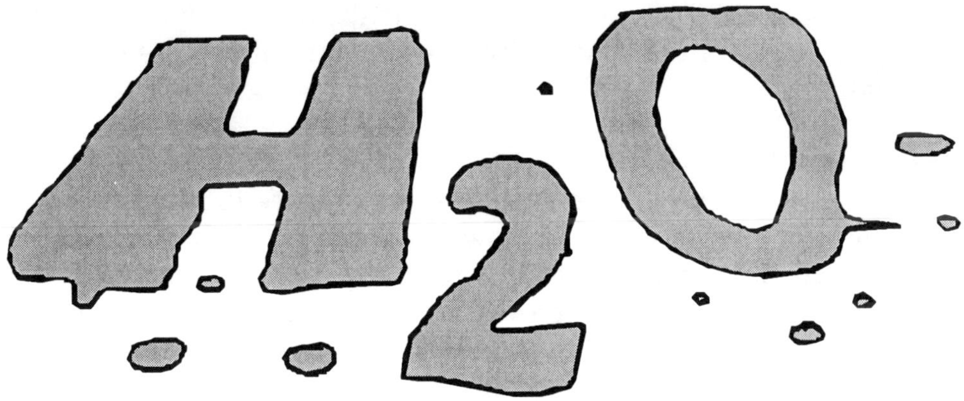

Topic: MAKING A WATER FILTER

Grade Level: 3 – 6 **Activity Time:** 2 days

Materials Needed (per group):

1. Two-liter drink bottle
2. Beaker (600 ml. or larger) for bottom of filter
3. Beaker (graduated, 250 – 400 ml.) for water
4. 600 ml. of play sand (toy-store variety)
5. 350 ml. of aquarium pebbles
6. 350 ml. of aquarium charcoal (or ground-up pieces of charcoal briquettes)
7. 350 ml. of soil
8. 250 ml. of water (dirty water, pond water, etc.)
9. 2 x 2 (5cm. x 5cm.) piece of window-screen material
10. Cotton
11. Rubber band

Objectives:

As a result of this activity, the learner will:

- make a water filtration system.
- explain how water is filtered as it travels in the ground.

Introduction:

1. Focus on how the Earth is more than 70 percent water. However, salt water accounts for approximately 97 percent of this total. Only 3 percent of the water in the world is fresh water. Of this total, less than 1 percent is drinkable. *The Weather Book* by Jack Williams (*USA Today*) is an excellent resource here.
2. Indicate to your pupils how important it is to keep drinking water as clean as possible. Ask your pupils how the fresh water we drink can be cleaned (e.g., water treatment plants, the natural process of ground filtration).

Major Instructional Sequence:

1. Organize your pupils into small groups of three to four.
2. Demonstrate for your pupils how to cut the two-liter bottle: Insert the tip of the scissors to make a cut into the bottle approximately two-thirds distance from the top. Cut away the bottom one-third of the bottle and discard. If you do not have access to beakers, you could cut a two-liter bottle in half and use the bottom half for your beaker. You would need a graduated cylinder (100 ml. or larger) with which to measure your materials.

3. Instruct your pupils to wrap the prepared piece of screen material around the mouth of the bottle (the cap is removed). Use the rubber band to hold the screen in place. This is now the bottom of the filter.
4. Ask your pupils to invert the bottle and stuff the cotton into the bottom of the filter, next to the mouth.
5. Instruct your pupils to pour in half the sand and spread it out evenly. Tell them to save the remaining half to place on the top layer.
6. Ask your pupils to pour in all of the aquarium pebbles and smooth out the top layer.
7. Repeat this procedure with the soil and charcoal, respectively.
8. Finally place the remaining sand on the top layer.
9. Demonstrate for your pupils how to place the inverted filter carefully into the bottom beaker (collection device).
10. Instruct the pupils to take their pond water and slowly pour it into the top of the filter. If you do not have access to pond water, make your own "dirty water" by simply adding dirt or soil to the water supply you are using for the activity.
11. Ask your pupils to record what they observe.
12. If you have time, have your pupils pour the collected water back into the filter a second time and record their new observations.

Note: You could use a few drops of food coloring to simulate contamination of the water. Make sure each group filters the water several times. They could keep approximately 5 ml. of each filtrate in a separate test tube to help in their analysis.

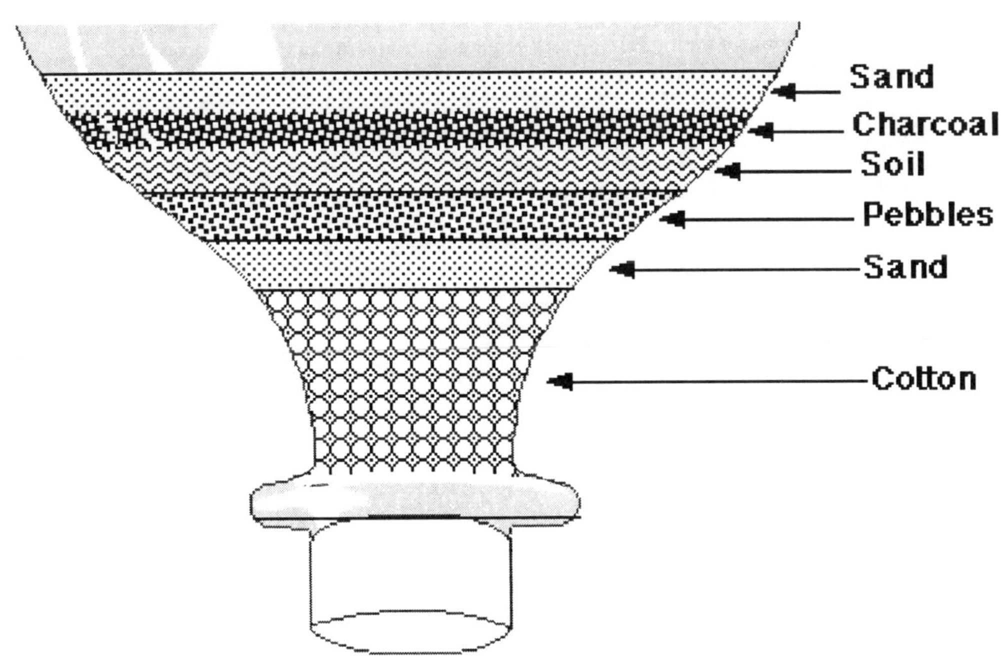

Closure or Evaluation:

1. Ask each group to share their results (conclusions) with the class. Don't forget to ask them to defend their conclusions (with evidence).
2. Prepare a write-up and description of the activity on a posterboard. Display the results in a prominent area of the school, complete with samples of filters and filtrates.

Topic: ADHESIVE PROPERTIES OF WATER

Grade Level: 3 – 6 **Activity Time:** 1 Day

Materials Needed (per group):

1. 2 beakers
2. Cotton twine
3. Scissors
4. Water

Objectives:

As a result of this activity, the learner will:

- demonstrate the property of adhesion.
- demonstrate measuring skills.

Introduction:

Review the concepts of adhesion and cohesion with your pupils. *Cohesion* involves water molecules clinging to one another. A water droplet is an example of this. *Adhesion* involves water molecules clinging to another substance. The substance being used in this activity will be the cotton twine. This activity will actually depend on both properties. Cohesion holds the water molecules together as they pass down the twine. Adhesion between the water molecules and the twine keeps the water attached to the twine as it travels to the bottom beaker.

Major Instructional Sequence:

1. Organize your pupils into small groups of three to four.
2. Instruct your pupils to cut an 18-inch (45 – 46 cm.) piece of twine.
3. Demonstrate for your pupils how to position the string and the beakers for the activity (one beaker held above and one below with the twine leading from one beaker to the other). Remind them to wet the twine first. This will enhance the adhesive properties of the twine and reduce spillage.
4. Before each group pours its water down the twine, make sure the pupils are holding the pre-wet twine tightly on the spout of the first beaker. Another pupil needs to be holding the twine tightly to the inside of the bottom beaker.

Closure or Evaluation:

Review with your pupils the properties of adhesion and cohesion.

Topic: WATER ON THE EARTH

Grade Level: 2 – 6 **Activity Time:** 1 Day

Materials Needed (per group):

1. A 1,000 ml. graduated cylinder
2. A 50 ml. graduated cylinder
3. A 10 ml. graduated cylinder
4. Three small medicine cups
5. A medicine dropper
6. Water source and plastic bucket

Objectives:

As a result of this activity, the learner will:

- compare and contrast the percentage of water contained in fresh water, salt water, glaciers, surface and ground water, and the atmosphere.
- demonstrate measuring skills.

Introduction:

1. Focus on how the Earth is more than 70 percent water. However, salt water accounts for approximately 97 percent of this total. Only 3 percent of the water in the world is fresh water. Of this total, 2.5 percent is found locked in glaciers and ice caps.
2. Ask your pupils if a city such as Los Angeles, located near the Pacific Ocean, could use salt water for households and industry.
3. Explain that desalinization is the removal of salt from seawater so that it can be utilized as fresh water. *Note: Much research has gone into finding efficient methods of removing salt from seawater. The most cost-efficient methods involve heating the seawater until it evaporates into steam. The steam then condenses and is drawn off as pure water.*
4. Explain to your pupils that they are going to participate in an activity that illustrates where the water on Earth is located.

Major Instructional Sequence:

1. Organize your pupils into small groups of three to four.
2. Instruct your pupils to pour 1,000 ml. of water into the 1,000 ml. graduated cylinder from a bucket of water. Use the 10 ml. graduated cylinder and the medicine dropper to get the water level to the 1,000 ml. line. This represents all of the water on Earth.
3. Tell your pupils to pour approximately 30 ml. of water into the 50 ml. graduated cylinder. This represents the total amount of fresh water on Earth.
4. Pour 5 ml. of water from the 50 ml. graduated cylinder into the 10 ml. graduated cylinder. This represents the groundwater component of

fresh water available on Earth.

5. Have each group use the medicine dropper to place two drops of water in one of the medicine cups. This represents the amount of fresh surface water available on Earth (e.g., lakes, rivers, streams).
6. Have each group place one drop of water in the second medicine cup. This represents the amount of fresh water available in the topsoil and atmosphere.

Closure or Evaluation:

1. Ask your pupils to tell you how much water is left in the 50 ml. graduated cylinder. Indicate that this represents the amount of fresh water locked up in the icecaps and glaciers of the Earth.
2. Discuss with your pupils the significance of each of the containers of water they have in front of them. Ask them where most of the fresh water on Earth is located. Can we use that source for our water needs? Tell pupils that the idea of chopping ice into large blocks and shipping or pushing (with tugboats) the ice to civilized areas of the Earth has been discussed many times, but is too expensive.
3. Ask your pupils to indicate why we must protect our fresh water supplies on Earth.

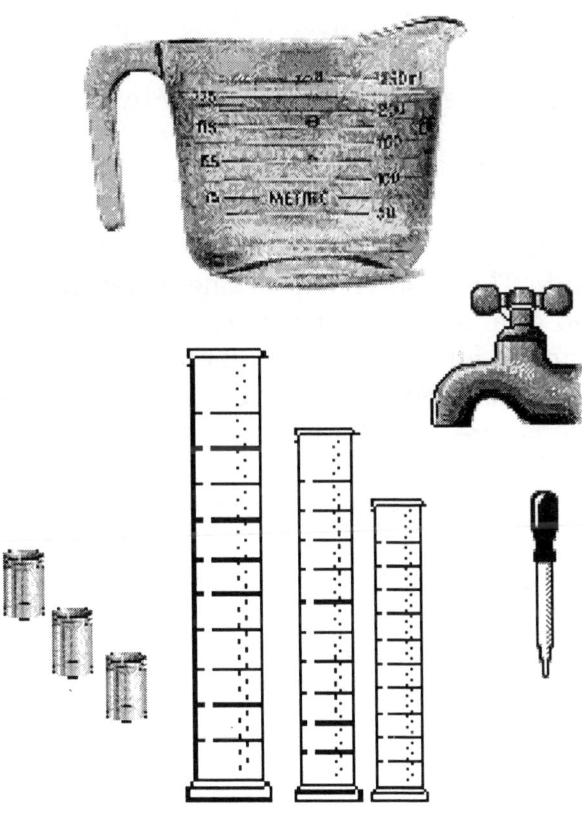

Topic: BUBBLES

Grade Level: K – 6 **Activity Time:** 1 – 2 Days

Materials Needed (per group):

1. Clean aluminum roasting pan
2. Liquid soap detergent (dish-washing soap)
3. Glycerin (obtainable in grocery stores and pharmacies)
4. Clean, fresh water
5. Metal coat hanger or pipe cleaners
6. Sewing needle
7. Drinking glass
8. Medicine dropper

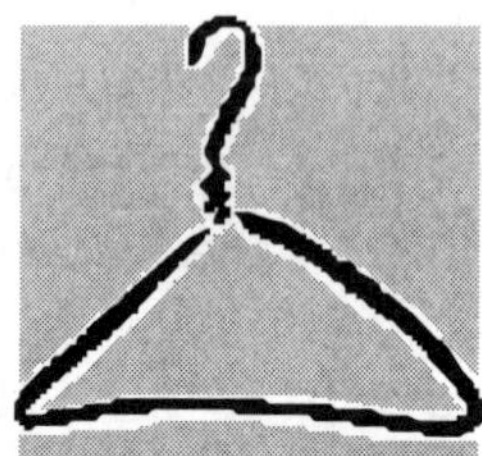

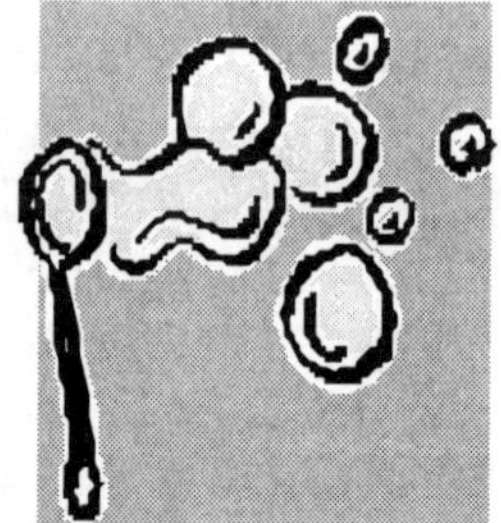

Objectives:

As a result of this activity, the learner will:

- relate why water does not normally form bubbles.
- explain how soap helps water form bubbles.
- see how light affects bubbles and makes them form colors.

Introduction:

1. Ask your pupils to explain what bubbles are and how they are formed.
2. Point out to your pupils that bubbles may be found in various places. We can make bubbles in our milk simply by blowing into a straw. Nearly everyone has blown bubbles through a small plastic wand dipped in a bubble-making solution. But what causes bubbles in the first place?
3. Bubbles are mainly made up of water molecules. These water molecules are bipolar, meaning that they are positive on one end and negative on the other end. The positive end of one water molecule is attracted to the negative end of another water molecule. You can see an example of water's attraction for itself when you observe its surface. You can add water to a full glass and actually exceed the top of the edge of the glass. The cohesive nature of water causes the surface to behave as if it possessed a "skin." This phenomenon is known as *surface tension*.
4. To demonstrate surface tension, carefully float a needle on the surface of a glass of water, using a fork to gently place the needle on the water's surface. The needle is actually held up by the bonding of the water molecules.
5. Soap can be used to break the surface tension of the water, thus reducing the pull of the water molecules on each other. Place a drop of liquid soap into the glass and the needle sinks because the surface tension was broken.
6. It is nearly impossible to blow bubbles in plain water because of the attraction the molecules have for one another. Soap, however, causes an expansion of the water's skin; it "breaks" the surface tension of the water.

Major Instructional Sequence:

1. Organize your pupils into small groups of three to four.
2. Instruct the pupils to make a wand out of the clothes hanger or pipe cleaners. Encourage them to experiment with different shapes besides a circle (e.g., square, triangle).
3. Assist the groups in making a soap solution. Add approximately 100 ml. of dish-washing detergent to 300 ml. of pure water. Add about 7 ml. of glycerin to the solution, particularly if you live in a fairly dry climate.
4. Have pupils dip their wands into the soap solution and wave the wands through the air to create bubbles.

Note: If you want to make larger bubbles, place a 60 cm. string through two hollow, plastic rods from a Tinkertoy™ set. Use the rods as handles to dip the string in the solution (make sure the ends of the string are tied together). Pull the string out of the solution and separate the loop. The result should be a much larger bubble. Pupils can experiment with different sizes of string loops.

Closure or Evaluation:

1. Ask your pupils to explain what is happening when they dip their wands into the soap solution and wave the wand through the air.
2. Discuss with your pupils the significance of having soap and glycerin in the bubble solution. (Both reduce the pull of the water molecules on each other.)
3. Investigate whether other geometric shapes of bubbles would be possible to make besides a sphere.
4. Instruct your pupils to look at the colors in the bubble, particularly if you are outside. The sun produces white light, yet the bubbles will contain a kaleidoscope of colors that are changing constantly.
5. Explain to your pupils that the white light (containing all the colors of the visible spectrum) penetrates the edge of the bubble and is bounced around off the inner surfaces of the bubble. The waves of light actually "run into" each other causing *interference*. Interference is the effect that occurs when two or more waves overlap or intersect. Interfering light waves are responsible for the colors seen in the soap bubbles.

Note: White light is made up of light waves of different wavelengths. The light waves that reflect off the inner surface of the bubble interfere with light waves of the same wavelength that reflect off the outer surface of the bubble. Since different wavelengths of light correspond to different colors, the light reflecting off the soap bubble appears colored.

Topic: WATER POLLUTION SIMULATION

Grade Level: 4 – 6 **Activity Time:** 1 – 2 Days

Materials Needed (per group):

1. Three cups, jars, or jugs (each approximately double the previous volume and made of transparent glass or plastic)
2. Red or blue food coloring
3. Graduated cylinder (50 – 100 ml.)
4. Water source
5. Stirring rod
6. Pencil and note pad

Objectives:

As a result of this activity, the learner will:

- relate how adding substances to water affects water pollution.
- explain why the amount of the pollutant becomes diluted.
- demonstrate measuring skills.

Introduction:

1. Ask your pupils to name some examples of water pollution they have seen.
2. Ask them why these are examples of water pollution.
3. Point out to your pupils that water pollution becomes diluted as the main source of the pollution travels down a stream or into a large volume of water (such as groundwater).
4. Explain that the pollutants diffuse from an area of greater concentration to an area of lesser concentration.
5. Point out that the damage or harm imposed by a water pollutant (or any pollution source) is dependent upon its concentration.
6. Explain to your pupils that they are going to participate in an activity to show how pollutants can be diffused, lessening their concentration.

Major Instructional Sequence:

1. Organize your pupils into small groups of three to four.
2. Instruct the groups to place their three cups, jars, or jugs in ascending order, based on increasing volume. Have them fill each based on a doubling of the volume of the previous container. (For example, if the first container requires 30 ml., the next container should contain 60 ml., and the last container 120 ml.)
3. Instruct your groups to add approximately 2 – 3 drops of pollutant (food coloring) to the first container. Ask them to stir the solution with the stirring rod provided. Encourage your pupils to record their observations.
4. Have your groups pour all but 5 ml. of the original solution into the

second container and stir, recording their observations.

5. Have the groups pour all but 5 ml. of their second solution into the third container, stir, and record their observations.

Closure or Evaluation:

1. Ask your groups to share their observations with the class. They should have noticed that the original color of the pollutant became diluted (reduced color and strength) as each container was mixed with the next.
2. Review with your pupils the reason for this color reduction. The molecules of the pollutant disperse and mix with the solvent. As more and more molecules of solvent are added to the solution, the color becomes lighter due to a spreading out of the molecules.

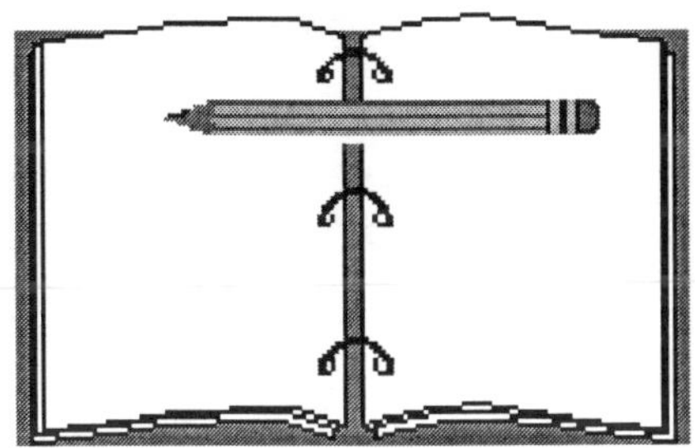

CHAPTER EIGHT
Weather

Weather is what we call the short-term changes in barometric pressure, rainfall, temperature, and humidity in the atmosphere. Weather takes place in the troposphere, the lower part of the atmosphere where living organisms are found. The troposphere is about seven miles thick. It is thinner at the poles (about five miles thick) and thicker at the equator (about ten miles thick). Weather patterns are dominated by air masses moving between low- and high-pressure areas.

Humans have been predicting the weather for centuries. The Weather Bureau was created in the late 1800s in the United States and became known as the National Weather Service in the 1970s. Most weather information today is gathered from space via satellites. Weather pictures of cloud movements seen on television and in newspapers are taken by cameras onboard satellites and transmitted to weather bureaus on Earth.

Topic: CONDENSATION: THE CLOUD IN THE BOTTLE

Grade Level: 2 – 5 **Activity Time:** 1 Day

Materials Needed:

1. Two-liter soda bottle
2. Rubber stopper w/ a small plastic tube inserted through the center
3. Bicycle pump that attaches to the valve stem with a clamp
4. Matches
5. Water

Objectives:

As a result of this activity, the learner will:

- be able to illustrate that clouds form when air expands and cools.

Introduction:

It is important for your pupils to understand the mechanism by which clouds form. Clouds form in the atmosphere from rising air. As the air rises, it expands because air pressure on it is less at higher altitudes. When air expands, it uses up energy by pushing back against the surrounding air. This results in a loss (or decrease) in temperature. When the temperature gets low enough, water vapor condenses, forming a cloud. Water droplets form more easily on tiny particles called *condensation nuclei* (e.g., dust particles). The atmosphere is full of many naturally occurring condensation nuclei. This substantially reduces the amount of cooling necessary for condensation and cloud formation to occur.

Major Instructional Sequence: (Demonstration)

1. Invert the soda bottle over a lighted match so smoke particles (condensation nuclei) from the match can rise into the bottle. *Note: The particles will be barely (if at all) visible, so don't panic if you don't see anything in the bottle!*
2. Explain to your pupils that the condensation nuclei are important for clouds to form and that there are natural particles in the air at all times.
3. Put some water (a squeeze bottle works well) into the bottom of the bottle and seal it with the rubber stopper. This ensures that the humidity is high enough for the cloud to form.
4. Attach the bicycle pump to the tube in the rubber stopper. Pump the handle several times (Caution: don't pump too hard, you may burst the bottle).
5. Quickly release the pressure in the bottle by opening the clamp. The air should rush out of the bottle with an audible sound, and a cloud should form in the bottle.

Closure or Evaluation:

1. Explain to your pupils that clouds form in the atmosphere when air expands and cools. Even though the expansion takes place more slowly in the atmosphere, the basic process is the same.

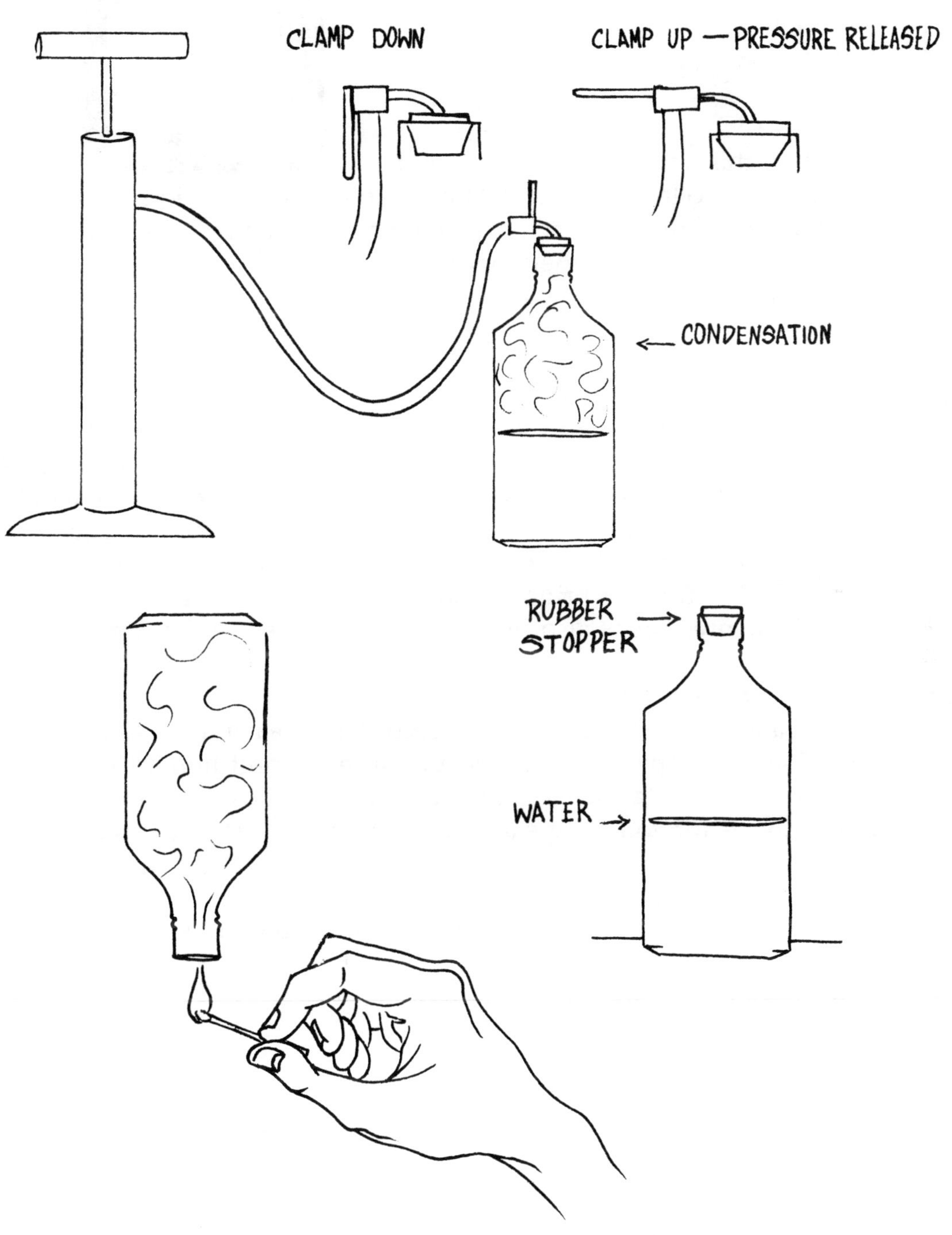

Topic: CAN YOU PREDICT WEATHER?

Grade Level: 3-6

Activity Time: 1-3 months

Materials Needed:

1. TV/VCR setup (cable if possible)
2. Bulletin Board or posterboards

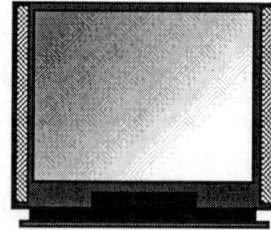

Objectives:

As a result of this activity, the learner will:

- observe and collect weather data over an extended period (1-3 months).
- compare wind direction, wind speed, barometric pressure and percent humidity to actual weather conditions.
- infer which weather variables are necessary for sunny, cloudy, or rainy days.

Introduction:

1. Introduce your pupils to the concepts of *wind direction, wind speed, barometric pressure* and *percent humidity.* Point out how wind direction may play a role in weather. In the southeastern United States winds from the south bring moisture from the Gulf of Mexico. The opposite would be true for states like Indiana or Illinois, where northerly winds blowing across the Great Lakes bring moisture to the state. Point out that barometric pressure is also important, as well as percent humidity.

Major Instructional Sequence:

1. Assign a different pupil the role of recorder for each day's data (wind direction, wind speed, barometric pressure, percent humidity, and actual weather). This data can be gathered by pupils via TV or newspaper. An alternative is for you to tape a local weather forecast or a cable station (*The Weather Channel* is highly recommended) and broadcast the tape to your pupils each day (See Table 8.1).
2. Assign your pupils to groups of 3-4 and ask them to look for similarities between the variables collected, particularly barometric pressure and percent humidity, and the actual weather for each day.

Closure or Evaluation:

1. Ask each group to present their conclusions to the class.
2. Record each group's conclusions on the blackboard/overhead.
3. Ask the class to analyze and critique the conclusions and come to a possible consensus as to possible relationships between the variables (data) collected and the actual weather observed.

Table 8.1
Weather Data for Montgomery, Alabama
March 11-April 6, 1997

Date	Wind	Barometric Pressure	Humidity	Actual Weather
March 11	NE8	30.51	50%	Fair
March 12	Calm	30.25	73%	Fair
March 13	S5	30.18	82%	Fair
March 14	SW10	30.12	100%	Partly Cloudy
March 15	SSW3	29.99	83%	Partly Cloudy
March 16	SW16	29.83	68%	Mostly Cloudy
March 17	SW10	29.73	97%	Rain
March 18	E10	29.74	100%	Rain
March 19	WNW23	29.65	79%	Cloudy/Windy
March 20	WSW10	29.95	73%	PC/PM Rain
March 21	NW10	30.02	79%	Fair
March 22	NW8	30.07	82%	PC/Fair
March 23	NW10	30.09	83%	Sunny
March 24	NW8	30.05	88%	Partly Cloudy
March 25	ESE5	30.04	90%	MC/Th. Storms
March 26	N10	30.17	54%	Partly Cloudy
March 27	E14	30.00	93%	PC/PM Rain
March 28	Calm	29.94	100%	Rain
March 29	Calm	29.99	81%	Partly Cloudy
March 30	Calm	30.02	96%	Sc. Th. Storms
March 31	NW16	29.86	100%	AM Rain/PC
April 1	NW13	29.93	74%	PC
April 2	NNW6	30.14	67%	PC/Sunny
April 3	S10	30.13	89%	Fair
April 4	SSE5	30.03	93%	Cloudy
April 5	N8	30.07	90%	Cloudy
April 6	N7	30.05	89%	Cloudy

The data in Table 8.1 was given to a group of sixth graders to analyze. The class consensus was as follows:

1. The percent humidity exceeded 90 in seven out of eight cases of rain.
2. The barometric pressure was 30.04 or less in all eight cases of rain.
3. The percent humidity exceeded 74 in 18 of 21 cases of rainy/cloudy days.
4. The barometric pressure was 30.07 or less in 19 of the 21 cases of rainy/cloudy days.
5. The percent humidity ranged from 50 to 89 on sunny/fair days.
6. The barometric pressure ranged from 30.02 to 30.51 on sunny/fair days.

The class concluded that when the barometric pressure was close to or below 30.00, and the percent humidity was 75–100%, the chances for clouds or rain increased.
The class also concluded that when the barometric pressure was above 30.00, and the percent humidity decreased from 80–75, the chances for fair or sunny weather improved.

Topic: THERMOCLINES

Grade Level: 2-5 **Activity Time:** 1 day

Materials Needed (per group):

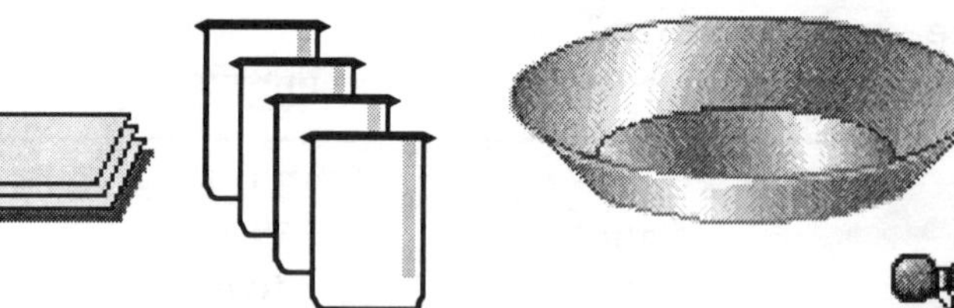

1. 4 baby food jars
2. Water source
3. Food coloring
4. Laminated 3 x 5 cards
5. Hot plate with pan (or other source for heating water)

Objectives:

As a result of this activity, the learner will:

- describe what a thermocline is.
- determine that hot and cold water have different densities.
- relate the movement of hot and cold water to the movement of hot and cold air in the atmosphere.

Introduction:

1. Ask pupils whether air rises or sinks. Ask them *why* hot air rises and cold air sinks. (The hot-air balloon activity on page 9.19 would work well here.)
2. Introduce the terms density and thermocline. *Density* involves the amount of matter in a given space. If something is lighter than another object, it will float. If something is heavier than another object it will sink. *Thermoclines* result when different levels of water or air have different densities. Sometimes layers of air or water with different densities can occur (e.g., a layer of warm water or a layer of cooler water).
3. Explain to your pupils that they are going to be involved in an activity that illustrates how different water densities react to each other. Point out to your pupils that the same basic principle applies to different densities of air.

Major Instructional Sequence:

1. Arrange your pupils into small groups of three to four.
2. Instruct designated pupils from each group to obtain four baby food jars and laminated 3 x 5 cards from the central supply area.
3. Have each group fill two jars with cool water and two jars with warm (hot) water.
4. Ask each group to pour one or two drops of food coloring in *one* cool-water jar and *one* warm-water jar.
5. Instruct each group to place a jar of cold water (with food coloring added) upside down on top of a jar of warm water (without food coloring added). This is accomplished by placing a laminated card over the mouth

of the jar before placing it upside down on the other jar. The laminated card is now between the two jars of water. Tell pupils that they will carefully remove the cards at a designated time. This will be called Experiment 1. (You may need to demonstrate this procedure for the groups, using plain water.)

6. Instruct each group to place a bottle of warm water (with food coloring added) on top of a bottle of cold water (without food coloring added). Instruct your pupils to place a laminated card between the jars again. This will be called Experiment 2.
7. Ask each group to predict what will happen when they "mix" the levels of water (by removing the laminated cards at the designated time).
8. At the designated time, instruct each group to carefully remove the laminated card between the jars in Experiment 1 and observe as the liquids mix. Tell them to record their observations (see Figure 8.1).
9. Instruct each group to repeat the same procedure for Experiment 2.

Closure or Evaluation:

1. Ask each group to present their findings to the class. Ask them to explain why the result of each experiment occurred as it did. In Experiment 1, the cold water (with food coloring) sank. This caused the water in both bottles to have roughly the same tint. In Experiment 2, the warm water (with the food coloring) stayed on top. This resulted in colored water on top and plain water on the bottom. Density was the key to both. In Experiment 1, the denser cold water sank. In Experiment 2, the lighter warm water stayed on top.
2. Ask pupils to relate this activity to the relationship between hot air and cold air (weather). Point out that some turbulent weather, like thunderstorms, results from excessive heating of air in particular places. In addition, high-pressure and low-pressure areas are determined somewhat by the temperatures of the air.

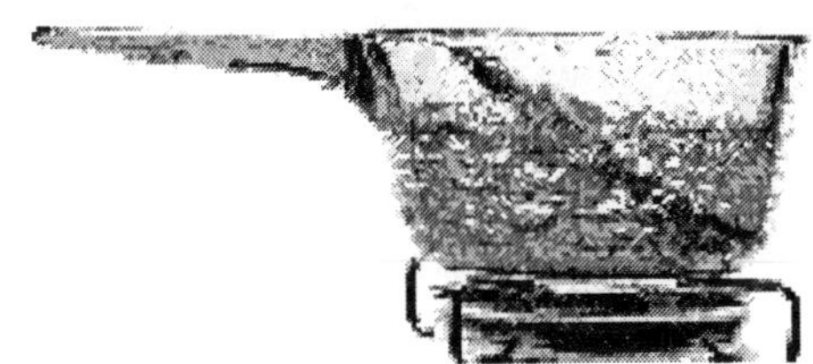

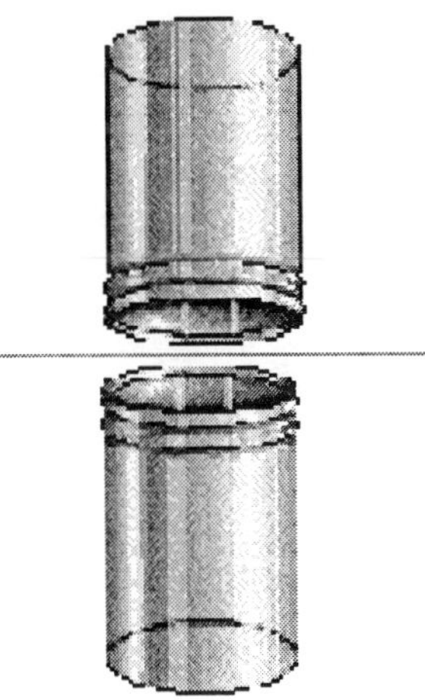

Figure 8.1

DENSITY WORKSHEET

1. What happened in Experiment 1 when you added the cold water (with food color) to the hot water? What could have caused this?

2. What happened in Experiment 2 when you added the hot water (with food color) to the cold water? What could have caused this?

3. Would it be possible to create several layers of water in a container? How? (Optional)

4. If cold water is more dense, why does ice form on the surface of the water and not sink? (Optional)

Topic: GRAPHING TEMPERATURE VARIATIONS

Grade Level: 3 – 6 **Activity Time:** 1 day

Materials Needed (per group):

1. Weather data set (collected previously)
2. Bulletin board or posterboard
3. Watercolors, markers, or crayons
4. Rulers and scissors

Objectives:

As a result of this activity, the learner will:

- observe and collect weather data over an extended period (1 – 2 months).
- graph the high and low temperatures for an extended period (1 – 2 months).
- compare the graph to actual weather conditions that occurred during the time period of data collection.

Introduction:

1. Remind your pupils that the data they have been collecting and recording on the bulletin board (or posterboard) will be used for different activities during the year (See Table 8.2).
2. Refresh their memory as to what a bar graph looks like.

Major Instructional Sequence:

1. Organize your class into small groups of 3 – 4 pupils.
2. Give each group a portion of the data collected.
3. Instruct each group to construct one or more "bars" representing highs and lows for particular days.
4. If you are using the bulletin board to create the bar graph, instruct your pupils to create bars based on the following dimensions:
   (a) if you are using 30 or more days in your graph, each bar will be one inch wide and the length will be based on 1/4 inch equaling 1 degree (or one inch equaling 4 degrees).
   (b) if you are using fewer than 30 days in your graph, each bar will be two inches wide (the length will be the same as in (a).
5. You will need to designate the point of origin for the bar (based on the normal temperature ranges for the region). In the South, there would probably be no need to start below -10 degrees F (Fahrenheit). However, in some locations in the North, the low could exceed -10 degrees F.
6. Once your pupils have constructed their high and low bars, ask them to place them in the appropriate location on each graph. You may want to have two separate graphs (one for the highs and one for the lows).

Note: As an alternative, simply graph the high and low temperatures each day over a given period of time, and have one pupil place the corresponding data on the bulletin board or posterboard provided (a line graph would probably be more appropriate here).

Closure or Evaluation:

1. Once your pupils have finished placing their bars on the appropriate graph, ask them to look for trends between the high/low temperatures and the actual weather for the day.
2. You may also want to compare one graph with another graph. Provided you have the data, your pupils can compare one month in a given year with the same month in a previous year. You could also compare two or more different months within the same year.

Date	Act. High	Act. Low
18-Mar	68	59
19-Mar	50	44
20-Mar	44	34
21-Mar	55	34
22-Mar	63	35
23-Mar	68	42
24-Mar	74	50

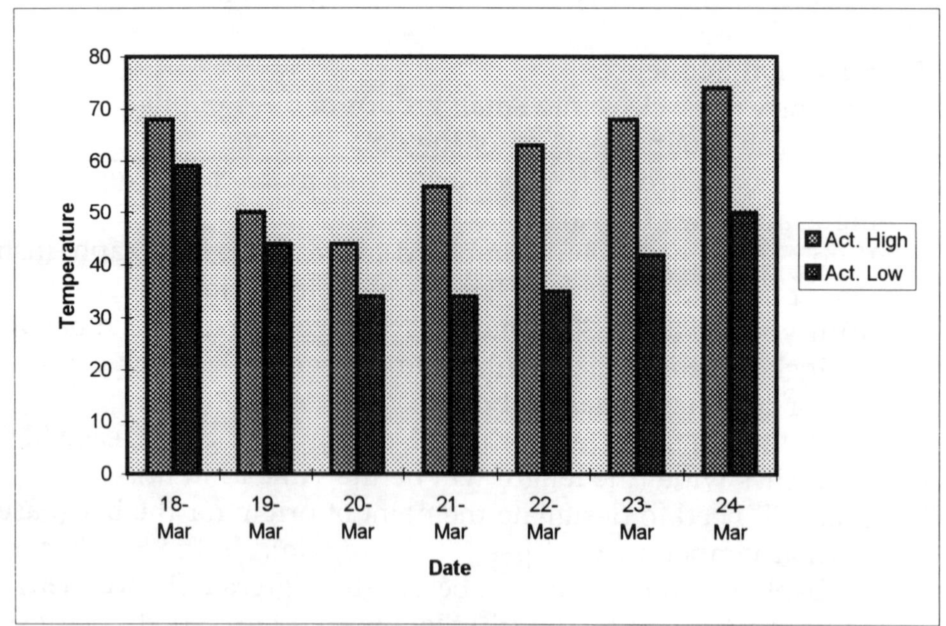

Table 8.2
A Comparison of the Five-Day Forecast
With the Twenty-four-Hour Forecast
March 18-March 24, 1996

Date	Pred. High (5-Day)	Act. High	+/-	Pred. High (24 Hr.)	Act. High	+/-
March 18	68	68	0	70	68	-2
March 19	64	50	-14	54	50	-4
March 20	47	44	-3	45	44	-1
March 21	54	55	+1	53	55	+2
March 22	65	63	-2	63	63	0
March 23	69	68	-1	65	68	+3
March 24	73	74	+1	75	74	-1

Note: The average difference between predicted and actual highs was 3.14 for the five-day forecast and 1.86 for the twenty-four-hour forecast.

Date	Pred. Low (5 Day)	Act. Low	+/-	Pred. Low (24 Hr.)	Act. Low	+/-
March 18	62	59	-3	60	59	-1
March 19	47	44	-3	43	44	+1
March 20	35	34	-1	35	34	-1
March 21	26	34	+8	33	34	+1
March 22	34	35	+1	35	35	0
March 23	37	42	+5	35	42	+7
March 24	45	50	+5	46	50	+4

Note: The average difference between predicted and actual lows was 3.71 for the five-day forecast and 2.14 for the twenty-four-hour forecast

Topic: CHARTING THE WEATHER

Grade Level: K – 2 **Activity Time:** ongoing

Materials Needed:

1. Copy of a calendar (any month)
2. Crayons or markers (various colors)

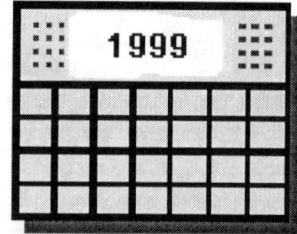

Objectives:

As a result of this activity, the learner will:

- draw and label a representation of the weather for each day of the month.
- determine the number of days in the month that were cloudy, rainy, snowy, sunny, or windy.
- determine what type (or types) of weather was/were more prominent for the month.

Introduction:

1. Introduce your pupils to the concepts of cloudy, rainy, snowy, sunny, and windy.
2. Acquaint your pupils with the monthly calendar and what it represents.

Major Instructional Sequence:

1. Pass out the blank calendars for the month you have chosen. The calendar should contain only the numerical days of the week and the name and a set of questions for the pupils. A sample set of questions might include the following:
   (a) How many cloudy days were there in *April?* ____
   (b) How many rainy days were there in *April?* ____
   (c) How many snowy days were there in *April?* ____
   (d) How many sunny days were there in *April?* ____
   (e) How many windy days were there in *April?* ____
   (f) Which type of weather did you see the most?
2. Pass out a chart listing the type of weather for a particular month (see Table 8.3 on page 8.14).
3. Instruct your pupils to draw a picture depicting the weather for each day (e.g., if April 1 was a cloudy day, then they should draw clouds in the space marked April 1).
4. Ask your pupils to answer the questions below the calendar. If necessary, you can read the question for them and have them record their numerical response in the appropriate space.

Closure or Evaluation:

Once your pupils have finished drawing/coloring their depictions of each day's weather and have answered the questions, ask several pupils to present their findings to the class.

Note: You might want to draw an outline of a calendar on a large piece of posterboard, which may be displayed on the bulletin board, and have each pupil decorate a particular day (e.g., April 14 was rainy, so the pupil would draw a depiction of rain in the square representing April 14).

Table 8.3
Sample Data Sheet

Date	Pred. High	Act. High	+/-	Pred. Low	Act. Low	+/-	Pred. Weather	Act. Weather
March 12	65	67	+2	30	33	+3	Sunny	Sunny
March 13	75	71	-4	36	40	+4	Sunny	Sunny
March 14	75	78	+3	46	46	0	Cloudy	Cloudy
March 15	75	76	+1	54	51	-3	Cloudy	Cloudy
March 16	75	78	+3	54	53	-1	Rain	Cloudy
March 17	70	72	+2	56	56	0	Rain	Rain
March 18	68	68	0	62	59	-3	Rain	Rain
March 19	64	50	-14	47	44	-3	Windy	Windy
March 20	47	44	-3	35	34	-1	Windy	Rain
March 21	54	55	+1	26	34	+8	Sunny	Sunny
March 22	65	63	-2	34	35	+1	Sunny	Cloudy
March 23	69	68	-1	37	42	+5	Sunny	Sunny
March 24	73	74	+1	45	50	+5	Cloudy	Cloudy
March 25	76	72	-4	63	59	-4	Rain	Rain
March 26	73	59	-14	60	49	-11	Rain	Cloudy
March 27	64	57	-7	53	48	-5	Rain	Rain
March 28	74	73	-1	55	53	-2	Rain	Rain
March 29	76	75	-1	55	57	+2	Cloudy	Cloudy
March 30	75	73	-2	56	55	-1	Rain	Rain
March 31	72	71	-1	53	54	+1	Sunny	Cloudy
April 1	68	60	-8	45	48	+3	Sunny	Cloudy
April 2	74	74	0	45	38	-7	Sunny	Sunny
April 3	75	75	0	45	43	-2	Sunny	Sunny
April 4	71	77	+6	54	53	-1	Cloudy	Cloudy
April 5	65	67	+2	48	50	+2	Cloudy	Cloudy
April 6	64	63	-1	46	43	-3	Rain	Cloudy
April 7	56	65	+9	44	39	-4	Windy	Sunny
April 8	55	72	+17	36	42	+6	Cloudy	PC/Sunny
April 9	64	65	+1	45	43	-2	Cloudy	Cloudy
April 10	68	68	0	45	37	-8	Sunny	Sunny
April 11	75	78	+3	45	36	-9	Sunny	Sunny
April 12	75	76	+1	54	46	-8	Cloudy	Cloudy
April 13	81	81	0	56	52	-4	Th.Show.	Cloudy
April 14	76	79	+3	65	64	-1	Th.Show.	Th.Show.
April 15	65	73	+8	55	62	+7	Windy	Rain/Cloudy
April 16	66	72	+6	44	42	-2	Sunny	Sunny
April 17	76	81	+5	46	43	-3	Sunny	Sunny
April 18	75	76	+1	55	56	+1	Cloudy	Cloudy
April 19	82	81	-1	55	63	+8	Cloudy	Cloudy
April 20	84	85	+1	57	60	+3	Th.Show.	Cloudy
April 21	84	84	0	64	70	-6	Th.Show.	Cloudy
April 22	84	84	0	64	58	-6	Th.Show.	Cloudy
April 23	80	78	-2	65	64	-1	Th.Show.	Th.Show.
April 24	75	75	0	53	44	-9	Sunny	Sunny
April 25	83	82	-1	55	48	-7	Th.Show.	Cloudy
April 26	80	82	+2	56	67	+11	Th.Show.	Th.Show.
April 27	78	76	-2	56	46	-10	Cloudy	Sunny
April 28	75	88	+13	54	54	0	Cloudy	Sunny
April 29	77	83	+6	63	67	+4	Cloudy	Cloudy/Rain
April 30	68	68	0	63	62	-1	Rain	Rain
May 1	66	77	+11	46	45	-1	Sunny	Sunny
May 2	75	81	+6	53	50	-3	Sunny	Sunny
May 3	81	79	-2	56	56	0	Cloudy	Cloudy
May 4	85	88	+3	58	67	+9	Cloudy	PC/Sunny
May 5	85	83	-2	65	67	+2	Cloudy	Sunny
May 6	81	89	+8	64	64	0	Sunny	Sunny

Topic: HOW ACCURATE IS THE FIVE-DAY FORECAST?

Grade Level: 4 – 6 **Activity Time:** 1 – 3 months

Materials Needed:
1. TV/VCR setup (cable if possible)
2. Bulletin board or posterboards

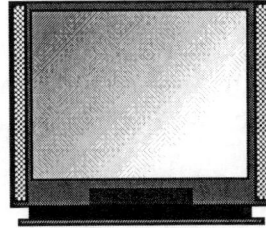

Objectives:

As a result of this activity, the learner will:
- observe and collect weather data over an extended period (1 – 3 months).
- compare the predicted highs and lows over an extended period with the actual highs and lows.
- compare the predicted five-day weather forecasts with the actual weather over an extended period (1 – 3 months).
- compare the predicted five-day weather forecasts with the 24-hour weather prediction for accuracy over an extended period (1 – 3 months).
- construct graphs that reflect the accuracy of both five-day and 24-hour weather prediction.

Introduction:
1. Start by introducing the idea of weather prediction.
2. Ask your pupils to explain how people actually can forecast the weather before it has happened. Showing some film clips from *The Weather Channel* or the weather report from local stations would help, particularly when pupils see maps indicating fronts, cloud formations, the jet stream, etc. Clippings of weather maps from the local paper or *USA Today* would also help reinforce any particular concepts you wish to use.
3. Construct your bulletin board or posterboard. You might want to set up your board based on the "data sheet" format for Montgomery, Alabama (See Table 8.4 on page 8.16).

Major Instructional Sequence:
1. Ask a different one of your pupils to write down the data collected for each day. This information may come from TV or newspaper sources.
2. As you proceed with this activity, you may want to ask for pupil comments concerning the accuracy of the forecasts.
3. Have your pupils determine the +/- values between predicted and actual highs/lows.

Closure or Evaluation:
1. After collecting data for a given period of time (1 – 3 months), ask your pupils to calculate the average difference between predicted and actual

temperatures.

2. Ask your pupils to calculate the percentage of the time that the weather forecasters were correct or wrong in their five-day forecasts.
3. Ask them to speculate as to what factors might have caused the forecasters to be wrong.
4. Your pupils could even graph the data to help them visualize discrepancies in the data.

Variation:

Collect weather prediction data given 24 hours in advance and compare its accuracy to the five-day forecast. This would generate new information which might influence the pupils' original hypotheses concerning the problem of predicting the weather. A sample of this variation is inserted after the sample data sheets for weather collected between March 12 – May 6, 1996 (Refer back to Table 8.2).

Table 8.4
Weather Data for Montgomery, Alabama
March 11-April 7, 1996

Date	Wind	Barometric Pressure	Humidity	Actual Weather
March 11	NE8	30.51	50%	Fair
March 12	Calm	30.25	73%	Fair
March 13	S5	30.18	82%	Fair
March 14	SW10	30.12	100%	Partly Cloudy
March 15	SSW3	29.99	83%	Partly Cloudy
March 16	SW16	29.83	68%	Mostly Cloudy
March 17	SW10	29.73	97%	Rain
March 18	E10	29.74	100%	Rain
March 19	WNW23	29.65	79%	Cloudy/Windy
March 20	WSW10	29.95	73%	PC/PM Rain
March 21	NW10	30.02	79%	Fair
March 22	NW8	30.07	82%	PC/Fair
March 23	NW10	30.09	83%	Sunny
March 24	NW8	30.05	88%	Partly Cloudy
March 25	ESE5	30.04	90%	MC/Th. Storms
March 26	N10	30.17	54%	Partly Cloudy
March 27	E14	30.00	93%	PC/PM Rain
March 28	Calm	29.94	100%	Rain
March 29	Calm	29.99	81%	Partly Cloudy
March 30	Calm	30.02	96%	Sc. Th. Storms
March 31	NW16	29.86	100%	AM Rain/PC
April 1	NW13	29.93	74%	PC
April 2	NNW6	30.14	67%	PC/Sunny
April 3	S10	30.13	89%	Fair
April 4	SSE5	30.03	93%	Cloudy
April 5	N8	30.07	90%	Cloudy
April 6	N7	30.05	89%	Cloudy
April 7	NNE5	30.01	70%	PC/Sunny

Topic: HOW FAR AWAY IS THE THUNDERSTORM?

Grade Level: K – 6 **Activity Time:** 1 day

Materials Needed:

1. Stopwatch
2. Flashlight and audiocassette tape or CD of thunderstorm
3. Portable tape or CD player

Objectives:

As a result of this activity, the learner will:

- predict his/her proximity to the thunderstorm.
- determine if the storm is coming toward or moving away from him/her.

Introduction:

1. Introduce your pupils to the concepts of thunder and lightning. *Lightning* occurs when electricity travels between areas of opposite electrical charge within a cloud, between clouds or from a cloud to the ground. We hear claps and rumbles of *thunder* because some of the tremendous energy of the lightning bolt is transformed into heat. The heat causes a quick expansion and contraction of air around the lightning bolt, which starts air molecules moving back and forth, producing sound waves.
2. Acquaint your pupils with the distance light and sound travel in a second. Light travels approximately 186,000 miles per second, while sound travels approximately 1 mile in 5 seconds (quite a difference!).

Major Instructional Sequence:

1. Indicate to your pupils that the flashlight will represent the lightning and the audiotape or CD will represent the thunder. Another option to this activity could be the use of a camcorder to record the actual lightning and thunder of a real storm. The pupils could still predict the distance of the storm and its subsequent movement from what they observe on the TV screen.
2. Instruct one pupil to start the stopwatch when the lightning occurs and stop the timer when the sound of thunder is heard.
3. Ask the pupil for the elapsed time. Have another pupil record the time on the board or overhead.
4. Ask your pupils to calculate how far away the storm was (i.e., if the time between the lightning and thunder was 10 seconds, dividing 10 by 5 [the time sound travels a mile] will produce an answer of 2 miles).

5. Repeat the activity using different time intervals. A longer interval would indicate that the storm was moving away from the observer. A shorter time interval would indicate that the storm was moving toward them.

Note: Since sound travels approximately 1 mile in 5 seconds, you may need to introduce decimals or fractions into the lesson; i.e., 3 seconds would indicate the storm was approximately 0.6 miles or 3/5 of a mile from your position.

Closure or Evaluation:

1. Ask your pupils to explain how to determine the proximity of a thunderstorm and whether the storm is moving toward them or away from them.
2. Whenever a real thunderstorm occurs near your school, ask your pupils to determine the proximity of the storm and direction of its movement.

CHAPTER NINE
Chemical Properties

Chemistry is one of the physical sciences, the sciences which deal with inanimate matter or energy. Other physical sciences include physics, geology, and astronomy. Chemistry is the scientific study of the composition, structure, and properties of matter and its changes. It is the science which deals with the composition and properties of substances, and with the reactions by which substances are produced or converted into other substances. Chemistry is very important to the other sciences because it includes all materials in the universe. Chemists study the composition of gases in far-off stars as well as the complex structures of the components within living cells. It is an all-encompassing science.

The roots of chemistry are found in alchemy, a practice that probably started with the Taoists in China and the Pythagoreans in Greece after the sixth century B. C. In alchemy, people sought ways to change or transmute one substance into another substance, such as ordinary metals into gold. Alchemists learned much about the nature of substances. They heated liquids into gases and then turned them back into liquids again, inventing the chemical process of distillation. Alchemists also invented many of the specially shaped bottles, flasks, and funnels seen in a modern scientific laboratory.

Chemists of today are able to probe matter with more advanced techniques that have led humankind to greater understandings of the structure of the atom, but at the same time, raised larger questions about the nature of matter itself.

Topic: OSMOSIS AND THE CHICKEN EGG

Grade Level: 3 – 6 **Activity Time:** 2 or 3 days

Materials Needed: (per group)

1. Two raw chicken eggs
2. Four wide-mouth canning or preserving jars
3. Clear vinegar
4. Karo™ Light corn syrup
5. Source of water (faucet or sprinkling can), distilled if possible
6. Large spoon

Objectives:

As a result of this activity, the learner will:

- explain the direction of flow (of water) through the semipermeable membrane of the eggs used in this experiment.
- relate this activity to other (osmotic) situations.

Introduction:

1. Divide your pupils into groups of three.
2. Have each group pour enough vinegar into each canning jar to cover a raw egg (there should be two eggs — one in each of two canning jars).
3. Have each group secure a lid on the canning jars.
4. After 48 hours, ask each group to remove the eggs carefully from their jars with a large spoon, and wash the eggs with a gentle sprinkling of water. Remind them that a thin membrane is holding the egg together — be careful not to break it.
5. Have each group pour their vinegar carefully into a jar or container for reuse.

Major Instructional Sequence:

1. Upon examination, pupils should see two raw eggs with the outside shells dissolved away (due to the acidic action of the vinegar).
2. Pupils should place one egg in a jar filled with tap water (distilled water would be better), and one egg in a jar filled with light Karo™ syrup.
3. After 48 – 72 hours, pupils should observe the difference in the raw eggs. They should notice that the egg in the water seems to have grown larger and the egg in the syrup seems to have shrunk slightly.

4. The difference between the eggs will become more apparent over time, particularly with the egg in the syrup, which will start to form ridges similar to those of a prune.

Closure or Evaluation:

1. Ask the pupils to explain what they think might have happened to the eggs.
2. Relate the discussion to the concept of *osmosis* (the movement of water through a semipermeable membrane from an area of high concentration to an area of low concentration). In the case of the egg in the water, water moved through the semipermeable membrane from the area of higher concentration (the water) to that of the lesser concentration (the egg). The increase in water caused the egg to swell. In the case of the egg in the syrup, the concentration of water was higher inside the egg than in the syrup. Water moved through the semipermeable membrane from the egg into the syrup. The decrease in water inside the egg caused the egg to shrink.
3. Relate the experiment to other things such as how raisins and prunes are made. (See activity on page 4.6.)
4. Ask pupils to decide what would happen if they were out on the ocean on a lifeboat with no water. Would they drink ocean water? Why or why not? What would happen to the cells in their bodies if they did?

Topic: MAGIC MARKER CHROMATOGRAPHY

Grade Level: 3 – 6 **Activity Time:** 2 or 3 days

Materials Needed:

1. Eight to ten permanent (black) markers [at least 4 – 5 different brands]
2. Fifty #6 cone-style coffee filters (Mr. Coffee, Melitta, etc.)
3. Two quarts of 70% isopropyl rubbing alcohol
4. 40 – 50 semi-rigid, plastic 9 oz. cups
5. 40 – 50 Popcicle or construction sticks (available in hobby & art stores)
6. Rulers, pencils, Scotch™ tape and scissors for 8 – 10 groups
7. Video or film on chromatography

Objectives:

As a result of this activity, the learner will:

- observe that the pigments in different markers will travel a measurable and predictable distance on the filter paper (from the starting point).
- observe that each particular brand of black permanent marker produces distinct and predictable color patterns on the filter paper.
- relate this activity to crime lab and drug detection situations.

Introduction:

1. Show the video or film on chromatography.
2. Divide your pupils into groups of three.
3. Have the pupils cut the coffee filters into four-inch long strips (approximately one inch wide). Each group will need 4 – 5 strips, depending on how many pens you will be analyzing.
4. Pupils should place a thin, one-half inch horozontal mark approximately one inch from the bottom of the filter paper. *Note: it is important for the pupils to be consistent with the actual placement of the marks to improve accuracy.*
5. Pupils will tape the top of the strip (the side opposite the marked area) to the Popcicle or construction stick.
6. Have pupils prepare their cups by pouring in enough alcohol to measure approximately one-half of an inch from the bottom. *Note: the actual amount must reach the bottom of the strip when it is placed in the alcohol but must not reach the marked area.*
7. Have pupils place all of their prepared strips (one per cup) into the cups in a particular sequence or order. (They should rest the sticks on top of the cups to suspend the strips in the alcohol.)
8. After thirty minutes, have your pupils remove the strips in the same order that they placed them in the cups. *Note: the first strip in needs to be the first strip out, etc.*

Major Instructional Sequence:

1. Pupils should see that their strips produced particular pigment patterns.
2. Ask your pupils to record the colors produced and their respective distances from the starting point.
3. Have each group record data on the board or an overhead sheet. *Note: let them compare results for similarity.*

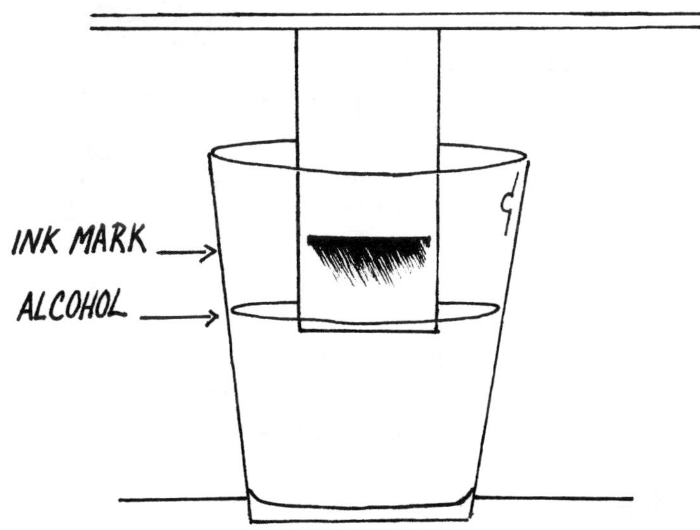

Closure or Evaluation:

1. Ask the pupils to explain the differences between the different brands of permanent markers.
2. Which types of markers produced the greatest variety of colors? The least?
3. Which type of marker produced pigments that traveled the farthest from the starting point? The least?
4. Ask the pupils to determine if the results produced any predictable information regarding chromatography. What were they?
5. Ask the pupils if there are any practical uses for this type of procedure. Relate this procedure to the basic drug chromatography tests done in labs for criminal investigations and for drug detection situations. The procedure is somewhat accurate, however additional tests are done to substantiate (and validate) positive drug tests.

Variation:

Have the pupils try different solvents, such as water or oil, to see if the substances being tested will always move in the same manner. They will see that "like dissolves like." Some substances may be attracted to the alcohol but not to water, for instance. You could even try to design some sort of fictitious crime based on the scenario of permanent markers (a whodunit!).

Topic: UNDERSTANDING DENSITY AND SPECIFIC GRAVITY

Grade Level: Grades 2 – 6 **Activity Time:** 1 day

Materials Needed (per group):

1. One large, transparent plastic container (e.g., vegetable oil container)
2. Vegetable oil
3. Light Karo™ corn syrup or honey
4. Glycerin
5. Water w/ food coloring added
6. Objects to place in the different layers such as: grapes, small plastic toys (rings, etc.), dried pasta
7. Dark-colored construction paper and scissors
8. Beakers, clear glass or plastic containers

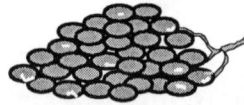

Objectives:

As a result of this activity, the learner will:

- explain why different liquids can float on top of one another.
- predict the order in which liquids will occur together.
- relate the concept of specific gravity to density.

Background Information:

Density is the amount of matter an object possesses within a given volume. In other words, the density of an object is determined by dividing its mass by its volume. *Specific gravity* is essentially the density of the material divided by the density of water at four degrees Celsius. (i.e., syrups usually have a specific gravity of 1.1, water 1.0, and vegetable oil 0.9. Therefore, syrups will be on the bottom and oils will be on top.)

Introduction:

1. Review with your class the concept of density.
2. Ask your pupils if all objects have the same mass. Produce various examples of materials that have similar volumes but different masses (weights).

Major Instructional Sequence:

1. Organize your class into groups of three or four.
2. Have one pupil in the group cut out a strip of construction paper (dark) long and wide enough to tape all around the group's container. The object of this is to prevent the group from initially seeing where each liquid layer ends up.
3. Ask one member of each group to slowly pour about 1/2 cup of each of the four liquids into the container. Make sure each group predicts where the liquid will form (which layer).

4. Once all the liquids have been poured into the container, have a member of the group remove the paper. Ask the group to draw and label a picture illustrating the layers in the container. Ask them to compare the results with their predictions.
5. Ask each group to drop several of the objects provided into the container. Make sure they predict where the object will end up *before* they actually drop it in the container. This should cause some cognitive dissonance because some of the objects will not float at the top of the first layer or sink to the bottom of the last layer.

Closure or Evaluation:

1. Ask your pupils to present their findings to the class. Have a pupil record the results (data) on the board or overhead.
2. Ask your pupils why the various liquids were in particular layers. Were their predictions correct? Why or why not? Review the concept of density with them.
3. Ask the members of each group if they predicted the location of each object correctly. Engage your pupils in a discussion as to why the objects fell into particular layers (e.g., the grape will sink in most layers but will float on top of the syrup layer). Relate this discussion to the concept of specific gravity.

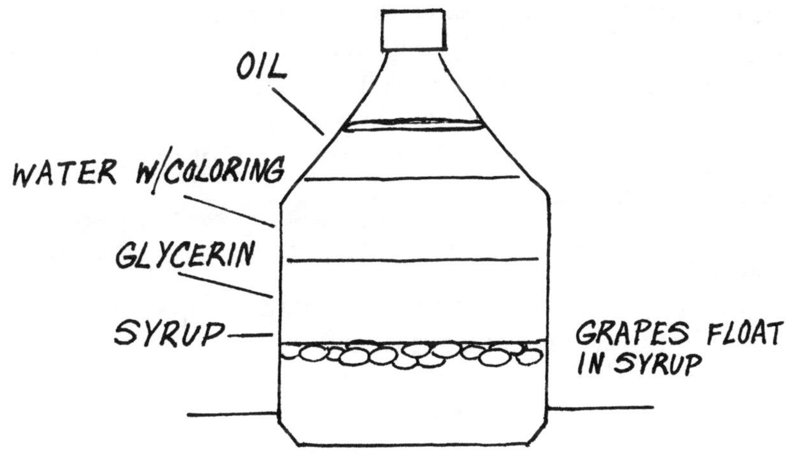

Topic: SURFACE TENSION AND COHESION: IS THE GLASS FULL?

Grade Level: Grades 4 – 6 **Activity Time:** 1 day

Materials Needed:

1. One transparent glass per group *or* one glass (teacher demo)
2. Paper clips or pennies (plan on 50+ per group, depending on the diameter of the glass)

Objectives:

As a result of this activity, the learner will:

- explain the concept of surface tension.

Introduction:

1. Divide your pupils into groups of two or three.
2. Have each group fill its glass with water until it appears to be full (level with the rim).
3. Ask your pupils to predict how many paper clips (or pennies) they can add to the water before it spills over the side of the glass.

Major Instructional Sequence:

1. Have each group add one paper clip (or penny) at a time. Caution them to drop them into the glass as vertically as possible.
2. Ask your pupils to record how many paper clips (or pennies) they can add to the glass of water before it overflows.
3. Ask your pupils to observe the shape of the water surface as they are placing paper clips (pennies) into the glass of water. The convex surface is called the *meniscus*.

Closure or Evaluation:

1. Ask the groups to report how many paper clips (pennies) they were able to place in the water before it overflowed.
2. Ask what they "discovered" about this activity.
3. Ask your pupils to brainstorm why some groups got higher numbers than others (followed directions, steady hand dropping the paper clips, etc.).
4. Discuss with your class the idea of *cohesion*. There are forces that attract molecules of water to each other. On the surface of the water the molecules are attracted in a "downward fashion."
5. Discuss with your class the idea of *surface tension*. The combined cohesion of the water molecules on the surface cause a thin "skin" to form on the water. This is surface tension. If the "skin" remains unbroken (this is why you drop the paper clips or pennies slowly in a

vertical fashion), the attractive forces can overcome the effect of gravity pulling the molecules apart. However, the pupils should note that there is a point where the gravitational forces overcome the surface tension forces. That is the exact point where the water starts to overflow.

Variation:

You could have the pupils experiment with different liquids besides water and compare their surface tension to that of water. Your pupils could also try adding solutes such as liquid detergent to the system and analyze their effect on surface tension.

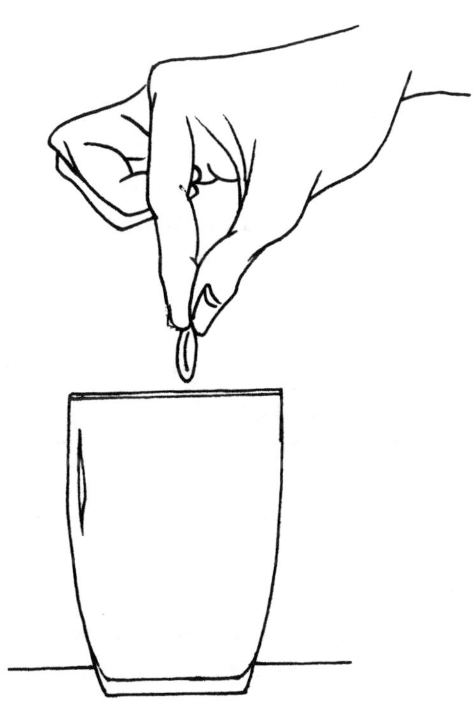

Topic: MAKING AN ANTIFREEZE

Grade Level: Grades 3 – 6 **Activity Time:** 1 day

Materials Needed (per group):

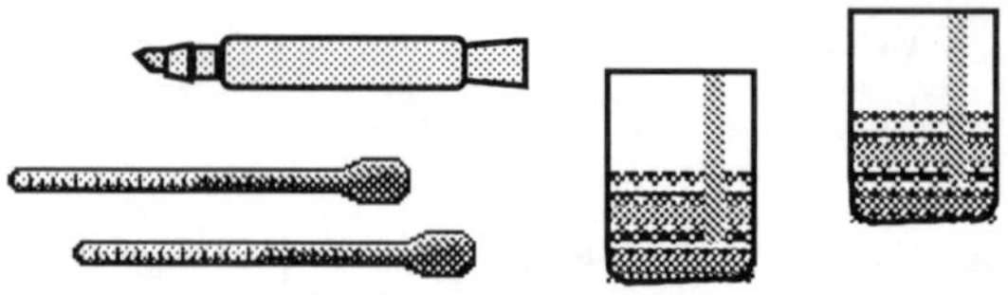

1. Two paper or plastic cups
2. Container of salt
3. Spoons (plastic or metal)
4. Thermometers
5. Thin-point permanent marker
6. Freezer unit available (lunchroom or home economics classroom)
7. Materials and freezer for homemade ice cream (optional)

Objectives:

As a result of this activity, the learner will:

- explain how adding salt to water can alter its freezing point.
- explain how salt can be used to remove road ice.
- illustrate how salt is instrumental in making homemade ice cream (optional).

Introduction:

1. Divide your pupils into groups of two or three.
2. Assign a number to identify each group (e.g., group 1, group 2).
3. Have the groups write their identifying group number on their two cups with the marker.
4. Ask each group to mark one of the two cups with the letter "s."

Major Instructional Sequence:

1. Have each group fill its two cups with water. Instruct them to make the volumes as similar as possible. A graduated cylinder would be useful here.
2. Ask each group to dissolve two spoonfuls of salt into the cup marked "s".
3. Have the groups place both cups into the freezer.
4. Check on the cups every 30 – 60 minutes. It would be best to let the cups sit for several hours to observe any real differences between the cups. The groups can place thermometers into the cups during the first hour or two and observe that there is a slight temperature difference between the two cups.

Closure or Evaluation:

1. Ask your pupils to present their findings to the class.
2. Ask them *why* it took longer for the salt water to freeze.

Variation:

Fill two Styrofoam cups about two-thirds to three-fourths full of ice. Place a tablespoon of salt on the ice in one cup and mix. Have your pupils determine the melting point of the ice with a thermometer. They should find that the "salted" ice will melt more quickly because the salt (solute) lowers the freezing point of water. You could use this activity to indicate why salt or sand is used to remove road ice.

Note: This activity could lead to making homemade ice cream in the classroom. Ice cream salt (calcium chloride) is used to lower the freezing point of the ice mixture around the ice cream container.

Topic: RADIANT ENERGY

Grade Level: 3 – 6 **Activity Time:** 2 days

Materials Needed (per group):

1. Two identical tin cans w/o the top lid
2. Two identical thermometers
3. Black spray paint
4. Newspapers for painting
5. Aluminum foil
6. Graduated cylinder and water

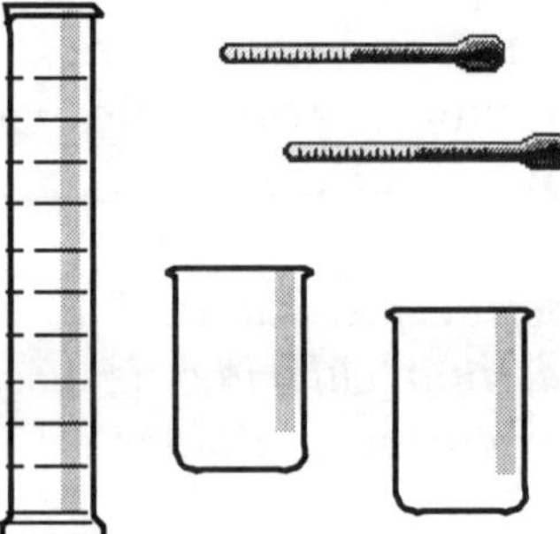

Objectives:

As a result of this activity, the learner will:

- explain how dark (black) surfaces absorb heat and shiny surfaces reflect heat.
- gather and graph data collected in an experiment.
- demonstrate competency in using scientific equipment.

Introduction:

1. Ask your pupils how color makes a difference in the absorption of heat. Ask them for specific examples. They will probably be able to relate to clothing and cars.
2. Ask them if the reflective nature of the material makes any difference in the absorption of heat. Tell them to defend their answers.
3. Indicate that they will be conducting an experiment to determine if their hypotheses are correct.

Major Instructional Sequence:

1. Divide your pupils into groups of three or four. Have each group prepare the two cans for the experiment.
2. Ask the groups to spread out some newspapers outside and paint one of the two cans entirely black on the outside. Let the can sit overnight in the classroom to dry.
3. Demonstrate for the class how to properly use the graduated cylinders and thermometers (if needed). Ask each group to demonstrate for you their competence in using the scientific equipment.
4. Ask each group to pour between 100 – 200 ml. of water into each can. The key factor here is uniformity. Each can must contain the same amount of water. A typical vegetable can has a volume of 400 – 500 ml.
5. Instruct the group to cover the open top with some aluminum foil. Ask one group member to punch a small opening directly in the middle of the foil with the sharpened end of a pencil. Have them place a thermometer through the hole of the can. Repeat the procedure for the other can.

6. Instruct each group to place their two cans in a place where sunlight will shine directly on the cans. A heating lamp or high-intensity lamp can be used in the classroom as an alternative to moving the cans outside.
7. Ask the groups to read the thermometers in both cans and record their results at ten-minute intervals. The amount of time you run the experiment depends on the amount of time you have available. The pupils will need a minimum of thirty minutes to gather enough data to use for graphing (50 – 60 minutes would be optimal).

Closure or Evaluation:

1. Instruct your groups to present their data. Have a pupil record the data on the board or overhead.
2. Ask the pupils to explain the differences between the thermometer temperatures in the two cans. Reinforce the concepts of absorption, reflectivity, and radiant energy.

Topic: MAKING A CARTESIAN DIVER

Grade Level: Grades 2 – 4 **Activity Time:** 1 day

Materials Needed: (per group)

1. Two-liter clear plastic soda bottle
2. Medicine dropper
3. Sink area (or plastic tub)
4. Black waterproof paint w/small brush

Objectives:

As a result of this activity, the learner will:

- demonstrate how water pressure affects density and buoyancy.

Introduction:

1. Take a medicine dropper and paint it completely black with waterproof paint. Remember to remove the rubber portion before painting. Replace rubber portion after dropper is dry.
2. Fill a two-liter bottle completely full of water.
3. Once the medicine dropper has dried, place it in the two-liter bottle full of water. Screw on the cap.
4. Present the bottle, complete with black medicine dropper, to your pupils.
5. Tell them that you have a magic bottle, and in the magic bottle is a dropper that rises when they have been good and falls when they have been bad, for example (you can use any line you wish: it rises or falls when pupils have been nice, polite, good, worked hard, etc.)
6. Walk around and place the bottle near various pupils. Remember to carefully squeeze the bottle when you want the dropper to sink. Try to avoid being seen squeezing the bottle.
7. Ask your pupils if this bottle is really magic. If any of them indicate it isn't magic, ask them to explain how the bottle works. They will probably indicate that you squeezed the bottle.

Major Instructional Sequence:

1. Explain to the class that the bottle contains a medicine dropper painted black so that they could not see what was occurring inside the dropper.
2. Take out another bottle (already prepared) with a clear medicine dropper.
3. Ask them to observe what happens in the medicine dropper when you squeeze on the bottle. They should see the air bubble in the dropper rising and falling when you squeeze and release pressure on the bottle.
4. Arrange your pupils into groups (3 – 4 people per group).
5. Give each group a bottle and a medicine dropper.
6. Tell them to fill the bottle with water to the very top. Make sure they

understand to let it slightly overflow so as to prevent air bubbles from accumulating. You will probably need a plastic tub or sink to keep spills to a minimum.

7. Instruct the pupils to squeeze a few ml. of water into the medicine dropper before dropping it (bulb end up) into the water.
8. Ask each of your pupils to squeeze the bottle and observe what they see happening. Call their attention to the level of water in the dropper while they are squeezing the bottle.
9. Instruct each group to discuss their findings and come to a consensus as to what is occurring.

Note: It might be best for you to have several bottles, complete with divers, already prepared if sink area is not available.

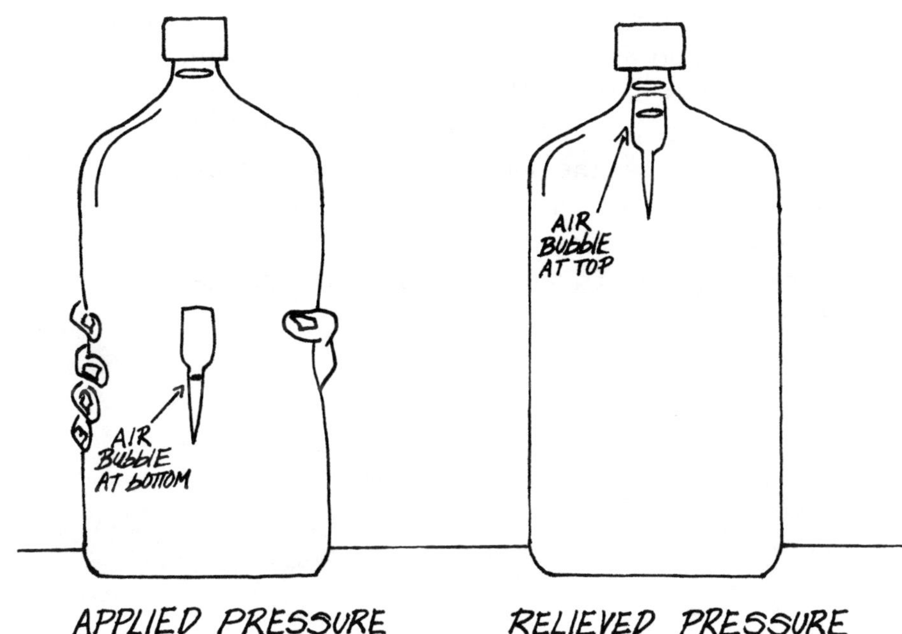

Closure or Evaluation:

1. Ask your pupils again what caused the diver to go up and down. They should indicate that the level of the water rises in the dropper as they squeeze on the bottle and the level sinks when they release pressure.
2. Remind them of the terms density and buoyancy. *Density* refers to the amount of mass per unit volume, and *buoyancy* refers to the "upthrust" of a fluid on an object. Materials with densities less than water float because the "upthrust" overcomes the weight of the material in the water (see the submarine activity on p. 9.25).
3. Make sure they understand that when you squeeze on the bottle, the pressure of the water causes the level of water to rise in the diver. This causes the weight (mass) to increase, subsequently increasing the density of the diver. Because it is more dense than water it will sink. The more water you place in the diver, the further it will sink. It is possible to have the diver "hover" in one position (i.e., the middle) for an extended time by simply applying the same amount of pressure. Practice makes perfect! When you release the pressure on the bottle, the air pressure becomes great enough to push the water back out of the diver. This causes the density to become less than water, allowing the diver to float back to the surface. If you have any problems with the device, simply unscrew and remove the top for a few seconds and then replace it tightly. This usually solves the problem!

Topic: CREATE YOUR OWN PH INDICATOR

Grade Level: 5 – 6 **Activity Time:** 1 – 2 days

Materials Needed (per group):

1. 5 ounces of cut-up red cabbage (fresh)
2. Knife and cutting board
3. Saucepan and sieve (strainer)
4. Hot plate and water
5. Various size jars (clean baby food jars work nicely)
6. Various materials to test (fruit juices, fruits, vinegar, baking soda, ammonia cleaner, etc.)
7. A commercially-made pH indicator (litmus paper, methyl orange, methyl red, or phenolphthalein (Most high school and college chemistry classes have these indicators available.)

Objectives:

As a result of this activity, the learner will:

- explain how indicators are used to determine if substances are acids or bases.
- explain the value of using indicators to determine the acidity or alkalinity of a substance.
- make his or her own indicator from red cabbage juice.
- test various substances to determine if they are acids or bases.

Introduction:

1. Explain to your pupils what acids and bases are (include pH).
2. Indicate that many substances with which they are familiar are acids or bases. Remind them that alkalis are bases.
3. Show your pupils some materials and ask them if they are acids or bases. Ask them to tell you why they think they are acids or bases.
4. Explain what indicators are and what they do.
5. Inform your pupils that they are going to make a natural indicator (optional) and test whether the substances (in No. 3) are acids or bases.

Major Instructional Sequence:

1. Place the pieces of red cabbage into a saucepan filled with approximately 100 – 200 ml. of water (distilled would be best but is not absolutely necessary).
2. Heat the mixture until it boils.
3. Drain off the liquid portion of the mixture into several clean jars (or test tubes if you have them).

Note: This portion of the activity is somewhat hazardous due to the cutting and boiling processes. You may wish to have the indicator already made and simply illustrate for the class how you made it. If you decide to let them make the indicator, then caution your pupils to be careful when cutting and boiling the cabbage.

4. Arrange your pupils into small groups of three or four.
5. Ask them to test each of the items you have provided for acidity or alkalinity.
6. Remind them that acids will turn the solution various shades of red and bases will turn the solution various shades of blue to green.

Note: Illustrate for them the proper procedure for mixing an unknown material with the indicator solution.

Closure or Evaluation:

1. Ask each group to report its findings to the class. Have a pupil record the data on the board or overhead.
2. Remind your pupils that there are commercially-made indicators that test certain pH ranges. Some examples might include: litmus paper, methyl orange, methyl red, and phenolphthalein.
3. Instruct your pupils to test the items with the commercially-made indicator you have provided and compare these results with the previous data.
4. Ask each group to tell how the indicators compared.

Topic: THE HOT-AIR BALLOON

Grade Level: 4 – 6 **Activity Time:** 1 day

Materials Needed:

1. One plastic "hangup" bag from the dry cleaners (per group)
2. Scotch™ tape
3. Spool of thread
4. Sterno™ and matches

Objectives:

As a result of this activity, the learner will:

- explain how hot air causes a balloon to rise.
- relate density and weight to buoyancy (see the submarine activity on p. 9.25).

Introduction:

1. Discuss with your pupils how hot air and cold air respond to each other in nature. Hot air rises and cold air sinks.
2. Explain to your pupils that hot air is less dense than cold. The accelerated movement of the heated air molecules results in fewer molecules occupying a given volume. This results in a reduced density (less mass per volume). Conversely, cooler air results in less movement and therefore has more molecules occupying a given volume.

Note: If you could film (with a camcorder) some hot-air balloons flying, it could help demonstrate the principles you are trying to teach (density and buoyancy).

Major Instructional Sequence:

1. Make sure there are no openings in the top of the plastic (dry cleaning) bag.
   If there are openings, seal them with a minimal amount of scotch tape. Do not make the bag too top-heavy.
2. Instruct your pupils to tape the ends of four pieces of thread (18 inches long) to the bag. Do not use a lot of tape (added weight).
3. Light the Sterno™ can and direct the pupils to stand around the can with the opening of the bag nearest the Sterno™. *Make sure they are cautious around the Sterno™. Keep the opening of the bag 12 – 18 inches above the Sterno™* You should hold the top of the bag while four of your pupils hold the threads, keeping the bottom of the bag opened wide.
4. As the bag fills with hot air, make sure the pupils are not holding the bag too tightly with the threads. Instruct them to release enough tension for the bag to start rising. Make sure they hold on to the threads so the bag doesn't tip over, spilling the hot air out.

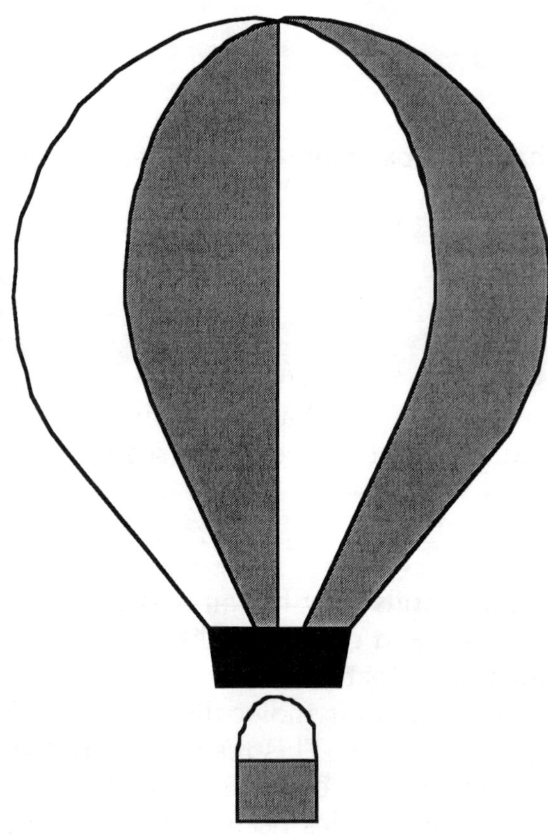

Closure or Evaluation:

1. After all groups have flown their balloons, place the metal lid of the Sterno™ can over the flame, extinguishing it. You should extinguish the Sterno™ can yourself.
2. Have the groups disassemble their balloons.
3. Once the pupils are back in their seats, ask them what they observed.
4. Ask them to explain the mechanism behind the balloon's flight. Remind them that the warmer air rose because it is less dense than the cooler air surrounding it.

Note: If you really feel industrious, you might try to attach the bottom of an aluminum tart pan (approximately 3 inches in diameter) to the bottom of the balloon. You will need to arrange it in the center of the opening using picture-hanging wire. This wire can be unraveled, leaving very thin but strong pieces of wire. Once you have rigged this apparatus, you can place a tablespoon-sized piece of Sterno in the tart pan (make sure you cut the sides down to approximately 0.5 inches) and light it. If you hold the sides of the plastic bag out (so it doesn't melt) you should be able to see it fly. You might want to do this outside with a string attached to the "balloon" to prevent it from sailing away.

Topic: THE CRUSHED CAN

Grade Level: K – 6 **Activity Time:** 1 day

Materials Needed:

1. Empty soft-drink can
2. Hot plate
3. Water bath (plastic tub filled with ice water)
4. Oven mitts or tongs

Objectives:

As a result of this activity, the learner will:

- explain how differences in air pressure can cause a structure to collapse.
- explain how this demonstration/activity relates to the real world.

Introduction:

1. Present your pupils with an empty soft-drink can.
2. Ask them to brainstorm ways they can cause the can to be crushed.
3. Have a pupil record these on the board or the overhead.
4. Once they have seemingly exhausted themselves of possibilities, ask them if air can crush the can.
5. Alert them that you are going to demonstrate how this can be done.

Major Instructional Sequence:

1. Place a few milliliters of water into the empty soft-drink can.
2. Turn on the hot plate. After a few minutes, place the soft-drink can on the hot plate.
3. Continue to heat the can until steam noticeably escapes from the open spout.
4. Using a pair of oven mitts or tongs (which can be borrowed from any high school chemistry teacher), pick up the can and invert it into the ice bath.
5. Ask your pupils to record what they observe.

Closure or Evaluation:

1. Ask the pupils to explain what they observed. It is important to try to guide them through the process. Make sure they understand that the number of air molecules present in the can is important. The heating of the water in the can will result in molecules of air and water moving faster and expanding the distance between neighboring molecules. The production of steam, as water molecules gain enough energy to escape into the atmosphere, results in a net loss of air molecules as well. Some of these molecules are pushed out of the opening of the can by the rising steam (convection current). When the can is placed in the ice bath, the

steam filling the inside of the can starts to condense, resulting in a lower pressure (fewer molecules pushing back). The outside pressure is greater than the inside pressure, resulting in a crushed can.

2. Ask them how this demonstration/activity might relate to things they have seen in the real world (submarines, air pumps, aerosol bottles, tires, etc.).

Note: You may want to conduct this activity in conjunction with the Power of Air, Submarine, or Hot Air Balloon activities.

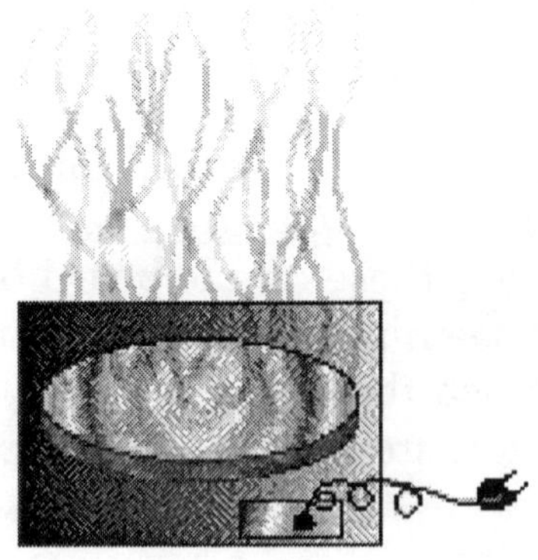

Topic: THE POWER OF AIR

Grade Level: 3 – 5 **Activity Time:** 1 day

Materials Needed:

1. Six or eight 4-gallon (15 L) garbage bags *or* two 30 gallon garbage bags
2. Two identical lightweight tables (about 30 " x 72")

Objectives:

As a result of this activity, the learner will:

- explain how compressed air can be used to make work easier.
- compare this activity to real-life situations involving air pressure.

Introduction:

1. Ask your pupils to explain why a balloon can be inflated. Reinforce the idea that the pressure in the balloon has to be greater than the pressure of the outside atmosphere around them.
2. Ask your pupils to name other things that can be inflated (e.g., bicycle and car tires, footballs).
3. Ask your pupils what these things have in common with a balloon.
4. Issue your pupils a challenge: "Can you lift a heavy table with only air?"

Major Instructional Sequence:

1. Ask for six to eight pupil volunteers (who are good at blowing up balloons). Give each of them a garbage bag.
2. Have each pupil open their garbage bag and then flatten it (remove the air) onto the table. Make sure that they spread out along the table.
3. Ask your pupil volunteers to grasp the opening of the garbage bags so that they will be able to blow air into the bag (same principle as blowing up the balloon).
4. Ask for pupil volunteers to help you lift one of the tables, turn it upside down, and place it onto the top of the other table. Make sure the table tops fit flush to one another. *Caution: Make sure that the fingers of the pupils holding the balloons are away from the edge of the table as the second table is placed on the first.*
5. Have four pupils ready to sturdy the top table by holding gently to the four table legs protruding into the air.
6. Instruct your pupil volunteers to blow into their bags.
7. The top table should rise.

Closure or Evaluation:

1. Ask the pupils to explain how the balloons can lift a table.
2. Invite your pupils to construct experiments/activities which could be used to illustrate the power of air. Older children (grades 3 – 5) could go to K – 2 classrooms to demonstrate the power of air to younger children.

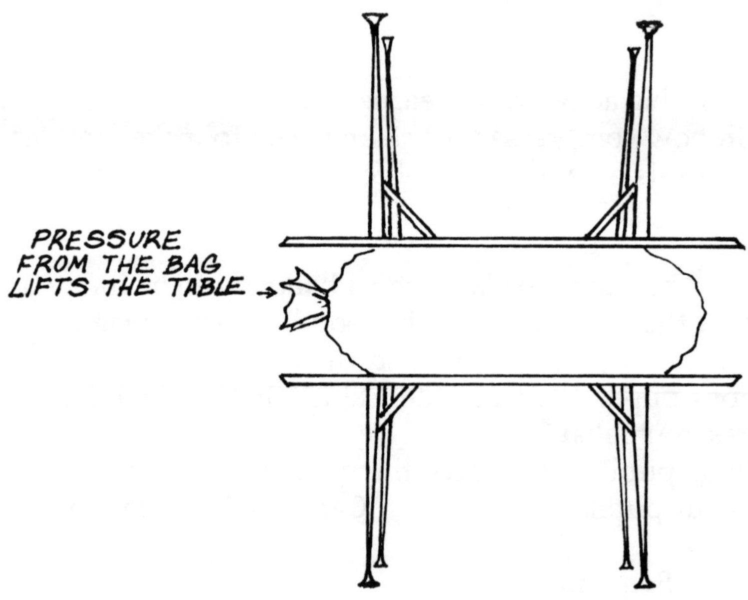
PRESSURE
FROM THE BAG
LIFTS THE TABLE

Topic: THE SUBMARINE

Grade Level: 3 – 6 **Activity Time:** 1 Day

Materials Needed (per group):

1. One 12 oz. plastic "mineral water" bottle
2. Two metal washers (approximately 1 inch in diameter)
3. Approximately 25 inches of plastic tubing (aquarium)
4. Modeling clay
5. Scotch tape
6. Scissors or sharp object (to punch holes in the water bottle)
7. One or two aquariums (in which to test the submarines)

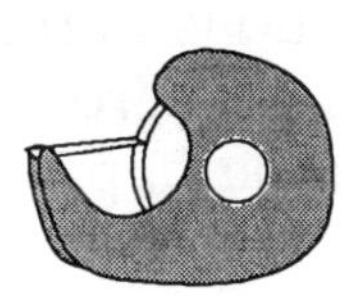
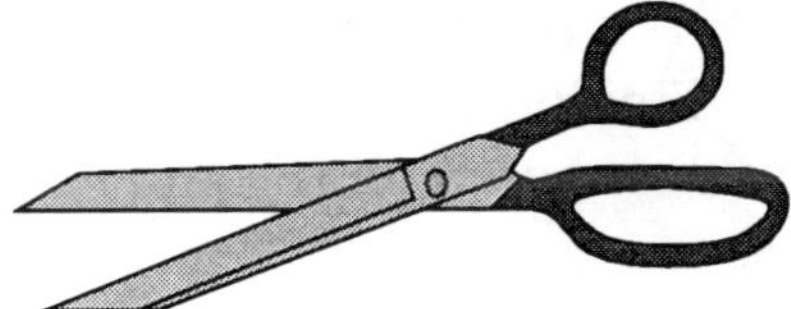

Objectives:

As a result of this activity, the learner will:

- explain how submarines are able to rise and sink in water.
- explain how density affects buoyancy.
- relate this activity to other situations involving density and buoyancy.

Introduction:

1. Start with a review/discussion of the terms, density and buoyancy. *Density* is the amount of mass a substance possesses in a particular volume. You need to be careful using the term "weight" instead of mass, because weight is based on "gravitational pull." In other words, if a pupil was placed on the moon, that pupil would weigh only a fraction of what they would weigh on Earth. Their mass did not change, only their weight. *Buoyancy* is more of an "upthrust" of a fluid on an object. The water pushes with a force equal to the "weight" of water displaced. Materials with densities less than that of water float because the "upthrust" can overcome the weight of the material in the water. Even though they are quite heavy, submarines float because they are full of air, which is less dense than water.

Major Instructional Sequence:

1. Divide your pupils into groups of three or four.
2. Have the pupils cut 25-inch long lengths of aquarium tubing.
   Note: Depending on the time available and the age of your pupils, you may want to precut the lengths for them.

3. Instruct one pupil from each group to punch four holes approximately 0.5 cm. in diameter and at least 2 – 3 cm. apart in the bottle (teacher should demonstrate).
4. Instruct your pupils to wrap three metal washers with tape around the center of the bottle.
5. Have your pupils insert approximately 8 cm. (3 inches) of the tubing into the bottle. Instruct them to seal the opening with the modeling clay.
6. Instruct each group to take turns testing their submarines. They should place the submarine on the water and record their observations. Once this has been completed, one of the pupils in each group should push the submarine down into the water (remind them to push the submarine down with the air holes pointing upward). Ask the pupils to record their observations. Finally, instruct one person from each group to blow hard into the tubing of their group's submarine. Ask the pupils to record their observations.
7. Have each group remove its submarine and clean up the area.

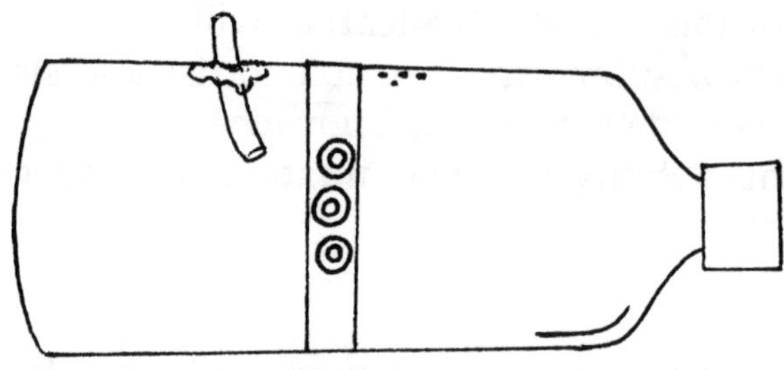

BOTTLE SUBMARINE

Closure or Evaluation:

1. Ask your pupils what they observed for each portion of the activity. Initially, they should have seen the submarine float on the surface. Next, they should have observed air bubbles escaping from the holes and water entering the submarine as it was pushed down into the water. Finally, they should have observed water being forced out as a pupil blew air into the submarine. This should have caused the submarine to rise to the surface.
2. Ask your pupils to tell you why the submarine floated initially. Encourage the use of the terms *density* and *buoyancy*.
3. Ask your pupils to tell you why water came in and air came out of the submarine when they pushed it down. The (more dense) water displaced the (less dense) air. This effect caused the submarine to be more dense and less buoyant.
4. Ask them to explain what happened when air was blown into the tubing. The air forced the water out (displacement) changing the density and weight of the submarine (making it less dense and more buoyant).
5. Ask your pupils to explain how submarines rise and sink in the water. Submarines use displacement to dive and to rise to the surface. Special tanks in the submarine can be alternately filled with air or water to alter the weight (and density) of the submarine.
6. Ask them to explain how density affects an object's buoyancy in water.
7. Relate this activity to other situations involving density and buoyancy (e.g., ships, canoes, people swimming in a pool, hot air balloons, Cartesian divers).

Topic: DETERMINING THE VOLUME AND WEIGHT OF A ROCK

Grade Level: 3 – 6 **Activity Time:** 1 – 2 days

Materials Needed (per group):
1. Rocks of various sizes
2. Coffee can
3. Large bowl or round baking pan
4. Spring balance for weighing
5. Graduated cylinder
6. String
7. Water

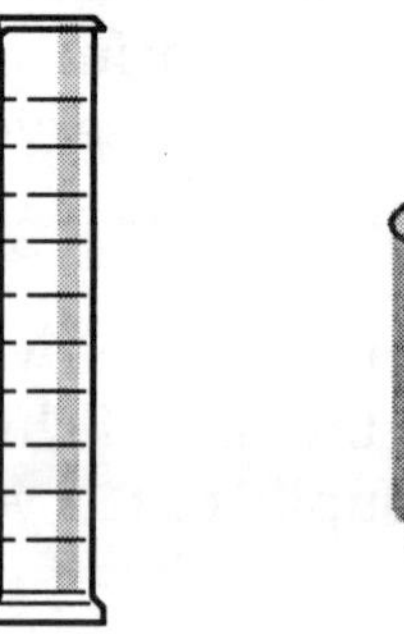

Objectives:

As a result of this activity, the learner will:
- discover the relationship between a physical body and the volume it displaces.
- describe why objects appear to feel lighter in water.
- graph the data collected and make appropriate inferences.

Introduction:
1. Tell your pupils the story of Archimedes, a Greek scientist who found a way to determine if the king's crown was made of solid gold.
2. Review for your pupils how Archimedes' principle works: When a body is placed in water, it will displace a volume of water equal to its own volume. The weight of the water displaced will also be equal to the apparent loss of weight in the object. (Bring up the concept of buoyancy here.)
3. Tell your pupils that they are going to conduct an experiment to determine if Archimedes' principle is true. It will be important to tell your pupils that one milliliter of water weighs approximately one gram. If their rock displaces 80 ml. of water, then the volume of the rock is 80 cubic centimeters or milliliters. If the rock weighs 125 grams on the spring balance before plunging in the water, it should weigh approximately 45 grams after placing it in the water.

Major Instructional Sequence:
1. Divide your class into groups of three or four pupils.
2. Have pupils place the coffee can in the bowl and fill it up to near the edge with water.
3. Instruct each group to tie a piece of the string to each rock.
4. Tell the groups to attach the end of the string to a spring balance and record the weight.

5. Instruct each group to gradually lower the rock into the water and record what happens. They should observe water being displaced by the rock. (Make sure they don't let go of the string.)
6. Ask the pupils to record the weight on the balance. They should notice that it has become lower.
7. Instruct them to record the weight and remove the rock.
8. Have one pupil in the group determine the amount of water displaced by pouring the water (in the bowl) into a graduated cylinder.
9. Ask them to pour the water back into the coffee can and repeat the experiment with a new rock (of different size and shape).

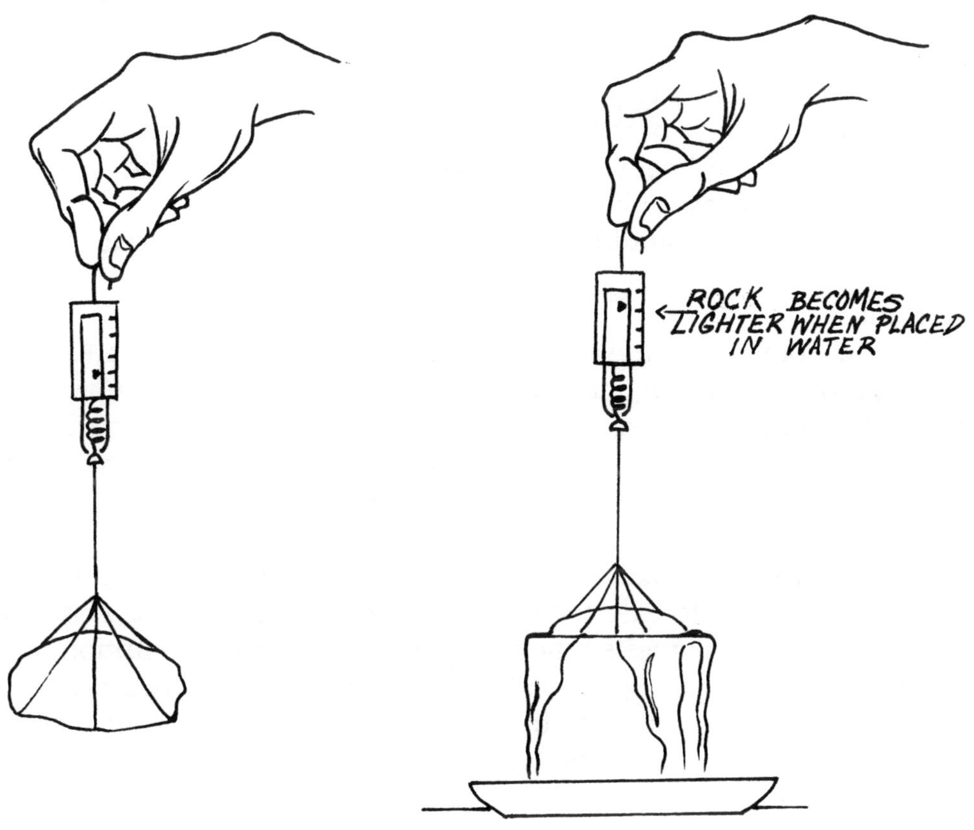
ROCK BECOMES
LIGHTER WHEN PLACED
IN WATER

Closure or Evaluation:

1. Ask the pupils to present their results (data) to the class. Have a pupil record the data on the board or overhead.
2. Instruct your pupils to graph their results.
3. Ask several pupils to review what the class found in their experiment.

Topic: HYPOTHESIS AND VALIDITY TESTING

Grade Level: 4 – 6 **Activity Time:** 2 – 3 days

Materials Needed:

1. Five coffee cups composed of various materials: ceramic, glass, metal, plastic and stoneware
2. Five Teflon-coated, mercury-filled thermometers (-10 to 150 degree Celsius range)
3. Tea kettle and hot plate
4. Stopwatch or digital timepiece
5. Graduated cylinder (100 ml. minimum)

Objectives:

As a result of this activity, the learner will:

- learn what an hypothesis is, and how to develop one.
- create an experiment designed to prove or disprove the hypothesis.
- learn the process of disciplined data gathering.
- test the validity of an hypothesis, using the data gathered.

Introduction:

1. Show your pupils the five different types of coffee cups and ask them what each of the cups are made of.
2. Ask the class to predict which of the cups they believe would retain heat for the longest and shortest periods of time. Do they think it makes any difference what the cup is made of? Ask them to explain/clarify their answers.
3. Your pupils will likely come to the conclusion that they do not have any facts on which to base their assumptions. Explain to the class that they are making an hypothesis when they make such an assumption, and tell them that they are going to learn how to test their hypotheses.
4. Arrange your pupils into five groups, and ask each group to come up with an hypothesis concerning which types of materials will retain the heat the longest. Ask them which types of materials will cool down fastest.
5. Ask the groups to come up with a way to test their hypotheses. Be sure to emphasize to them the need to run multiple tests on each cup. This is to ensure that the tests have a measure of validity.

Major Instructional Sequence:

1. Once your class has determined the parameters for the experiment, assign each group a portion of the experiment to perform (each group being assigned one type of cup to test).
2. Instruct the groups to fill their cups with 200 ml. of hot water from the kettle on the hot plate (keep the water at boiling point).

3. Instruct each group to place a thermometer into its cup and take an initial reading (within 30 seconds).
4. Instruct the groups to keep up with their times and record their temperatures at five-minute intervals (see sample activity sheet). The times can be modified if desired. Readings could be taken every two minutes and for less than 30 minutes, if you wish.
5. Once each group has completed its temperature readings, ask the pupils to determine their TC, or total (temperature) change.
6. Instruct them to run the test a second time to determine validity.
7. Ask them to calculate the average TC.

Note: With additional groups, cups, and thermometers you can collect more data in a given time. If you teach multiple science classes, you can have each class conduct the same experiment. This will provide your pupils with additional data to analyze.

Closure or Evaluation:

1. Ask the pupils to present their group's data. Have a pupil record the data for each cup on the board.
2. Ask your pupils which cup(s) was/were best. Be sure to ask them to defend (explain) their answers.
3. Ask your pupils to relate this experiment to real life. You might want to show them some copies of *Consumer Reports*. Explain to them how consumer groups test numerous products to determine which are the best value (most efficient, most effective).

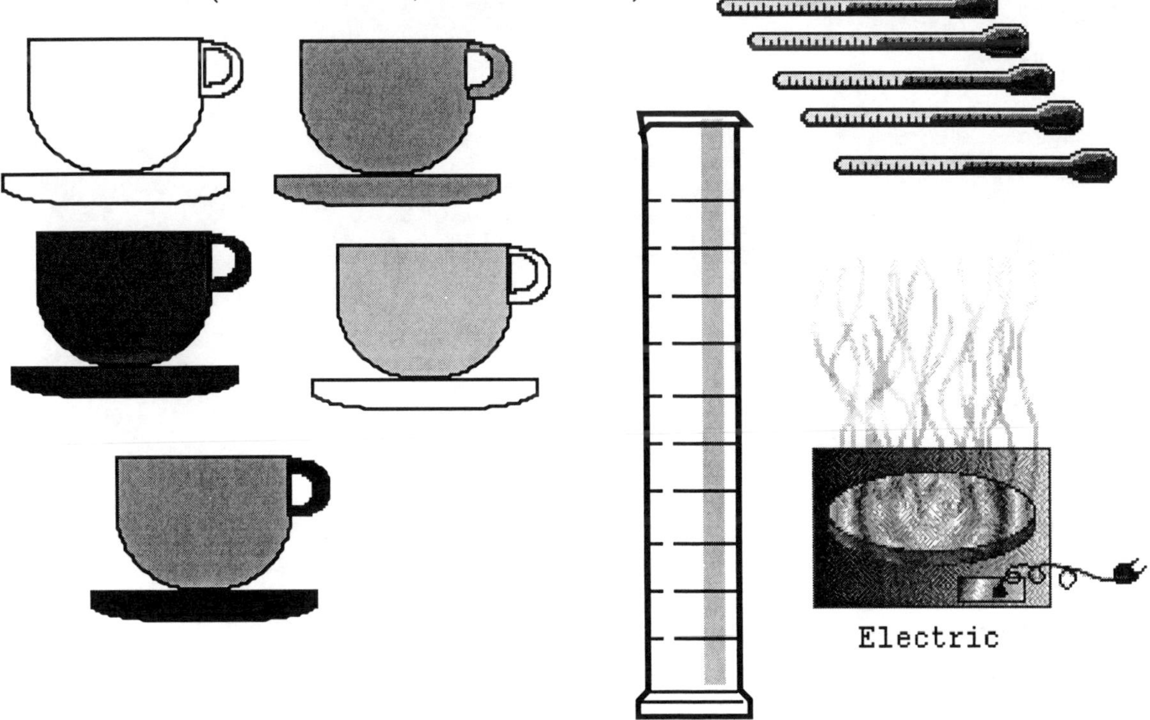

Figure 9.1
HEAT RETENTION DATA SHEET

MATERIAL TYPE	TIME 0	5	10	15	20	25	30	TC	AVG
Ceramic #1									
Ceramic #2									
Ceramic #3									
Ceramic #4									
Glass #1									
Glass #2									
Glass #3									
Glass #4									
Metal #1									
Metal #2									
Metal #3									
Metal #4									
Plastic #1									
Plastic #2									
Plastic #3									
Plastic #4									
Stoneware #1									
Stoneware #2									
Stoneware #3									
Stoneware #4									

Figure 9.2
HEAT RETENTION DATA SHEET (SAMPLE)

MATERIAL TYPE	TIME 0	5	10	15	20	25	30	TC	AVG
Ceramic #1	73	66	60	56	52	48	46	27	
Ceramic #2	70	66	59	55	52	48	46	24	
Ceramic #3	80	73	65	59	55	51	49	31	
Ceramic #4	73	67	61	57	53	49	47	26	27.00
Glass #1	78	71	63	59	55	51	48	30	
Glass #2	74	62	56	52	49	46	43	31	
Glass #3	71	64	58	54	49	47	44	27	
Glass #4	70	65	59	55	51	47	44	26	28.50
Metal #1	78	69	61	56	51	48	46	32	
Metal #2	76	63	56	52	49	46	43	33	
Metal #3	74	64	58	53	50	47	44	30	
Metal #4	78	71	63	57	52	49	46	32	31.75
Plastic #1	87	76	68	63	59	56	53	34	
Plastic #2	73	67	63	59	55	52	48	25	
Plastic #3	90	81	72	66	61	57	55	35	
Plastic #4	78	72	66	62	56	53	50	28	30.50
Stoneware #1	74	71	65	62	59	56	54	20	
Stoneware #2	70	66	62	59	56	53	50	20	
Stoneware #3	76	71	64	61	58	54	50	26	
Stoneware #4	74	69	64	61	58	54	48	26	23.00

Topic: MEASURING AIR

Grade Level: K – 3 **Activity Time:** 1 day

Materials Needed:
1. Balloons
2. Yardstick/meter stick
3. Thread and scissors
4. Needle or pin

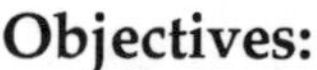

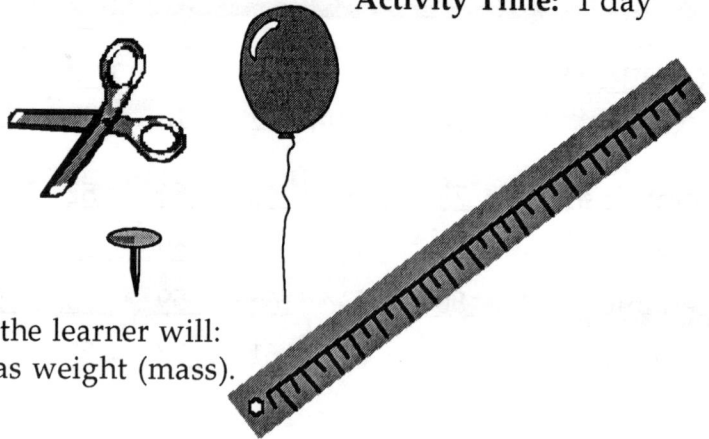

Objectives:

As a result of this activity, the learner will:
- demonstrate that air has weight (mass).

Introduction:
1. Review the concept that all matter has *mass*. Recalling the phrase, "Lighter than air," ask the class, "Does air have weight?"
2. Ask your pupils if they can design an experiment to determine if air has weight. Encourage them to use a balance scale to determine the weight.

Major Instructional Sequence (Demonstration):
1. Ask two pupils to blow up some balloons for you. Ask your pupils what they are putting into the balloons (air).
2. Before you tie off the balloons, make sure they are approximately the same size.
3. Tie a piece of thread (approximately 15 – 20 cm. long) to the center of your yardstick (or meter stick).
4. Tie the end of another piece of thread (approximately 10 – 12 cm. long) to one of the balloons. Repeat the process with the other balloon.
5. Tie the balloons to opposite ends of the yardstick/meter stick.
6. Adjust the balloons by moving the threads left or right until balance is achieved. You should be able to hold the stick from the central thread and have both balloons balanced (at the same level). You may wish to hang the balance from the ceiling. If so, use a longer piece of thread for the central piece (see No. 3 above).
7. Ask your pupils why the two balloons are balanced. (They have approximately the same weight.)
8. If you do not elect to hang the stick from the ceiling, instruct a pupil to hold the central point for you. You may wish to have the pupil stand on a desk or chair to elevate the balloons.

9. Ask the pupils what would happen to the balance if you popped one of the balloons.
10. Once you have obtained some answers (predictions), pop one of the balloons.

Closure or Evaluation:

1. Ask your pupils to discuss what they observed.
2. Ask the question again, "Does air have weight?"

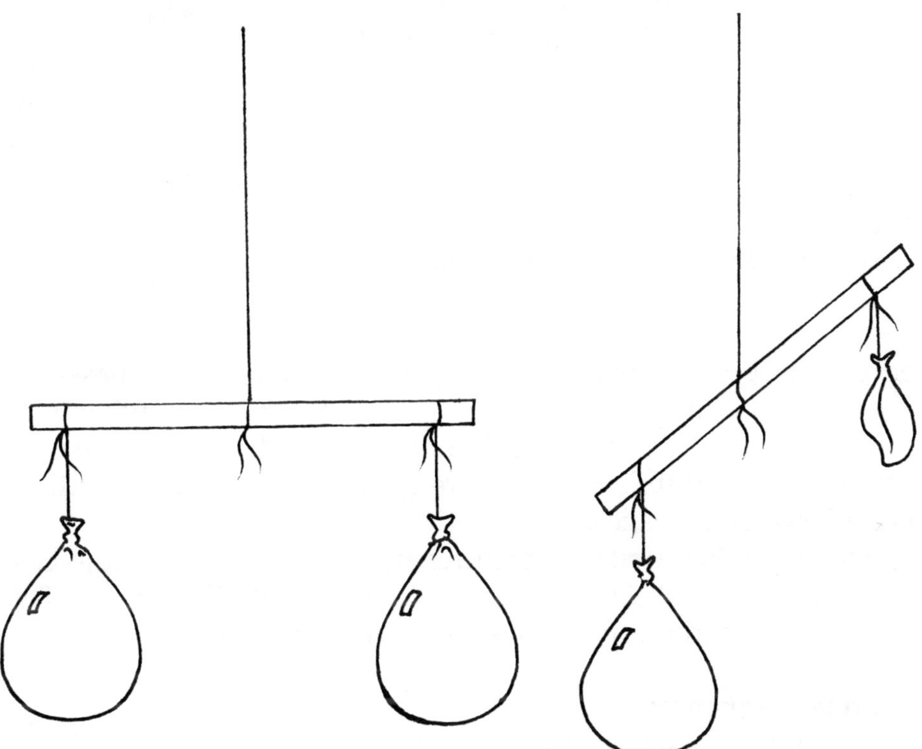

Topic: MAKING INVISIBLE INK

Grade Level: 1 – 3 **Activity Time:** 1 – 2 days

Materials Needed (per group):

1. Fresh lemon or lemon juice (grapefruit will also work)
2. Tiny (medicine) cups
3. Copy paper (unlined)
4. Fine-tip paint brushes (or cotton swabs)
5. Heat source (e.g., a light bulb, iron, candle)

Objectives:

As a result of this activity, the learner will:

- demonstrate that a chemical reaction occurs when certain fruit juices are heated.
- investigate which liquids work best as invisible ink.

Introduction:

1. Tell your pupils you will teach them how to send secret messages. These messages are sent using special inks that only show up when certain conditions are met. These conditions are called chemical reactions.
2. Indicate to your pupils that they are going to use some everyday materials to create secret messages.
3. The messages they write (or pictures they draw) using fruit juice can be seen when you heat the juice that has soaked into the paper. The fruit juice contains carbon, which darkens when heated.

Major Instructional Sequence:

1. Divide your pupils into pairs.
2. Instruct each pair to pour some lemon or grapefruit juice into a cup. They won't need much!
3. Have each pair take a brush (or cotton swab) and write a message or draw a picture on the blank copy paper. Each pupil should create his or her own message or picture.
4. Make sure each pair understands that their papers must dry. The drying process should take 3 – 5 minutes.
5. Instruct each pair to heat their messages or pictures near a 60 – 100 watt light bulb. Irons and candles work well, too, but are more dangerous. You might consider using older pupils or parent volunteers when heating the paper. The messages or pictures will develop slowly, over several minutes.

Closure or Evaluation:

1. Once each individual's message or picture has become recognizable, ask the partners to exchange their papers for interpretation.
2. Have each pair of pupils share with the class the secret messages and pictures that were revealed.
3. Review with your pupils the procedure for making the invisible ink messages.

Note: This would be a good activity for pupils to repeat at home with their parents.

Variation:

1. Pupils could try this activity with other types of liquids, such as milk, ginger ale, and the like. This would be a good way for pupils to find which liquids work and which do not.
2. Pupils (with adult help) might experiment with different types of heating sources to see if there are significant differences in "developing" time.

Magic Ink

Topic: BONES AND MINERALS

Grade Level: K – 4 **Activity Time:** 1 week

Materials Needed (per group):

1. Clean (empty) jelly jars w/ lids
2. Very clean raw chicken bones (legs work best)
3. Vinegar (clear, 5% acidity)
4. Water source

Objectives:

As a result of this activity, the learner will:

- explain that bones contain minerals, such as calcium, that make them strong (hard).
- explain that when minerals are removed from the bone, the bone gets softer.
- relate this activity to the need for minerals in the human diet (e.g., as from drinking milk).

Note: Before you do this activity with your pupils, you need to make sure that the chicken bones have had the meat on them removed as completely as possible and are absolutely clean.

Introduction:

1. Ask your pupils if they have any minerals in their bodies. Encourage them to tell you why they do and what job the minerals do.
2. Ask them to tell you what will happen if you don't drink milk or eat cheese, yogurt or other dairy products, or eat certain foods that contain minerals.
3. Explain that the following activity will demonstrate that minerals are present in bone.

Major Instructional Sequence:

1. Divide your pupils into groups of four.
2. Have the groups examine the "clean" chicken bones.
3. Instruct each group to place one chicken bone into the jar and fill the jar with vinegar. There should be enough vinegar in the jar to completely cover the chicken bone.

Note: Make sure your pupils wash their hands thoroughly with soap and water after touching the raw chicken bones because of potential Salmonella contamination.

4. The next day, ask the groups to take out their chicken bones and examine them. (Make sure they check the flexibility of the bone.) Have them record what they observe and replace the bone into the vinegar.
5. Instruct them to take out the bone after a week has passed and observe (and record) what they see. Make sure they again check the flexibility of the bone.

Closure or Evaluation:

1. Ask your groups to comment on what they observed from the experiment.
2. Explain to your pupils that the bones in their bodies start out rubbery like the chicken bone (after the vinegar took out most of the calcium) and become harder as the process of calcification increases with age.

Variation:

Ask your pupils to develop a way to determine if temperature has any effect on the speed of the reaction (the effect of the acid on the calcium in the bone). You could heat some vinegar or place the vinegar in an area that would be warm. You could place some other jars of vinegar in a cooler, or refrigerator, and determine which works faster over time.

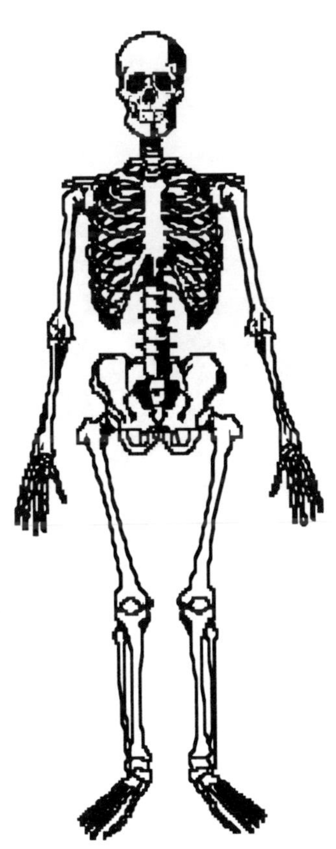

CHAPTER TEN
Physical Properties

Perhaps you have wondered what happens when you turn on a flashlight. How does the electricity in the battery become a beam of light? Why is it easier to pull something in a cart with wheels than to pull it across the ground? What makes an airplane fly? What makes wood float but a brick sink? Physics is the science which holds the answers to questions such as these. Physicists find out how things work by studying and experimenting with matter and energy.

Physics began in ancient Greece, where philosophers attempted to understand the physical world. Later scientists, notably Galileo, invented the scientific method wherein the researcher develops an hypothesis and tests it. The ultimate test of the validity of a scientific hypothesis, however, depends on its consistency with the totality of other aspects of the scientific framework and not just a single test. The scientific community as a whole judges the work of its members by the objectivity and rigor with which their work has been conducted. In this way, the scientific method prevails.

Today, much of physics deals with the behavior of matter (matter is anything that has mass and occupies space). Physics seeks to discover the laws of the universe which govern the behavior of matter and energy.

Topic: SOUND VIBRATIONS

Grade Level: K – 4 **Activity Time:** 1 day

Materials Needed (per group):

1. One metal pie pan (6 – 12 inch diameter) (Hard pans work better than disposable aluminum pie pans.)
2. Salt, sand or rice
3. One metal teaspoon
4. One magnifying glass
5. Fish, frogs, toads, lizards, etc. (in an aquarium)

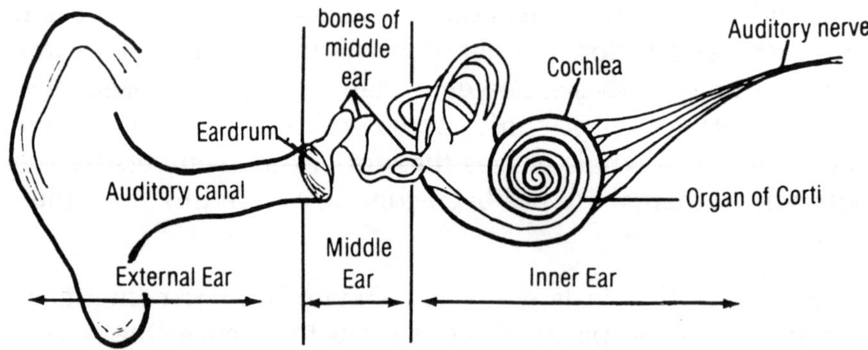

Objectives:

As a result of this activity, the learner will:

- explain how some animals that do not appear to have external ears, like an alligator, lizard, or toad, can hear.

Introduction:

1. Point out to your pupils that some animals don't appear to have ears. Ask them if they can name any animals that don't appear to have ears (alligators, lizards, frogs, toads, etc.).
2. Explain that these animals don't have *external* ears. Point to several pupils' ears to illustrate what external ears are.
3. Ask them if animals can have ears even though they don't appear to have them. Depending on the developmental stage of your pupils, point out the components of the human ear, particularly the fact that the mechanism of the ear that actually "hears" is inside the skull. Explain that humans have eardrums, or *tympanic membranes,* which are connected to small bones inside the skull. When the ear drum moves from "sound vibrations" hitting it, it causes movement in the adjacent three bones. Each bone amplifies the effect, making the next bone vibrate more. The vibrations of the last bone shake up the fluid contained in a snail-like structure called the *cochlea.* Tiny hair bristles are contained

here. When the fluid vibrates, it causes some of the hairs to respond accordingly. These hairs are connected to tiny *neurons* (nerve cells) which send the message to particular centers of the brain, where the message is received as a "sound." Although the ears of animals may differ physiologically, the same basic concept applies. Even animals that do not appear to have ears can hear sounds through the vibrations picked up by the bones (sound induction).

Major Instructional Sequence:

1. Divide your pupils into groups of three to four.
2. Ask each group to obtain a metal pan and a metal teaspoon.
3. Instruct them to obtain one teaspoon full of salt, sand or rice.
4. Tell each group to place the pie pan upside down.
5. Have your pupils spread the material around the upside-down pie pan. Make sure they spread it out thinly, so they can see individual grains.
6. Ask one pupil in each group to periodically tap the pie pan. Instruct the other members of the group to watch what happens to the individual grains. Ask them to record their results. Encourage them to watch the grains under a magnifying glass, which will amplify the effect.
7. Ask your pupils to take turns putting their heads down on a table (metal works best), being sure to rest one ear directly on the table, while a pupil carefully taps the table with the metal spoon. Once a pupil has heard the sound, ask him or her to raise his or her head and listen to the same tapping. Ask the pupils in each group to discuss what they observed and record it.

Closure or Evaluation:

1. Ask some of the groups to report their findings to the class. (The vibrations from the tapping caused the grains to move.)
2. Ask your pupils how this same process might allow an animal to hear. (The vibrations could travel through bones to an internal ear.)
3. Ask your pupils to compare their findings regarding the sounds they heard with their ears on the table and with their ears removed from the table. They should have heard a more distinct sound when their ears were on the table. Indicate that the bones can amplify a sound, just like the metal in the table.

Note: You could demonstrate that animals not possessing external ears can hear by using a frog, toad, or lizard in an aquarium. Simply tap a spoon carefully behind the organism and observe its response. If the children cannot see or if the collective sound of 25 – 30 children is disturbing the animal, you might want to videotape your demonstration using only one pupil, and play it back for your class(es). Fish swimming in an aquarium can also be used to demonstrate how animals respond to vibrations.

Topic: THE STRAW TOWER CHALLENGE

Grade Level: 4 – 6 **Activity Time:** 1 day

Materials Needed (per group):

1. Twenty-five straws (.635 cm. diameter)
2. Scotch™ tape
3. Measuring tape and timer
4. Pictures or samples of structures noted for their strength

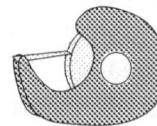

Objectives:

As a result of this activity, the learner will:

- explain how certain geometric shapes, particularly the triangle, are important in support strength.
- hypothesize and experiment with different tower constructions.

Introduction:

1. Show the class some pictures of buildings and bridges. You could also show them various examples of boxes.
2. Ask them what makes the building, bridge, or box so strong.

Major Instructional Sequence:

1. Organize your pupils into small groups of three to five.
2. Have each group obtain the materials needed for this activity from a prearranged central location.
3. Explain to your pupils that they will have thirty minutes to build the tallest tower they can from the straws and tape provided.
4. Remind them that they cannot tape the straws to the table (or floor), nor can they tape the tower to or from the ceiling. The tower must stand on its own!

Note: You can adjust the amount of time or the number of straws used to construct the tower. The main idea is that every group is on the "same playing field." Although it is best for all groups to start at the same height (table or floor), you can easily adjust to varied elevations with the "official tape measure."

Closure or Evaluation:

1. Ask your pupils to explain what they observed when constructing their towers. What problems did they encounter? How did they overcome these problems?
2. Review what they learned about the various strengths of geometric shapes (particularly the triangle).

Variation:

Pupils could experiment with alternative designs that could be used to support a given weight. The weight could be anything from a standard size (and weight) book to a standard size (and weight) board. The straw tower could also become a straw bridge, with a few modifications. Encourage pupils to stick a portion of each straw into the adjoining straw for added strength. Another option is to utilize an alternative material to Scotch™ tape, such as paper clips.

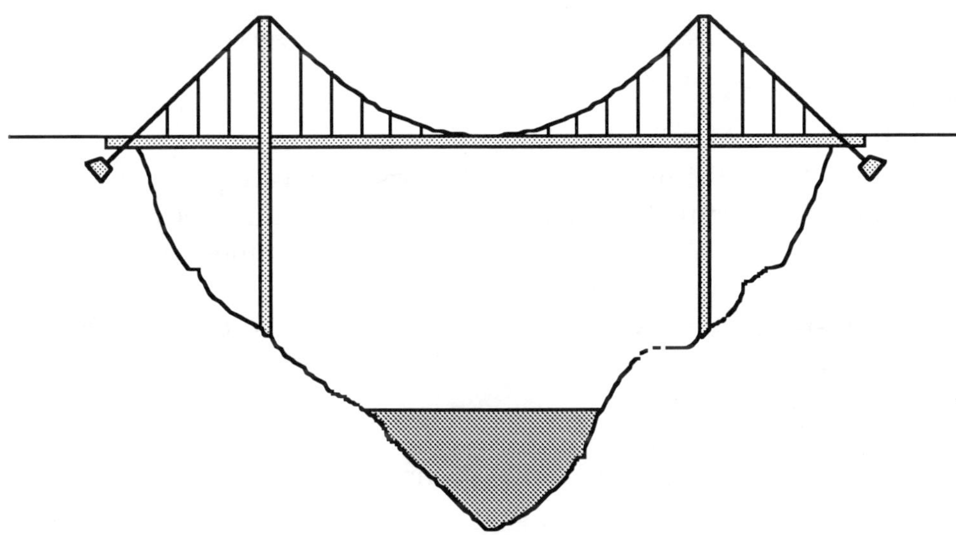

Topic: WHY DO WE HAVE TWO EARS?

Grade Level: 2 – 6 **Activity Time:** 1 day

Materials Needed (per group):

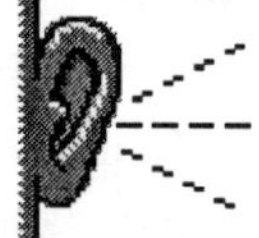

1. Scarf (for blindfold)
2. Plastic toy clacker or two marbles
3. Cardboard tube (from paper towel roll or toilet paper roll)
4. Worksheet

Objectives:

As a result of this activity, the learner will:

- explain why humans need two ears for detecting the source of sounds.
- relate this activity to how other animals detect sounds.

Introduction:

1. Ask your pupils why they have two ears.
2. Point out that the brain needs both ears for locating sound. Sounds closer to one ear reach that ear a split second sooner than they do the other ear. The brain receives this information and determines the direction from which the sound is coming.
3. Demonstrate (with two pupil volunteers) how to conduct the sound experiment.

Major Instructional Sequence:

1. Divide your pupils into groups of three.
2. Instruct one pupil in each group to blindfold one of their partners.
3. Have one pupil click the clacker or marbles at various points around the blindfolded subject. Make sure they produce sounds directly over the subject's head, directly in front of subject, directly behind subject, and to either side. Tell them to mix the sequence up and even repeat some of the positions. After each sound occurs, the subject should attempt to indicate from which direction the sound came.
4. Instruct the third pupil in the group to record the results.
5. Have the subject place the cardboard tube next to one ear (his or her choice).
   Conduct the experiment again and tell the groups to note any differences in data.
6. Ask your pupils to repeat steps 2 – 4, switching roles with the other two pupils. Everyone should have a turn being the subject, the experimenter, and the recorder.

Note: This activity should probably be conducted outside, in the lunchroom, or in an auditorium so the sounds of all the groups don't become intermingled. If this is not possible, you might want to simply conduct a class demonstration.

Closure or Evaluation:

1. Ask each group to present its data. Record the data on the board.
2. Ask some of your pupils to explain why the sounds were easy to determine (locate) on either side of the head but hard to locate in front, behind, or above the head. Split-second difference and an increase in volume on one side make the sounds easy to locate. The other sounds are more difficult to determine (locate) because the sounds reach both ears at the same time.
3. Ask them to explain why the cardboard tube interfered with their results. (The cardboard tube increased the distance the sound had to travel to that ear.)
4. Have a pupil summarize how the ears determine (locate) sound.
5. Point out how animals use their ears to locate potential predators or prey.

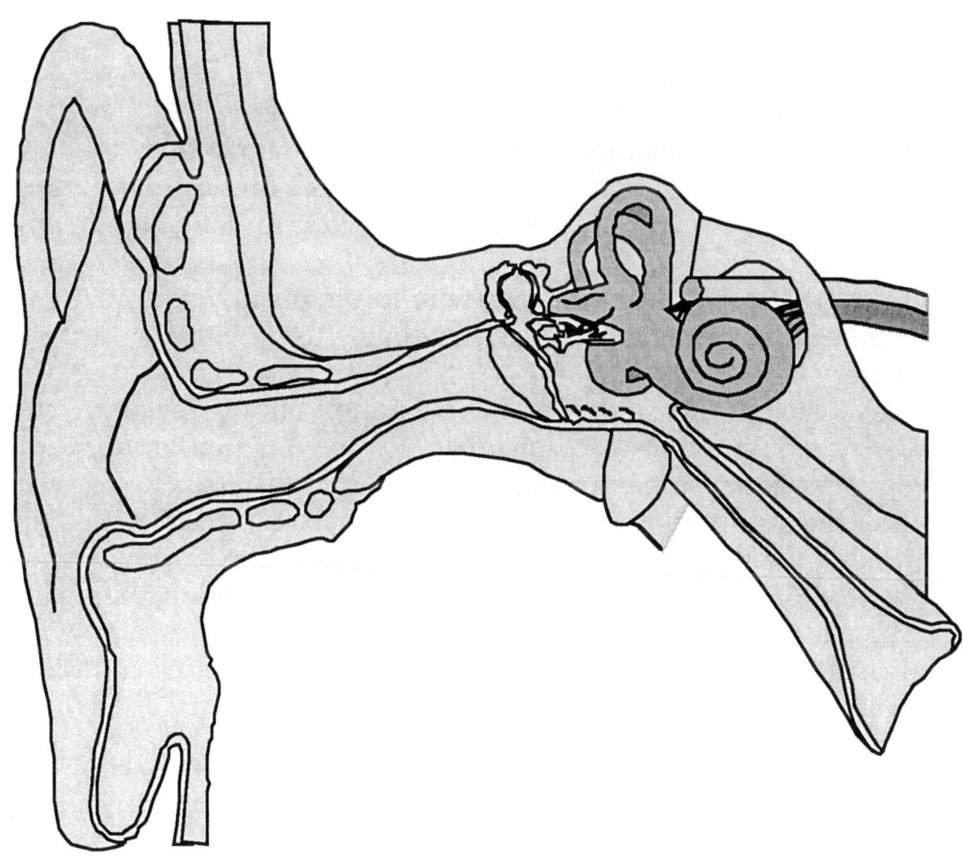

Topic: THE ELECTROMAGNET

Grade Level: 2 – 6 **Activity Time:** 1 – 2 days

Materials Needed (per group):

1. Several batteries (1.5 – 9 volts)
2. Bell wire
3. Long nail (over three inches long)
4. Paper clips

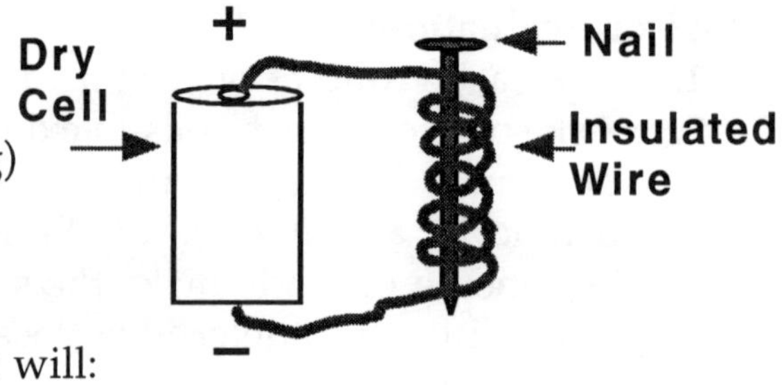

Objectives:

As a result of this activity, the learner will:

- explain what factors might influence the strength of an electromagnet.
- explain how an electromagnet works.

Introduction:

1. Ask your pupils if they know how an electromagnet works. The answer will probably be negative!
2. Tell them that they will be involved in a series of activities that will help them understand the principle.

Major Instructional Sequence:

1. Separate the pupils into groups of three or four.
2. Have one group member wrap the bell wire about 18 – 20 times around the nail, covering approximately two-thirds of it. Younger pupils may need some help with this. It might be better to demonstrate how to coil the nail.
3. Instruct a pupil to connect one wire to the positive terminal and one to the negative terminal of the battery being used. Start with the smallest battery (1.5 volts).
4. Have each group determine the maximum number of paper clips that can be picked up by the electromagnet. Repeat this step for each additional battery. Make sure your pupils record their results.
5. Ask the group to unwrap their nails and rewrap them with a piece of wire double the length of the original bell wire. Make sure they wrap the nail tightly (36 – 40 times). They still need to have approximately one-third of the nail bare.
6. Instruct them to repeat step 3, using different batteries and recording the results.

Closure or Evaluation:

1. Ask each group to present its data to the class. Have a pupil record the data on the board or overhead. This is another golden opportunity for graphing. Discuss conclusions which might be made from the data.

Topic: MAKING A CIRCUIT

Grade Level: 5 – 6 **Activity Time:** 1 – 2 days

Materials Needed (per group):

1. One D-cell battery
2. One bulb (1.25 or 1.50 volt)
3. Two pieces of copper or aluminum wire (each approximately 20 cm. long)
4. Reference materials or pictures of circuits

Objectives:

As a result of this activity, the learner will:

- assemble a circuit that functions to light a small bulb.
- explain the set-up of the circuit.
- draw a diagram of the circuit (optional).

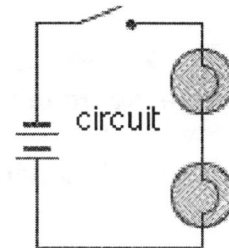

Introduction:

1. Introduce your pupils to batteries, bulbs and wires.
2. Define *circuit* for the class (a pathway for electric current to flow out from an energy source and back again).
3. Indicate the basic explanation for how circuits function.

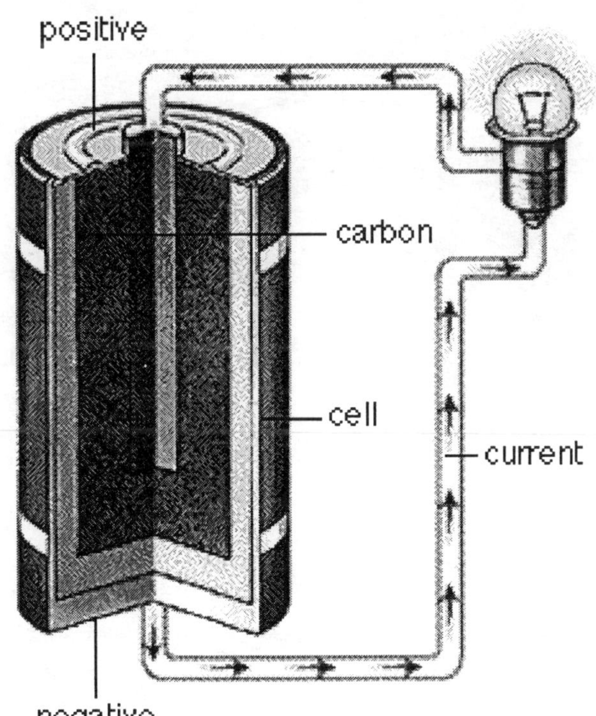

Major Instructional Sequence:

1. Separate pupils into groups of three or four.
2. Provide each group with the materials needed.
3. Instruct each group to experiment with their materials and construct a functional circuit. Remind them to look at reference books and pictures (illustrations) provided. Circulate among the groups, checking for understanding and providing assistance as needed. Caution them not to stick their wires into any outlets in the room.
4. Ask pupils to draw diagrams illustrating their circuits.

Note: You may wish to provide the pupils with additional bulbs and wire to see if they can figure out a two-bulb circuit.

Closure or Evaluation:

1. Ask each group to share its results with the class, including ideas that did not work. Ask the group or the class to determine why these designs did not work. Indicate to your pupils that scientists learn valuable information from designs that do not work, just as the class did.

Topic: INCLINED PLANES

Grade Level: 4-6

Activity Time: 1 or 2 days

Materials Needed (per group):

1. One flat piece of plywood or wooden board
2. One 20-cm. length of 2″ x 4″ board
3. One matchbox car
4. One stopwatch or watch with digital timer
5. Meter stick
6. Masking tape
7. Data Table (see Table 10.1)

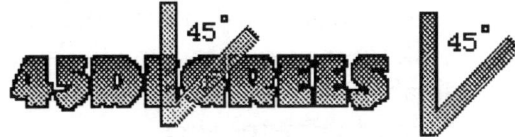

Objectives:

As a result of this activity, the learner will:

- explain the meaning of mechanical advantage.
- illustrate how to measure the mechanical advantage of an inclined plane.
- discover how the mechanical advantage of an inclined plane affects the acceleration of an object moving down the incline under the influence of gravity.
- explain how the weight of the object moving down the incline does not influence its acceleration.

Introduction:

1. Introduce the topic of simple machines to your pupils. Explain that when an object rests on an inclined plane, only a fraction of its weight is directed down the incline and that fraction is related to the mechanical advantage of the inclined plane. When the fraction is small the mechanical advantage is said to be large, since only a small fraction of the object's weight must be balanced to move the object up the incline. Tell pupils that the mechanical advantage of an inclined plane may be determined by dividing the elevation of its high end by its length.
2. Explain that, when friction is small, falling objects and objects moving down an inclined plane will accelerate because of the force of gravity. Tell pupils that the distance that the object travels in a given period of time is a measure of its acceleration. Objects with large accelerations will cover a larger distance than those with smaller accelerations. The distance an object travels down the incline starting from rest is also a measure of the mechanical advantage of the incline. The larger the distance, the larger the fraction of the weight is directed down the incline and the smaller the mechanical advantage of the incline.

Major Instructional Sequence:

1. Organize your pupils into groups of three or four.
2. Use the meter stick to mark a starting line one meter from the end of the plywood. Also measure the total length of the plywood.
3. Ask your pupils to elevate the plywood with the 2" x 4" board so that it is about 20 cm. above the floor. Have them measure the exact elevation using the meter stick.
4. Have each group release the matchbox car from rest at the starting line and measure the time for the car to reach the bottom of the incline.
5. Change the elevation of the incline by proping up the plywood with the 4" side of the 2" x 4" board. Have the pupils measure the actual elevation using the meter stick.
6. Guide pupils to find a new starting line so that the car will travel to the bottom of the incline in the same length as that measured in step 4. Mark the starting point for each trial with masking tape. Once the new starting line is located, measure the distance along the incline from the bottom of the plywood to the new starting line.

Closure or Evaluation:

1. Tell the groups to calculate the mechanical advantages of the two inclined planes by dividing the length of the plywood by the elevation of its end.
2. Look in Table 2 to find the distance that an object will fall under the action of gravity if it is allowed to fall for the time measured in step 4 of the procedure.
3. Divide the distance you found in Table 2 by one meter. Notice that this is equal to the mechanical advantage of the steepest inclined plane. This is because the distance traveled down the incline in a given time depends on the fraction of the car's weight that is directed down the incline. For an object in free fall, all of the object's weight causes it to accelerate. When the object is on an incline only that fraction of its weight directed down the incline will cause it to accelerate. Therefore, an object will cover a larger distance down the incline when the incline is steep and the mechanical advantage is small. Also find the mechanical advantage of the less steeply sloped inclined plane using the starting line located in step 6 of the procedure.

Variation:

Have pupils measure the time to travel down the incline when the car has a lump of clay attached to it. Pupils will find that the acceleration of the car does not depend on its weight but only on the mechanical advantage of the incline. With guidance pupils may be able to conclude that all objects in free fall have the same acceleration regardless of weight.

Table 10.1

Inclined Plane Data Table

Steep Incline

Elevation =

Time to Reach Bottom =

Gentle Incline

Elevation =

Distance of Starting Line from Bottom =

Calculations

Steep Incline

Mechanical Advantage = Length / Elevation =

Free Fall Distance =

Free Fall Distance / Starting Distance =

Gentle Incline

Mechanical Advantage = Length / Elevation =

Free Fall Distance / Starting Distance =

Table 10.2

Time (seconds)	Free-Fall Distance (cm)
0.5	123
0.6	176
0.7	240
0.8	314
0.9	397
1.0	490
1.1	593
1.2	706
1.3	828
1.4	960
1.5	1103

Conclusions

1. Was the acceleration of the car greater for the steep incline or for the gentle incline?
2. How does the mechanical advantage of the incline affect the acceleration of the car down the incline?
3. How does the ratio of the free-fall distance to the distance of the starting line from the bottom of the incline compare with the mechanical advantage of the incline?

Topic: THE WHEEL AND AXLE

Grade Level: 2 – 6 **Activity Time:** 1 – 2 days

Materials Needed:

1. Pencil sharpener (attached to table or wall)
2. String (heavy tension)
3. Various materials within 1 – 5 kg. mass limits (e.g., two-liter bottle filled with water, brick)
4. Spring balance (5000 g. x 100 g.)
5. Pictures of various wheels and axles in the environment

Objectives:

As a result of this activity, the learner will:

- demonstrate the simple machine, the wheel, and axle.
- compare the effort of the wheel and axle to the effort of lifting an object by hand.
- graph the difference in effort between the wheel and axle and lifting the material by hand.

Introduction:

1. Introduce the concept of the wheel and axle to the class. (A solid disk or a rigid circular ring connected by spokes to a hub, designed to turn around an axle passed through the center.)
2. Ask them if they can name any wheel-and-axle examples around their homes, the school, the community, and the like.
3. Show them some pictures of typical wheel-and-axle units.
4. Ask your pupils if (and how) the wheel and axle is more efficient at lifting objects than manual lifting.
5. Point out to your pupils that there is a wheel and axle in the classroom, the manual pencil sharpener.
6. Indicate to them that they will devise an experiment to determine if the wheel and axle is superior to using your arm strength.

Major Instructional Sequence:

1. Remove the cover of the pencil sharpener.
2. Attach a string around the central axis of the sharpener. Make sure it is tight.
3. Attach the other end of the string to a material to be lifted (e.g., two-liter bottle filled with water).
4. Demonstrate how to use the wheel and axle.
5. Ask a pupil to lift the same (or a similar mass) with their arms.
6. Ask your pupils if there is a way that the effort of the lift can be determined for each.

7. Show your pupils the spring balance. Demonstrate how it works.
8. Tie a piece of string to the spring balance. Attach the other end of the string to the material to be lifted (e.g., bottle, book, brick).
9. Ask a pupil to come up to the front of the class and lift the material.
10. Instruct another pupil to observe the reading on the instrument.
11. Ask another pupil to record the data on the board (or overhead).
12. Disconnect the spring balance from the lifting material and attach the hook to the handle of the pencil sharpener.
13. Reattach the lifting material to the string on the pencil sharpener shaft.
14. Ask a pupil to pull the pencil sharpener handle around with the spring balance.
15. Instruct another pupil to observe the reading on the instrument.
16. Ask another pupil to record the data on the board (or overhead).
17. Repeat the procedure with several different types of materials.

Closure or Evaluation:

1. Ask your pupils to look at the data recorded on the board (or overhead).
2. Demonstrate how to make a simple bar graph indicating the data.
3. Instruct pupils to construct a simple bar graph to compare the data for manual lifting with the data for wheel-and-axle lifting.
4. Ask them to determine which of the two is the more efficient.

Variation:

Your class could construct a basic wheel-and-axle design using Tinkertoys™. Pupils could test their designs for different load capacities.

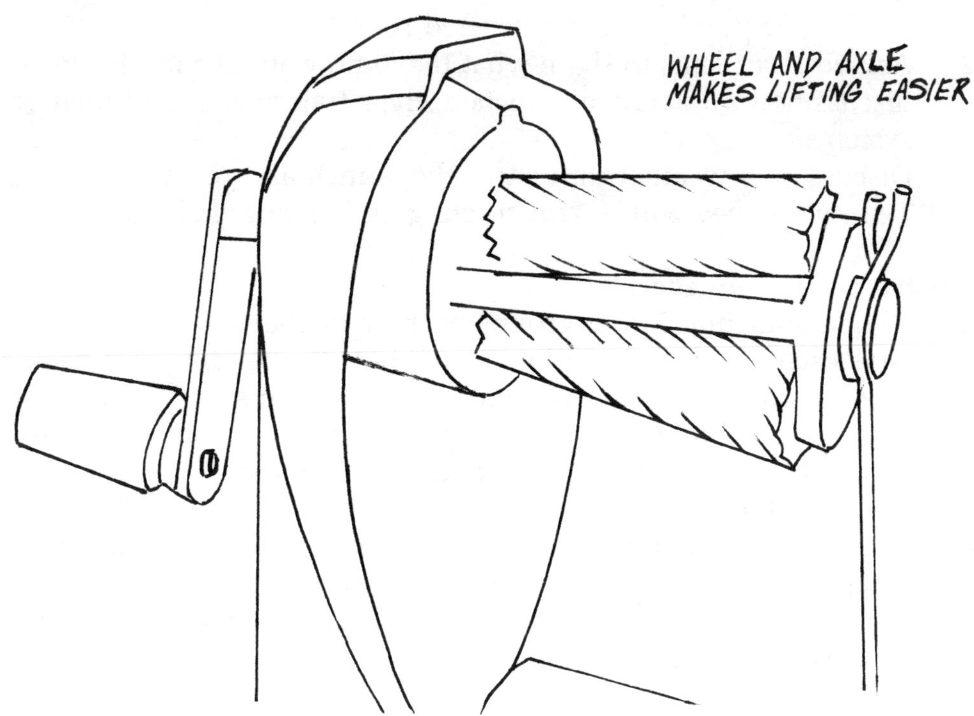
WHEEL AND AXLE
MAKES LIFTING EASIER

Topic: ROCKET PHYSICS

Grade Level: 5 – 6 **Activity Time:** 2 - 3 days

Materials Needed (per group):

1. *Estes* model rocket (*E2X* or *Beta* series recommended)
2. Rocket engines
3. Launch control device w/ extra batteries (AA)
4. Package of fireproof wadding
5. Plastic cement
6. Box cutter or utility knife
7. Pliers
8. Scotch tape, scissors, ruler, and pencil
9. Spray paint and permanent markers (optional)

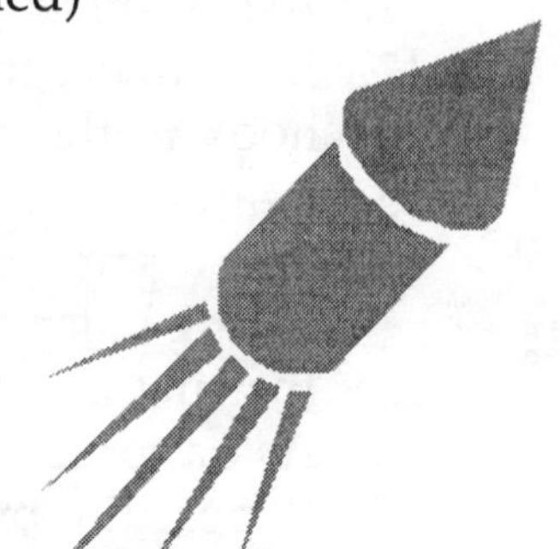

Note: Many of the materials listed can be purchased in bulk packages from Estes Industries. Their toll-free telephone number is 1-800-820-0202 and their toll-free fax number is 1-800-820-0203.

Objectives:

As a result of this activity, the learner will:

- develop a greater awareness for weather conditions during a launch.
- relate how a rocket is launched into space (technology in miniature).
- gather and graph data collected in an experiment.
- work together cooperatively.

Introduction:

1. Show your pupils a preconstructed rocket.
2. Ask your students to share what they know about rockets. Be sure to discuss how rockets are launched, their trajectories, and their recovery systems.
3. Discuss how weather influences the launch and recovery of a rocket.
4. Tell pupils they will be constructing and testing their own rockets.

Major Instructional Sequence:

1. Divide your pupils into groups of three or four.
2. Give each group a rocket kit, complete with wadding and engine.
3. Ask the groups to paint their rocket parts with spray paint or permanent markers (optional). They will need to paint the body tube, nose cone, and fins. Caution the groups to let the paint dry overnight before attaching the decals.
4. Instruct the groups to watch you demonstrate each of the following components: engine mount assembly, shock cord mount assembly, and parachute assembly. These can be worked on either on day one (while the paint is drying), or day two.

5. Once the components have been completed, demonstrate how to attach the engine mount into the body tube.
6. Instruct each group to tape the tube marking guide (provided in the kit) onto the bottom of the body tube.
7. Once the tube marking guide is firmly in place, demonstrate for each group how to glue the fins into place. You may wish to monitor the gluing process.
8. Once the fins are secure, instruct your pupils to glue the launch lug (provided in the kit) approximately 45 mm. from the bottom of the body tube. Allow time for the fins and launch lug to dry.
9. While the rocket components are drying, demonstrate for your pupils how to cut out and assemble the parachute.
10. Once you have inspected each group's rocket for stability, instruct them to attach the shock cord mount.
11. Attach the parachute and shock cord attachment to the nose cone.
12. The rockets are now ready for launching. Take the groups outside to an area with plenty of space (such as a school football field or softball field).
13. Attach the first group's rocket to the launch mechanism and fire.
14. Instruct your pupils to watch the launch from a safe distance (10 feet away) and record their observations. This would be an excellent time to record weather data prior to launch and discuss the influence of the weather on each launch and recovery.

Closure or Evaluation:

1. Ask each group to share the observations made on the launch and recovery of its rocket. Ask them to tell about the rocket's trajectory, the distance it traveled, and the parachute's descent.
2. If any of the rockets had trouble with the launch or recovery, ask your pupils to hypothesize what might have happened. Encourage them to fix the problem and relaunch the rocket.
3. Estes Industries sells an *Altitrak Altitude Finder* (part number EST 2232) which could be utilized by each group to determine peak altitude. With this instrument, pupils could experiment with different types of engines to determine if one is more efficient than another for height or distance.
4. Guide each group in a cooperative effort to calculate and graph the means (averages) of its launches, comparing rocket engines, trajectories and weather conditions.

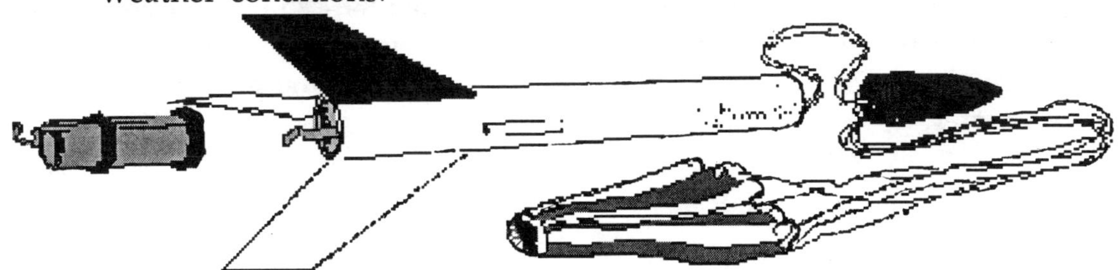

Topic: PRODUCING A COLOR SPECTRUM

Grade Level: K – 6 **Activity Time:** 1 – 2 days

Materials Needed (per group):

1. Tall, clear drinking glass
2. Note card (4 x 6) w/slit
3. Scissors or X-acto™ knife
4. Sheet of paper

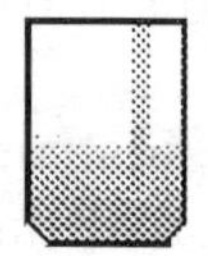

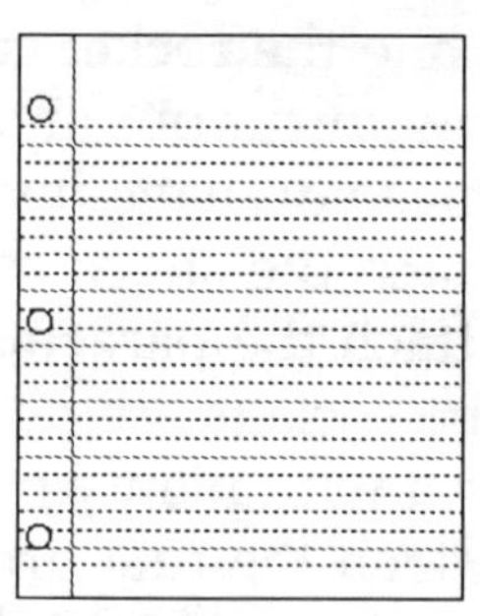

Objectives:

As a result of this activity, the learner will:

- construct an experiment that produces a color spectrum.
- explain how white light contains all the colors in the visible spectrum.

Introduction:

1. Ask your pupils to tell you what light is.
2. Tell them that white light contains colors and ask them to guess which colors are found in white light. Relate Newton's experiment with a prism (used to separate white light passed through it into a spectrum) to the discussion.
3. Inform your pupils that they will be constructing an experiment that will demonstrate that white light is made up of many different colors.

Major Instructional Sequence:

1. Divide pupils into groups of three or four.
2. Instruct the groups to place a tall glass, filled 80 – 85 percent with water, on top of the piece of paper, on a counter or window sill where sunlight can reach it. You will probably need to demonstrate the proper amount of water.

3. Assist each group in cutting a 5-cm.-long slit (1 cm. wide) into the six-inch side of the notecard with the knife (or scissors).
4 Instruct your groups to place the notecard (six-inch side up) next to the glass, where only a small portion of light can shine through the slit into the water of the glass.
5. Ask pupils to observe and record the pattern of the resulting color spectrum on the paper.

Closure or Evaluation:

1. Have each group share its observations with the class.
2. On the chalkboard or overhead, list the order of the color spectrum observed.
3. Point out that the sunlight was *refracted* by the water in the glass. Define refraction as the turning or bending of a light wave when it passes from one medium into another of different density (e.g., air to water).

Topic: STRAW TROMBONES

Grade Level: Grades K – 4 **Activity Time:** 1 – 2 days

Materials Needed:

1. Straight plastic straws and flexible plastic straws
2. Scissors

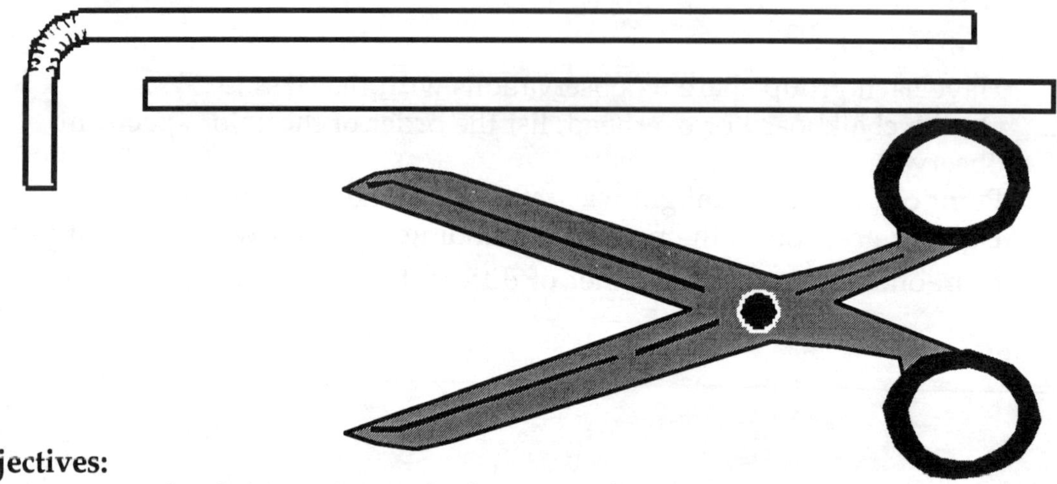

Objectives:

As a result of this activity, the learner will:

- demonstrate that sound is a rapid vibration of air.
- explain why the pitch (highness or lowness) of the sound produced by a wind instrument depends on the length of the instrument.

Introduction:

1. Explain how sound is a rapid vibration of air.
2. Describe how many musical instruments (clarinet, saxophone, and the like) use a wooden reed to produce the vibration. Brass instruments (trumpet, trombone, and the like) require the lips of the musician to form the reed. As the reed (or lips) vibrate, it alternately opens and closes a small opening through which air is blown into the instrument. When the reed is open, a puff of air is blown into the instrument through the opening. A low pressure is created in the opening by the fast-moving air, and the reed quickly snaps shut. As the air travels down the length of the instrument, most of the puff passes out the instrument. A small part is reflected back to the reed, causing it to open up again. The puffs of air travel up and down the length of the instrument, setting air into vibration and creating sound. The pitch depends on how rapid the vibrations are.
3. Tell your pupils that they will be constructing a trombone made of straws.

Major Instructional Sequence:

1. Give each pupil a straight straw.

2. Demonstrate how to cut one end of the straw so that it tapers to a point. The two triangular flaps of plastic created in your cut will form the reed of the instrument.
3. Slide the long end of the flexible straw over the uncut end of the straight straw. Bend the flexible end at a ninety degree angle. The flexible straw forms the slide of our instrument.
4. To play the instrument, pupils will need to flatten the two flaps of the reed with their fingers so that the opening between them is very small. Instruct your pupils to place the reed in their mouths, pressing the two flaps together with their lips. As they blow through the straw, the reed will vibrate, creating a sound similar to that of a kazoo. By sliding the flexible straw along the straight straw the pupils can change the length of the instrument.
5. Help your pupils discover how to make a sound using their instruments. Explain how sound is a vibration of the air and that the vibrations of the reed which they feel on their lips causes the air to vibrate.
6. Ask pupils to observe how the sound changes as the slide is moved in and out. Point out that the sound is lower when the instrument is longer and higher when it is shorter.

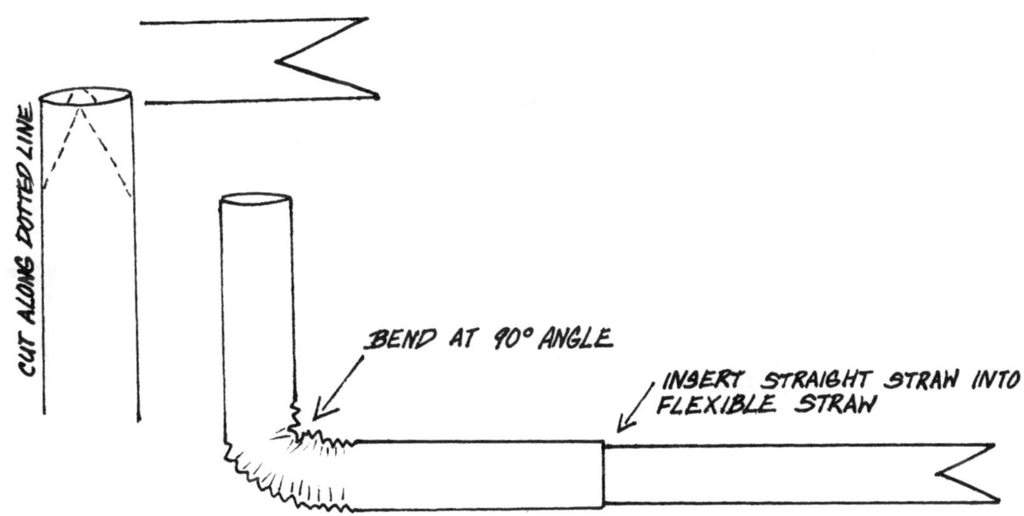

Closure or Evaluation:

1. Ask some of your pupils to demonstrate and explain the workings of their trombones.
2. Review how a long straw produces a lower sound than a short straw. Ask pupils to demonstrate this with their straw trombones.

Note: This would be a good activity for pupils to do at home with their parents.

The National Science Teachers Association

The National Science Teachers Association (NSTA) was founded in 1944 and is headquartered in Arlington, Virginia. It is the largest organization in the world committed to promoting excellence and innovation in science teaching. NSTA's current membership of more than 53,000 includes science teachers, science supervisors, administrators, scientists, business and industry representatives, and others involved in science education. To address subjects of critical interest to science educators, the Association publishes five journals, a newspaper, many books, a new children's magazine, called *Dragonfly*, and many other publications. NSTA conducts national and regional conventions that attract more than 30,000 attendees annually. NSTA provides many programs and services for science educators, including awards, professional development workshops, and educational tours. NSTA offers professional certification for science teachers in eight teaching-level and discipline-area categories. In addition, NSTA has a World Wide Web site with links to state, national, and international science education organizations, an on-line catalog of publications, and two "discussion rooms" to foster interaction and ongoing conversations about science education. NSTA's web address is http://www.nsta.org.

NSTA's newest and largest initiative to date, "Building a Presence for Science," seeks to improve science education and align science teaching to the National Science Education Standards nationwide. The Association serves as an advocate for science educators by keeping its members and the general public informed about national issues and trends in science education. NSTA disseminates results from nationwide surveys and reports and offers testimony to Congress on science education-related legislation and other issues. The organization has position statements on issues such as teacher preparation, laboratory science, the use of animals in the classroom, laboratory safety, and elementary and middle level science. NSTA is involved in cooperative working relationships with numerous educational organizations, government agencies, and private industries on a variety of projects.

Publications of the National Science Teachers Association:

NSTA Reports! (The newspaper of science education)
The Science Teacher (For high school science teachers)
Science & Children (For elementary teachers)
Quantum (The student magazine of math and science)
Dragonfly (A new science magazine for children)
Journal of College Science Teaching (For college science teachers)
Science Scope (For middle level science teachers)

Address: National Science Teachers Association, 1840 Wilson Boulevard, Arlington, Virginia 22201-3000. Phone: (703) 243-7100

The National Science Education Standards

View via WWW at http://www.nap.edu/nap/online/nses/

The National Science Education Standards envision change throughout the system and encompass the following changes in emphases:

LESS EMPHASIS ON	MORE EMPHASIS ON
Treating all students alike and responding to the group as a whole.	Understanding and responding to individual students' interests, strengths, experiences, and needs.
Rigidly following curriculum.	Selecting and adapting curriculum.
Focusing on student acquisition of information.	Focusing on student understanding and use of scientific knowledge, ideas, and inquiry processes.
Presenting scientific knowledge through lecture, text, and demonstration.	Guiding students in active and extended scientific inquiry.
Asking for recitation of acquired knowledge.	Providing opportunities for scientific discussion and debate among students.
Testing students for factual information at the end of the unit or chapter.	Continuously assessing student understanding.
Maintaining responsibility and authority.	Sharing responsibility for learning with students.
Supporting competition.	Supporting a classroom community with cooperation, shared responsibility, and respect.
Working alone.	Working with other teachers to enhance the science program.

Introduction to The National Science Education Standards

The National Science Education Standards are designed to guide our nation toward a scientifically literate society. Founded in exemplary practice and research, the Standards describe a vision of the scientifically literate person and present criteria for science education that will allow that vision to become reality. Why is science literacy important? First, an understanding of science offers personal fulfillment and excitement – benefits that should be shared by everyone. Second, Americans are confronted increasingly with questions in their lives that require scientific information and scientific ways of thinking for informed decision making. And the collective judgment of our people will determine how we manage shared resources – such as air, water, and national forests.

Science understanding and ability also will enhance the capability of all students to hold meaningful and productive jobs in the future. The business community needs entry-level workers with the ability to learn, reason, think creatively, make decisions, and solve problems. In addition, concerns regarding economic competitiveness stress the central importance of science and mathematics education that will allow us to keep pace with our global competitors.

Why National Science Education Standards?

The term "standard" has multiple meanings. Science education standards are criteria to judge quality: the quality of what students know and are able to do; the quality of the science programs that provide the opportunity for students to learn science; the quality of science teaching; the quality of the system that supports science teachers and programs; and the quality of assessment practices and policies. Science education standards provide criteria to judge progress toward a national vision of learning and teaching science in a system that promotes excellence, providing a banner around which reformers can rally.

A hallmark of American education is local control, where boards of education and teachers make decisions about what students will learn. National standards present criteria by which judgments can be made by state and local school personnel and communities, helping them to decide which curriculum, staff development activity, or assessment program is appropriate. National standards encourage policies that will bring coordination, consistency, and coherence to the improvement of science education: They allow everyone to move in the same direction, with the assurance that the risks they take in the name of improving science education will be supported by policies and practices throughout the system.

Some outstanding things happen in science classrooms today, even without national standards. But they happen because extraordinary teachers do what needs to be done despite conventional practice. Many generous teachers spend their own money on science supplies, knowing that students learn best by investigation. These teachers ignore the vocabulary-dense textbooks and encourage student inquiry. They also make their science courses relevant to students' lives, instead of simply being preparation for another school science course.

Implementation of the National Science Education Standards will highlight and promote the best practices of those extraordinary teachers and give them the recognition and support they deserve. School principals who find money in their budgets for field trips, parents whose bake-sale proceeds purchase science equipment, and publishers who are pioneering authentic assessments despite the market for multiple-choice tests will also be recognized and encouraged.

The Standards help to chart the course into the future. By building on the best of current practice, they aim to take us beyond the constraints of present structures of schooling toward a shared vision of excellence.

Goals for School Science

The goals for school science that underlie the National Science Education Standards are to educate students who are able to experience the richness and excitement of knowing about and understanding the natural world; use appropriate scientific processes and principles in making personal decisions; engage intelligently in public discourse and debate about matters of scientific and technological concern; and increase their economic productivity through the use of the knowledge, understanding, and skills of the scientifically literate person in their careers.

These goals define a scientifically literate society. The standards for content define what the scientifically literate person should know, understand, and be able to do after 13 years of school science. The separate standards for assessment, teaching, program, and system describe the conditions necessary to achieve the goal of scientific literacy for all students that is described in the content standards.

Schools that implement the Standards will have students learning science by actively engaging in inquiries that are interesting and important to them. Students thereby will establish a knowledge base for understanding science. In these schools, teachers will be empowered to make decisions about what students learn, how they learn it, and how resources are allocated. Teachers and students together will be members of a community focused on learning science while being nurtured by a supportive education system. Students could not achieve the standards in most of today's schools. Implementation of the Standards will require a sustained, long-term commitment to change.

History of the National Science Education Standards

Setting national goals and developing national standards to meet them are recent strategies in our education reform policy. Support for national education standards by state governments originated in 1989, when the National Governors Association endorsed national education goals. President George Bush immediately added his support by forming the National Education Goals Panel. The support for standards was continued by the new administration after the election of President William Clinton.

The first standards appeared in 1989, when mathematics educators and mathematicians addressed the subject of national standards with two publications: *Curriculum and Evaluation Standards for School Mathematics,* by the National

Council of Teachers of Mathematics (NCTM) (1989); and *Everybody Counts: A Report to the Nation on the Future of Mathematics Education,* by the National Research Council (1989). The NCTM experience was important in the development of other education standards, and it demonstrated that participation in the development of standards had to be open to all interested parties, especially those responsible for their realization.

The National Science Education Standards had several important precursors. In 1983, *A Nation at Risk* was published, calling for reconsideration and reform of the U.S. education system. In the 1980s, the American Chemical Society (ACS), the Biological Sciences Curriculum Study, the Education Development Center, the Lawrence Hall of Science, the National Science Resources Center (NSRC), and the Technical Education Resources Center all developed innovative science curricula. In 1989, the American Association for the Advancement of Science (AAAS), through its Project 2061, published *Science for All Americans,* defining scientific literacy for all high school graduates. Somewhat later, the National Science Teachers Association (NSTA), through its Scope, Sequence & Coordination Project, published *The Content Core.*

In the spring of 1991, the NSTA president, reflecting a unanimous vote of the NSTA board, wrote to Dr. Frank Press – president of the National Academy of Sciences and chairman of the National Research Council (NRC) – asking the NRC to coordinate development of national science education standards. The presidents of several leading science and science education associations, the U.S. secretary of education, the assistant director for education and human resources at the National Science Foundation, and the cochairs of the National Education Goals Panel all encouraged the NRC to play a leading role in the effort to develop national standards for science education in content, teaching, and assessment. Shortly thereafter, major funding for this project was provided by the Department of Education and the National Science Foundation.

To oversee the important process of standards development, the NRC established the National Committee on Science Education Standards and Assessment (NCSESA). The committee was chaired successively by Dr. James Ebert and (from November 1993) Dr. Richard Klausner. In addition, the Chair's Advisory Committee was formed, consisting of representatives from NSTA, AAAS, ACS, NSRC, the American Association of Physics Teachers, the Council of State Science Supervisors, the Earth Science Education Coalition, and the National Association of Biology Teachers. This group helped to identify and recruit staff and volunteers for all of the committees and working groups that were required.

The oversight committee (NCSESA) first met in May 1992, and the three working groups (content, teaching, and assessment) each held intense working sessions over the summer. An initial phase of standards development lasted through the fall of 1993. During that 18 months, input to the standards was solicited from large numbers of science teachers, scientists, science educators, and many others interested in science education. More than 150 public presentations were made to promote discussion about issues in science education reform and the nature and content of science education standards.

Late in 1993, work began on the production of a complete "predraft" of the science education standards. This predraft was released in May 1994 to a selected set of focus groups for their critique and review. Each organization represented on the Chair's Advisory Committee, joined by two additional organizations (NCTM and the New Standards Project), formed focus groups. In addition, the NRC convened five focus groups that were composed entirely of individuals who had not yet been involved in the project to critique the predraft. In this NRC-organized review, separate groups of experts reviewed the content, teaching, assessment, program, and system standards present in the predraft.

After the many suggestions for improving the predraft were collated and analyzed, an extensively revised standards document was prepared as a public document. This draft was released for nationwide review in December 1994. More than 40,000 copies of the draft National Science Education Standards were distributed to some 18,000 individuals and 250 groups. The comments of the many individuals and groups who reviewed this draft were again collated and analyzed; these were used to prepare the final National Science Education Standards.

The many individuals who developed the content standards sections of the National Science Education Standards made independent use and interpretation of the statements of what all students should know and be able to do that are published in *Science for All Americans* and *Benchmarks for Science Literacy*. The National Research Council of the National Academy of Sciences gratefully acknowledges its indebtedness to the seminal work by the American Association for the Advancement of Science's Project 2061 and believes that use of *Benchmarks for Science Literacy* by state framework committees, school and school-district curriculum committees, and developers of instructional and assessment materials complies fully with the spirit of the content standards.

Brief Overview of the Science Teaching Standards

Science teaching is a complex activity that lies at the heart of the vision of science education presented in the Standards. The teaching standards provide criteria for making judgments about progress toward the vision; they describe what teachers of science at all grade levels should understand and be able to do. To highlight the importance of teachers in science education, these standards are presented first. However, to attain the vision of science education described in the Standards, change is needed in the entire system. Teachers are central to education, but they must not be placed in the position of being solely responsible for reform. Teachers will need to work within a collegial, organizational, and policy context that is supportive of good science teaching. In addition, students must accept and share responsibility for their own learning.

In the vision of science education portrayed by the Standards, effective teachers of science create an environment in which they and students work together as active learners. While students are engaged in learning about the natural world and the scientific principles needed to understand it, teachers are working with their colleagues to expand their knowledge about science teaching. To teach science as portrayed by the Standards, teachers must have theoretical and practical knowledge and abilities about science, learning, and science teaching.

The standards for science teaching are grounded in five assumptions.

- The vision of science education described by the Standards requires changes throughout the entire system.
- What students learn is greatly influenced by how they are taught.
- The actions of teachers are deeply influenced by their perceptions of science as an enterprise and as a subject to be taught and learned.
- Student understanding is actively constructed through individual and social processes.
- Actions of teachers are deeply influenced by their understanding of and relationships with students.

Selected Highlights of the Science Teaching and Content Standards

Dividing science teaching into separate components oversimplifies a complex process; nevertheless, some division is required to manage the presentation of criteria for good science teaching, accepting that this leaves some overlap. In addition, the teaching standards cannot possibly address all the understanding and abilities that masterful teachers display. Therefore, the teaching standards focus on the qualities that are most closely associated with science teaching and with the vision of science education described in the Standards.

The teaching standards begin with a focus on the long-term planning that teachers do. The discussion then moves to facilitating learning, assessment, and the classroom environment. Finally, the teaching standards address the teacher's role in the school community. The standards are applicable at all grade levels, but the teaching at different grade levels will be different to reflect the capabilities and interests of students at different ages. A challenge to teachers of science is to balance and integrate immediate needs with the intentions of the yearlong framework of goals.

Teachers across the country will find some of their current practices reflected below. They also will find criteria that suggest new and different practices. Because change takes time and takes place at the local level, differences in individuals, schools, and communities will be reflected in different pathways to reform, different rates of progress, and different emphases. For example, a beginning teacher might focus on developing skills in managing the learning environment rather than on long-term planning, whereas a more experienced group of teachers might work together on new modes for assessing student achievement. Deliberate movement over time toward the vision of science teaching described here is important if reform is to be pervasive and permanent.

Teaching Standard A

Teachers of science plan an inquiry-based science program for their students. In doing this, teachers:

- develop a framework of yearlong and short-term goals for students.
- select science content and adapt and design curricula to meet the interests, knowledge, understanding, abilities, and experiences of students.
- select teaching and assessment strategies that support the development of student understanding and nurture a community of science learners.
- work together as colleagues within and across disciplines and grade levels.

Teaching Standard B

Teachers of science guide and facilitate learning. In doing this, teachers:

- focus and support inquiries while interacting with students.
- orchestrate discourse among students about scientific ideas.
- challenge students to accept and share responsibility for their own learning.
- recognize and respond to student diversity and encourage all students to participate fully in science learning.
- encourage and model the skills of scientific inquiry, as well as the curiosity, openness to new ideas and data, and skepticism that characterize science.

Teaching Standard C

Teachers of science engage in ongoing assessment of their teaching and of student learning. In doing this, teachers:

- use multiple methods and systematically gather data about student understanding and ability.
- analyze assessment data to guide teaching.
- guide students in self-assessment.
- use student data, observations of teaching, and interactions with colleagues to reflect on and improve teaching practice.
- use student data, observations of teaching, and interactions with colleagues to report student achievement and opportunities to learn to students, teachers, parents, policy makers, and the general public.

Teaching Standard D

Teachers of science design and manage learning environments that provide students with the time, space, and resources needed for learning science. In doing this, teachers:

- structure the time available so that students are able to engage in extended investigations.
- create a setting for student work that is flexible and supportive of science inquiry.
- ensure a safe working environment.
- make the available science tools, materials, media, and technological resources accessible to students.
- identify and use resources outside the school.
- engage students in designing the learning environment.

Teaching Standard E

Teachers of science develop communities of science learners that reflect the intellectual rigor of scientific inquiry and the attitudes and social values conducive to science learning. In doing this, teachers:

- display and demand respect for the diverse ideas, skills, and experiences of all students.
- enable students to have a significant voice in decisions about the content and context of their work and require students to take responsibility for the learning of all members of the community.
- nurture collaboration among students.
- structure and facilitate ongoing formal and informal discussion based on a shared understanding of rules of scientific discourse.
- model and emphasize the skills, attitudes, and values of scientific inquiry.

Teaching Standard F

Teachers of science actively participate in the ongoing planning and development of the school science program. In doing this, teachers:

- plan and develop the school science program.
- participate in decisions concerning the allocation of time and other resources to the science program.
- participate fully in planning and implementing professional growth and development strategies for themselves and their colleagues.

Content Standards for Grades K-4: Science as Inquiry

Content Standard A

As a result of activities in grades K-4, all students should develop:

- abilities necessary to do scientific inquiry.

- an understanding about scientific inquiry.

Content Standard B

As a result of the activities in grades K-4, all students should develop an understanding of:

- the properties of objects and materials.
- the position and motion of objects.
- light, heat, electricity, and magnetism.

Content Standard C

As a result of activities in grades K-4, all students should develop an understanding of:

- the characteristics of organisms.
- the life cycles of organisms.
- organisms and environments.

Content Standard D

As a result of their activities in grades K-4, all students should develop an understanding of:

- properties of earth materials.
- objects in the sky.
- changes in earth and sky.

Content Standard E

As a result of activities in grades K-4, all students should develop:

- abilities of technological design.
- understanding about science and technology.
- abilities to distinguish between natural objects and objects made by humans.

Content Standard F

As a result of activities in grades K-4, all students should develop understanding of:

- personal health.
- characteristics and changes in populations.
- types of resources.
- changes in environments.
- science and technology in local challenges.

Content Standard G

As a result of activities in grades K-4, all students should develop understanding of:

- science as a human endeavor.

Content Standards for Grades 5-8: Science as Inquiry

Content Standard A

As a result of activities in grades 5-8, all students should develop:

- abilities necessary to do scientific inquiry.
- understandings about scientific inquiry.

Content Standard B

As a result of their activities in grades 5-8, all students should develop an understanding of:

- properties and changes of properties in matter.
- motions and forces.
- transfer of energy.

Content Standard C

As a result of their activities in grades 5-8, all students should develop understanding of:

- structure and function in living systems.
- reproduction and heredity.
- regulation and behavior.
- populations and ecosystems.
- diversity and adaptations of organisms.

Content Standard D

As a result of their activities in grades 5-8, all students should develop an understanding of:

- structure of the Earth system.
- Earth's history.
- Earth in the solar system.

Content Standard E

As a result of activities in grades 5-8, all students should develop:

- abilities of technological design.
- understandings about science and technology.

Content Standard F

As a result of activities in grades 5-8, all students should develop understanding of:

- personal health.
- populations, resources, and environments.
- natural hazards.
- risks and benefits.
- science and technology in society.

Content Standard G

As a result of activities in grades 5-8, all students should develop understanding of:

- science as a human endeavor.
- the nature of science.
- the history of science.

The National Science Education Standards describe a vision and provide a first step on a journey of educational reform that might take a decade or longer. At this point, the easy portion of the journey is complete; we have a map. The scientific and education communities have labored to reach agreement on what students should understand and be able to do, how students should be taught, and means for assessing students' understandings, abilities, and dispositions in science. The Standards took an insightful and innovative step by suggesting that the responsibility for improving scientific literacy extends beyond those in classrooms and schools to the entire educational system. The real journey of educational reform and the consequent improvement of scientific literacy begins with the implementation of these standards.

Constructivism

In today's educational community, a theory known as *constructivism* is perhaps the most widely accepted view of how children learn. It proposes that children must be active participants in the development of their own understanding.

Deeply rooted in the cognitive theories of Piaget,[1] which date from the 1960s, constructivism rejects the notion that children's minds are blank slates awaiting something to be imprinted. Instead, constructivism suggests that children help create their own knowledge through the basic mental activities of *assimilation* and *accommodation*.

Stemming from the view that the mind constantly changes its structure to help us make sense of things that we perceive, Piaget described the shifting modifications in the mind as assimilation and accommodation. When things are familiar to us and fit well with what we already know from our previously developed understanding, we fit the new experiences into our existing ideas. Piaget called this process *assimilation*. When new experiences or perceptions do not fit with what we already know, however, Piaget said that we must appease the dissonance within our minds by modifying the new experience to make it fit. Piaget called this modifying process *accommodation*, a shift in our cognitive framework which permits assimilation of the new experience. Knowledge is built up by the learner as existing ideas are expanded, elaborated, and changed to allow a new idea to fit.

In the constructivist approach, then, learners actively build their own understanding through reflective thought. Reflective thinking is stimulated as learners brainstorm in an environment of encouragement (provided by the teacher), exploring the networks of ideas already existing in their minds. They integrate these networks, both within their own minds and by sharing with other learners through active reflective thought. The nextworks of ideas change, become rearranged, take on additions, and are modified as learning occurs. The more connections the learner can make with his/her existing network of ideas, the better that new experiences and ideas are understood (or learned).

Constructivist instruction is based on the supposition that the pupil is a naturally active learner who constructs new individual knowledge through linking prior knowledge with new knowledge. Constructivist learning involves an interactive and collaborative dialogue between the teacher, the pupil, and other learners. The teacher orchestrates the learning by providing a rich and supportive environment where assistance and direction allow the learner to construct his/her own knowledge. This construction of knowledge results in ownership by the learner and, thus, a deeper understanding of the new information. The teacher focuses on guiding the learner to achieve success. The learner is a proactive participant in the learning process and not a sponge waiting to absorb knowledge!

---

[1]Piaget, J. (1977). *The development of thought: Equilibrium of cognitive structures.* New York: Viking Press.

Using Bloom's Taxonomy

As teachers, we ask many questions to find out what a learner knows and to encourage thinking. Benjamin Bloom's Taxonomy of Educational Objectives provides us with a convenient framework for developing a solid questioning strategy. Questions at the lower level require answers based on knowledge, whereas those at the higher levels require the application of knowledge.

Level One - Knowledge

The Level of Simple Recall: Questions ask for factual information and answers are either right or wrong.

Example: Name a coniferous tree.

Level Two - Comprehension

The Level of Understanding: Questions ask for reasons. Answers are usually right or wrong.

Example: Where might one find coniferous trees?

Level Three - Application

The Level of Usage: Questions usually ask for ways to use knowledge and allow for individual creativity. There may be more than one correct answer.

Example: How can one identify a coniferous tree?

Level Four - Analysis

The Level of Relationships and Intent: Questions ask for comparisons to be made or for component parts of an idea. Answers are more divergent and personal.

Example: How does a coniferous tree differ from a deciduous tree?

Level Five - Synthesis

The Level of Ideas: Questions ask students for ideas for new or different solutions to problems. Answers are creative and divergent; there is no one correct answer.

Example: What changes would you make to coniferous and deciduous trees if you could?

Level Six - Evaluation

The Level of Judgment: Questions ask students to make value judgments about ideas of their own or others. Answers are very personal, divergent, and sometimes argumentative.

Example: Which type of coniferous tree is your favorite and why?

Multiple Intelligences

Howard Gardner[2] theorized that humans have multiple intelligences, and he identified seven: bodily-kinesthetic intelligence, interpersonal intelligence, intrapersonal intelligence, linguistic intelligence, logical-mathematical intelligence, musical intelligence, and spatial intelligence.

Bodily-kinesthetic intelligence, said Gardner, relates to physical movement and the ability to use and master one's bodily motions in highly skilled ways. Gardner identified **interpersonal intelligence** as ability and skill in person-to-person relationships such as understanding and dealing effectively with another person's moods, temperaments, behaviors, feelings, and motivations. **Intrapersonal intelligence** is the ability to know oneself, to be self-reflective, to understand ones own feelings, moods, and motivations. **Linguistic intelligence**, according to Gardner, deals with word sense and the capacity to use words powerfully in written and spoken language (for example, as in being particularly persuasive with words). **Logical-mathematical intelligence**, sometimes called scientific thinking, involves the ability to reason abstractly, order and reorder quantitatively, and recognize significant problems and solve them through inductive and deductive thinking. Gardner identified **musical intelligence** as the ability to recognize tonal patterns and to hear and use pitch that is rhythmically arranged as musical sound. Visualizing, creating, and recreating accurate mental images of the visual world as it is was described by Gardner as **spatial intelligence**.

Reporting on how the recognition of multiple intelligences and the application of multiple-intelligence theory at the New City School in St. Louis resulted in a revised curriculum, Hoerr[3] said, "We have found that multiple intelligences is more than a theory of intelligence; it is, for us, a philosophy about education with implications for how kids learn, how teachers should teach, and how schools should operate" (p. 29).

Enthusiastic about the use of multiple intelligences in developing an integrated curriculum, Armstrong[4] said,

> At times, I almost think of Gardner as an archeologist who has discovered the Rosetta stone of learning. One can use this model to teach virtually anything, from the "schwa" sound to the rain forest and back. The master code of this learning style model is simple: for whatever you wish to teach, link your instructional objective to *words, numbers* or *logic, pictures, music, the body, social interaction,* and/or *personal experience.* If you can create

[2] Gardner, H. (1993). *Multiple intelligences: The theory in practice.* New York: Basic Books.

[3] Hoerr, T. (1994). How the New City School applies the multiple intelligences. *Educational Leadership, 52* (3), 29-33.

[4] Armstrong, T. (1994). Multiple intelligences: Seven ways to approach curriculum. *Educational Leadership, 52* (3), 26-28.

activities that combine these intelligences in unique ways, so much the better!

When planning a lesson, ask the right questions! Certain questions help me look at the possibilities for involving as many intelligences as possible.
Linguistic: How can I use the spoken or written word?
Logical-Mathematical: How can I bring in numbers, calculations, logic, classifications, or critical thinking?
Spatial: How can I use visual aids, visualization, color, art, metaphor, or visual organizers?
Musical: How can I bring in music or environmental sounds, or set key points in a rhythm or melody?
Bodily-Kinesthetic: how can I involve the whole body, or hands-on experiences?
Interpersonal: How can I engage students in peer or cross-age sharing, cooperative learning, or large-group simulation?
Intrapersonal: How can I evoke personal feelings or memories, or give students choices? (pp. 26-27).

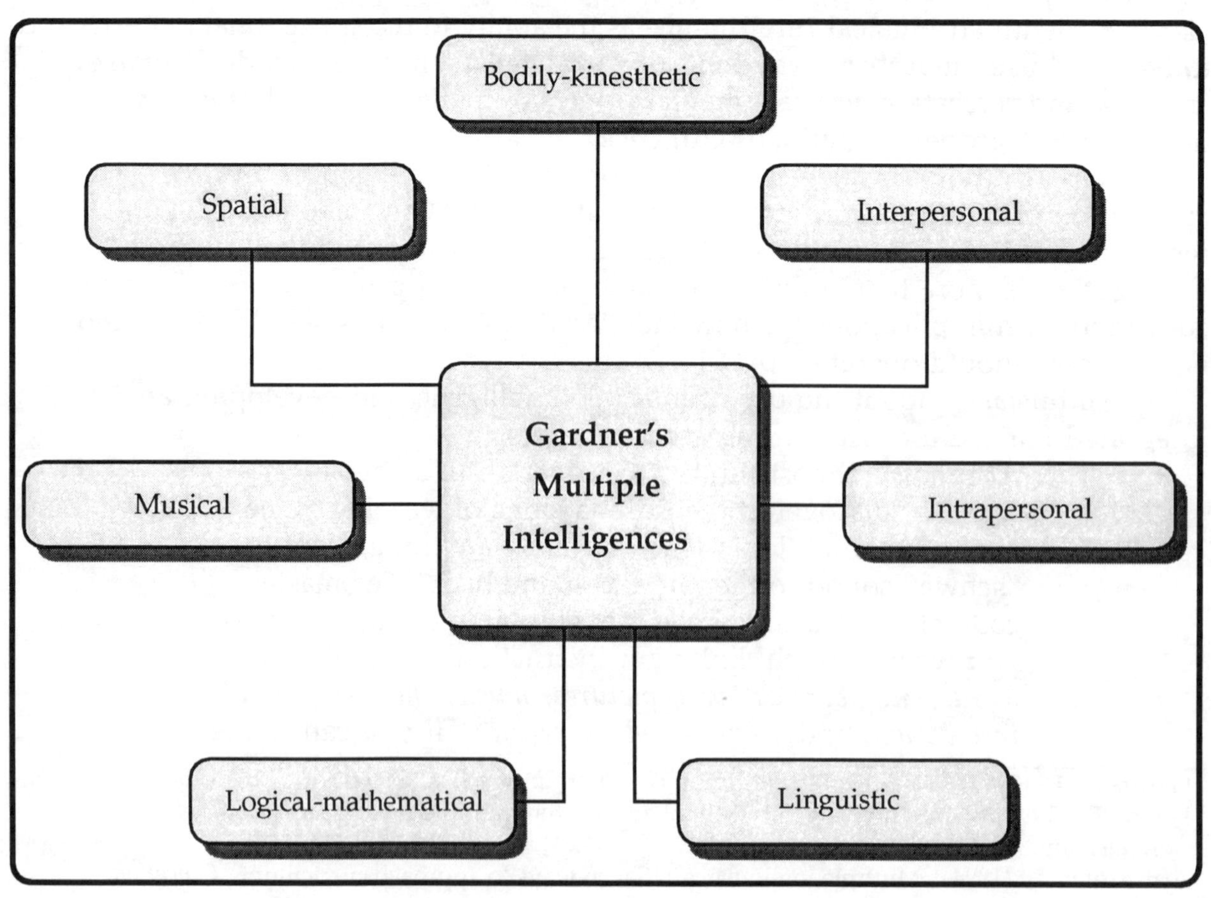

Adding An Eighth Intelligence[5]

Human intelligence continues to intrigue psychologists, neurologists, and educators. What is it? Can we measure it? How do we nurture it? Howard Gardner's theory of multiple intelligences sparked a revolution of sorts in classrooms around the world, a mutiny against the notion that human beings have a single, fixed intelligence. The fervor with which educators embraced his premise that we have multiple intelligences surprised Gardner himself. "It obviously spoke to some sense that people had that kids weren't all the same and that the tests we had only skimmed the surface about the differences among kids," Gardner said. Here Gardner brings us up-to-date on his current thinking on intelligence, how children learn, and how they should be taught.

How do you define intelligence?

- Intelligence refers to the human ability to solve problems or to make something that is valued in one or more cultures. As long as we can find a culture that values an ability to solve a problem or create a product in a particular way, then I would strongly consider whether that ability should be considered an intelligence. First, though, that ability must meet other criteria: Is there a particular representation in the brain for the ability? Are there populations that are especially good or especially impaired in an intelligence? And, can an evolutionary history of the intelligence be seen in animals other than human beings? I defined seven intelligences [see p. 11.16] in the early 1980s because those intelligences all fit the criteria. A decade later when I revisited the task, I found at least one more ability that clearly deserved to be called an intelligence.

That would be the naturalist intelligence. What led you to consider adding this to our collection of intelligences?

- Somebody asked me to explain the achievements of the great biologists, the ones who had a real mastery of taxonomy, who understood about different species, who could recognize patterns in nature and classify objects. I realized that to explain that kind of ability, I would have to manipulate the other intelligences in ways that weren't appropriate. So I began to think about whether the capacity to classify nature might be a separate intelligence. The naturalist ability passed with flying colors. Here are a couple of reasons: First, it's an ability we need to survive as human beings. We need, for example, to know which animals to hunt and which to run away from. Second, this

[5] Checkley, K. (1997). The first seven... and the eighth: A conversation with Howard Gardner. *Educational Leadership, 55* (1), 8-13. Reprinted with permission from the Association for Supervision and Curriculum Development.

ability isn't restricted to human beings. Other animals need to have a naturalist intelligence to survive. Finally, the big selling point is that brain evidence supports the existence of the naturalist intelligence. There are certain parts of the brain particularly dedicated to the recognition and the naming of what are called "natural" things.

How do you describe the naturalist intelligence to those of us who aren't psychologists?

- The naturalist intelligence refers to the ability to recognize and classify plants, minerals, and animals, including rocks and grass and all variety of flora and fauna. The ability to recognize cultural artifacts like cars or sneakers may also depend on the naturalist intelligence. Now, everybody can do this to a certain extent — we can all recognize dogs, cats, trees. But, some people from an early age are extremely good at recognizing and classifying artifacts. For example, we all know kids who, at age 3 or 4, are better at recognizing dinosaurs than most adults. Darwin is probably the most famous example of a naturalist because he saw so deeply into the nature of living things.

Are there any other abilities you're considering calling intelligences?

- Well, there may be an existential intelligence that refers to the human inclination to ask very basic questions about existence. Who are we? Where do we come from? What's it all about? Why do we die? We might say that existential intelligence allows us to know the invisible, outside world. The only reason I haven't given a seal of approval to the existential intelligence is that I don't think we have good brain evidence yet on its existence in the nervous system — one of the criteria for an intelligence.

The Intelligences, in Gardner's Words

- *Linguistic intelligence* is the capacity to use language, your native language, and perhaps other languages, to express what's on your mind and to understand other people. Poets really specialize in linguistic intelligence, but any kind of writer, orator, speaker, lawyer, or a person for whom language is an important stock in trade highlights linguistic intelligence.

- People with a highly developed *logical-mathematical intelligence* understand the underlying principles of some kind of a causal system, the way a scientist or a logician does; or can manipulate numbers, quantities, and operations, the way a mathematician does.

- *Spatial intelligence* refers to the ability to represent the spatial world internally in your mind — the way a sailor or airplane pilot navigates the large spatial world, or the way a chess player or sculptor represents a more circumscribed spatial world. Spatial intelligence can be used in the arts or in the sciences. If you are spatially intelligent and oriented toward the arts, you are more likely to become a painter or a sculptor or an architect than, say, a musician or a writer. Similarly, certain sciences like anatomy or topology emphasize spatial intelligence.

- *Bodily kinesthetic intelligence* is the capacity to use your whole body or parts of your body--your hand, your fingers, your arms--to solve a problem, make something, or put on some kind of a production. The most evident examples are people in athletics or the performing arts, particularly dance or acting.

- *Musical intelligence* is the capacity to think in music, to be able to hear patterns, recognize them, remember them, and perhaps manipulate them. People who have a strong musical intelligence don't just remember music easily — they can't get it out of their minds, it's so omnipresent. Now, some people will say, "Yes, music is important, but it's a talent, not an intelligence." And I say, "Fine, let's call it a talent." But, then we have to leave the word intelligent out of all discussions of human abilities. You know, Mozart was extremely smart!

- *Interpersonal intelligence* is understanding other people. It's an ability we all need, but is at a premium if you are a teacher, clinician, salesperson, or politician. Anybody who deals with other people has to be skilled in the interpersonal sphere.

- *Intrapersonal intelligence* refers to having an understanding of yourself, of knowing who you are, what you can do, what you want to do, how you react to things, which things to avoid, and which things to gravitate toward. We are drawn to people who have a good understanding of themselves because those people tend not to screw up. They tend to know what they can do. They tend to know what they can't do. And they tend to know where to go if they need help.

- *Naturalist intelligence* designates the human ability to discriminate among living things (plants, animals) as well as sensitivity to other features of the natural world (clouds, rock configurations). This ability was clearly of value in our evolutionary past as hunters, gatherers, and farmers; it continues to be central in such roles as botanist or chef. I also speculate that much of our consumer society exploits the naturalist intelligences, which can be mobilized in the discrimination among cars, sneakers, kinds of makeup, and the like. The kind of pattern recognition valued in certain of the sciences may also draw upon naturalist intelligence.

Annotated Bibliography of Children's Books for Elementary Science

Key: E = easy book; P = picture book.

Alvin, Virginia and Robert Silverstein. *Plants.* New York: Twenty-First Century Books, 1996. For more mature upper-elementary school pupils, this is an excellent, well-illustrated beginning book for exploring the world of plants.

Anderson, Margaret J. *Issac Newton: The Greatest Scientist of All Time.* New York: Enslow, 1996. Nicely illustrated with photographs and drawings, the life, work, and goals of Isaac Newton are described. A descriptive chapter of experiments on color, paddle wheels, and gravity motivates children to think and explore, as Newton did.

Arnold, Caroline. *Bat.* Illustrated with photographs by Richard Hewett. New York: Morrow, 1996. Relates the fascinating life history of American bats, with special emphasis on Mexican free-tailed and big brown bats. Facts dispel many myths and superstitions about these nocturnal flying mammals. Excellent photographs in full color.

Arnosky, Jim. *All About Deer.* New York: Scholastic, 1996. Illustrated by the author, this delightful book gives young children a close-up look at deer. It describes their physical characteristics, what they eat, how they raise their young, how they travel, and the dangers they face from predators. E, P

Atwell, Debby. *Barn.* New York: Houghton/Lorraine, 1996. A 200-year-old New Hampshire barn tells the story of its raising, decline, and resurrection. Beautiful folk-art paintings record the changing seasons, activities, and times. E

Bash, Barbara. *Ancient Ones: The World of the Old-Growth Douglas Fir.* San Francisco: Sierra Club, 1994. Watercolor paintings are used in depicting the life cycle of the Douglas fir tree and its place in the ecology of the forest.

Bash, Barbara. *Shadows of Night: The Hidden World of the Little Brown Bat.* San Francisco: Sierra Club, 1993. A well illustrated description of the day-to-day life of the brown bat.

Bonnet, Bob and Dan Keen. *Science Fair Projects with Electricity and Electronics.* New York: Sterling, 1996. For those boys and girls in the upper-elementary grades who are looking for science fair projects which deal with electricity, this is an ideal, easy-to-follow resource.

Booth, David. *The Dust Bowl.* Illustrated by Karen Reczuch. Toronto: Kids Can Press Ltd., 1996. This is a tale of the great drought of the 1930s. It captures readers' attention from the very beginning with its colorful illustrations and wonderfully large print.

Booth, Jerry. *You Animal!* Illustrated by Nancy King. San Diego: Gulliver Green/Harcourt Brace, 1996. Well-described activities, from collecting and observing slime molds to testing human ability to differentiate odors, encourage children to creatively explore their world. An enticing narrative compares human senses to those of animals.

Brandenburg, Jim. *To the Top of the World: Adventures with Arctic Wolves.* New York: Walker, 1993. This book is a personal account of the author's observations of an Arctic wolf pack, complete with marvelous color photographs.

Brooks, Bruce. *Making Sense: Animal Perception and Communication.* New York: Farrar, 1993. This book is a penetrating examination of how animals use their senses to perceive their world and for communication.

Challoner, Jack. *The Visual Dictionary of Chemistry.* New York: DK Publishing,

1996. The typical, wonderfully illustrated, eye-appealing, irresistible kind of book that you expect from DK. Elementary pupils will contemplate this magnificent resource for hours on end.

Chandler, Gary and Kevin Graham. *Alternative Energy Sources.* New York: Twenty-First Century Books, 1996. A logical look at options for common resources for energy production.

Cherry, Lynne. *A River Ran Wild.* San Diego, CA: Harcourt, 1992. The Nashua River in New England is the subject of this book which explores the river's history and what effect human influence has had on the river and nature in general.

Chinery, Michael. *How Bees Make Honey.* Tarrytown, NY: Benchmark Books, 1997. A well-illustrated, fascinating little book that will interest less-mature pupils in the upper-elementary grades and introduce them to the intricacies of honey-bee society.

Cobb, Cathy and Harold Goldwhite. *Creations of Fire: Chemistry's Lively History from Alchemy to the Atomic Age.* New York: Plenum Press, 1995. An engaging chronology of the development of chemistry, from the spooky exploits of alchemists to the incredible accomplishments of atomic scientists. For more mature upper-elementary pupils.

Cole, Joanna. *The Magic School Bus Inside the Earth.* Illustrated by Bruce Degen. New York: Scholastic, 1987. Ms. Frizzle takes her class on a field trip to the Earth's center for an investigation of geology.

Cone, Molly. *Squishy, Misty, Damp & Muddy: The In-between World of Wetlands.* New York: Sierra Club, 1996. Provocative photographs enhance this story of the diversity of wetlands and the abundant life they support. It also speaks of their precarious future and the importance of preservation. Richly innovative text is enhanced by touches of alliteration and an almost poetic cadence. E

Couper, Heather and Nigel Henbest. *Black Holes.* Illustrated with various drawings and diagrams by Luciano Corbella. New York: DK Publishing, 1996. The text and superb illustrations describe the role that black holes play in our universe and bring the reader to the frontier of scientific knowledge.

Dingus, Lowell and Mark A Norell. *Searching for Velociraptor.* New York: HarperCollins, 1996. Retraces the 1920s explorations of Roy Chapman Andrews, who was searching for human fossils in Mongolia but instead discovered the first dinosaur eggs. Illustrated with color photographs.

Doherty, Paul, Dan Rathjen, and the Exploratorium Teacher Institute. *The Cool Hot Rod and Other Electrifying Experiments on Energy and Matter.* New York: Wiley, 1996. A great resource for exciting experiments, demonstrations, and investigations in physical science.

Esbensen, Juster. *Echoes for the Eye: Poems to Celebrate Patterns in Nature.* Illustrated by Helen K. Davie. New York: HarperCollins, 1996. Illustrated with pastel drawings, these "poems to celebrate patterns in nature" introduce observation and integrate several subject areas.

Farris, Katherine. *You Asked? Over 300 Great Questions and Astounding Answers.* Toronto: Owl Books, 1996. One of those wonderful question-and-answer books that can entrance upper-elementary children for hours on end.

Fitzgerald, Karen. *The Story of Oxygen.* New York: Franklin Watts/Grolier, 1996. Illustrated with various photographs, prints, and diagrams, this book goes from myth and mystery to discovery and explanation, chronicling the discovery of oxygen. The book describes the unique characteristics of oxygen, such as its importance to life, chemical behaviors, and abundance, and tells the stories of many scientists and their contributions.

Fox, Mary Virginia. *Satellites.* Tarrytown, NY: Benchmark Books, 1996. This book will help boys and girls in the upper-elementary grades develop an understanding of what satellites are and how they are employed in today's world.

Funston, Sylvia and Jay Ingram. *A Kid's Guide to the Brain.* Illustrated by Gary Clement. Toronto: Greey de Pencier, 1994. A fascinating compendium of facts about the function of the human brain. The book is divided into four major sections: senses, emotions, memory, and thinking. Simple enough for upper-elementary children but fascinating even for adults.

Gibbons, Gail. *The Milk Makers.* New York: Macmillan, 1985. This delightful picture book shows how dairy cows produce milk and the steps involved in getting the milk to the market. P

Gibbons, Gail. *Spiders.* New York: Holiday House, 1993. This picture book looks at different kinds of spiders and examines their characteristics. P

Glaser, Linda. *Compost! Growing Gardens From Your Garbage.* Illustrated by Anca Hariton. New York: Millbrook, 1996. Learn about the wonderful world of composting through the eyes of a little girl. She narrates what composting is, what her family puts into the composting bin, how they maintain it, and how they use it to fertilize their garden. Richly illustrated with watercolors. P

Guiberson, Brenda Z. *Into the Sea.* Illustrated by Alix Berenzy. New York: Holt, 1996. Magnificent underwater seascapes, a compelling text, and a dramatic sense of danger describe the real-life trials of a female sea turtle. E

Heilgman, Deborah. *From Caterpillar to Butterfly.* Illustrated by Bari Weissman. New York: HarperCollins, 1996. Butterfly growth stages are seen through the eyes of children in a primary classroom. Illustrations are large, bright, and detailed. Includes a guide to common butterflies. P

Hickman, Pamela. *The Kids Canadian Bug Book.* Illustrated by Heather Collins. Toronto: Kids Can Press, 1996. Different topics are considered in each section of this delightfully illustrated book. Topics include insects at night, insect migration, giant moths, and the like. E, P

Hickman, Pamela. *The Kids Canadian Plant Book.* Illustrated by Heather Collins. Toronto: Kids Can Press, 1996. Sections of this book deal with different topics, like pollination, surviving winter, and plant defenses. Some sections have suggested activities and experiments. E, P

Hodge, Deborah. *Bears: Polar Bears, Black Bears and Grizzly Bears.* Illustrated by Pat Stephens. Toronto: Kids Can Press Limited, 1996. An information book about the grizzly bear, the polar bear and the black bear. To make research about this popular animal easy and enjoyable for children, the author organized the information into fourteen two-page chapters, such as "Bear Food", "How Bears are Born", "How Bears Protect Themselves", "Bears and People" and "Bears Around the World". E

Iritz, Maxine Haren. *Super Science Fair Sourcebook.* New York: McGraw-Hill, 1996. For boys and girls in the middle-school grades, this is an excellent resource for finding suitable science fair projects.

Jackson, Donna M. *The Bone Detectives: How Forensic Anthropologists Solve Crimes and Uncover Mysteries of the Dead.* Illustrated with photographs by Charlie Fellenbaum. Boston: Little, Brown, 1996. This intriguing book details the investigative processes used by forensic anthropologists to determine the sex, race, height, and weight of a person by studying the bones and teeth.

Jenkins, Steve. *Big & Little.* New York: Houghton, 1996. Illustrations by the author and exciting cut-paper collages reveal the similarities and differences among creatures great and small; the long and the short of the animal kingdom.

Johnson, Jinny. *Simon & Schuster Children's Guide To Birds.* New York: Simon and Schuster, 1996. Beautiful photographs, drawings, and fact-packed text take the reader soaring through the air with the American golden plover or diving with the king penguin in this engaging and informative one-volume encyclopedia on birds.

Johnson, Sylvia. *Raptor Rescue! An Eagle Flies Free.* Photographs by Ron Winch. New York: Dutton, 1995. This book describes the work of the Gabbert Raptor Center at the University of Minnesota in caring for and rehabilitating injured birds.

Kaufman, Allan and Jim Flowers. *Technology Projects for the Classroom.* Ann Arbor, MI: Prakken, 1996. More mature upper-elementary pupils with a penchant for today's high-tech sophistication will engage in these technology projects with enthusiasm.

Keeler, Patricia A., and Francis X. McCall, Jr. *Unraveling Fibers.* New York: Atheneum, 1995. Natural fibers from plants and animals and man-made, synthetic fibers are explored in this book which is illustrated with color photographs.

Lasky, Kathryn. *Sugaring Time.* Photographs by Christopher Knight. New York: Macmillan, 1983. A family farm in Vermont is the setting for this book which uses photographs to enhance the description of what happens at maple sugar time.

Lasky, Kathryn. *Surtsey: The Newest Place on Earth.* New York: Hyperion, 1992. The creation of Surtsey, a volcanic island off the coast of Iceland, is the subject of this book.

Lauber, Patricia. *Hurricanes: Earth's Mightiest Storms.* New York: Scholastic, 1996. Illustrated with various photographs, diagrams, and maps, hurricanes is an amazing work that uses narrative very effectively in weaving the story of these powerful storms. Clearly written and relevant text combined with impressive photographs and informative illustrations enhance this excellent upper-elementary book.

Lauber, Patricia. *The News About Dinosaurs.* New York: Bradbury, 1989. This book examines how new discoveries by scientists are challenging what was previously believed about dinosaurs.

Lauber, Patricia. *Seeing Earth from Space.* New York: Orchard, 1991. This book uses NASA photographs as enhancements to provide a unique perspective about the Earth.

Lauber, Patricia. *Summer of Fire: Yellowstone 1988.* New York: Orchard, 1991. A description of the 1988 fire at Yellowstone National Park and how plants and animals have returned to the forest ecology in the burned areas of the park.

Lauber, Patricia. *Volcano: The Eruption and Healing of Mount St. Helens.* New York: Bradbury, 1986. The 1980 eruption of Mount St. Helens and the aftermath is decribed in this book which is well illustrated with color photographs.

Lessem, Don. *Dinosaur Worlds: New Dinosaurs, New Discoveries.* New York: Boyds Mills, 1996. Illustrated with various photographs, drawings, diagrams, and maps, this book contains the latest information about what the dinosaurs looked like, how they lived, how they died, and how they were discovered. This is a comprehensive reference about the Age of the Dinosaurs.

London, Jonathan. *Red Wolf Country.* Illustrated by Daniel San Souci. New York: Dutton, 1996. Two red wolves experience winter's hardships, evade enemies, and look for a good place to den. Lyrical prose and naturalistic watercolors make this an unforgettable survival story. E

Malam, John. *Highest, Longest, Deepest: A Foldout Guide to the World's Record Breakers.* Illustrated by Gary Hincks. New York: Simon and Schuster, 1996. Richly illustrated pages cover natural phenomena, such as the longest river, highest waterfall, and largest desert. Outline boxes highlight other fascinating facts. Foldout landscape pages are durable and increase the book's interest.

Markle, Sandra. *Science to the Rescue.* New York: Atheneum, 1994. This book addresses contemporary problems and the ways that modern science is solving them.

Moore, Patrick and Wil Tirion. *Cambridge Guide to Stars and Planets.* New York: Cambridge University Press, 1997. For more mature elementary pupils, this is an accurate and detailed book about the solar system, the universe, and the field of astronomy.

Oldfield, Sara. *Rain Forests.* New York: Lerner, 1996. This amazing book uses detailed text and excellent photographs to detail the many aspects of rain forests. It includes information about the people who inhabit the rain forests and their cultures, the uses and abuses of the land, and the future of rain forests.

Penny, Malcolm. *How Plants Grow.* Tarrytown, NY: Benchmark Books, 1997. This excellent, well-illustrated little book is an excellent beginning look at the world of plants for less-mature upper-elementary pupils.

Pringle, Laurence. *Fire in the Forest: A Cycle of Growth and Renewal.* Illustrated by Bob Marstall. New York: Atheneum, 1995. This book explains the fire cycle in the forest and its relationship to the ecology of the forest.

Ripley, Catherine. Do the Doors Open by Magic? And Other Supermarket Questions. Illustrated by Scot Ritchie. Toronto: Owl Book, 1995. A delightfully illustrated book that helps answer all sorts of questions about the supermarket, including how they get apples in the winter. E, P

Patent, Dorothy Hinshaw. *Biodiversity.* New York: Clarion, 1996. A look into the world of complexity, intricacy, and abundant variations in the biosphere.

Ripley, Catherine. *Why Is Soap So Slippery? And Other Bathtime Questions.* Illustrated by Scot Ritchie. Toronto: Owl Books, 1995. Deals with such bath-related questions as why some shampoos sting your eyes, how towels dry overnight and why fingers wrinkle in the tub. E, P

Sandeman, Anna. *Blood.* Illustrated by Ian Thompson. New York: Copper Beach/Millbrook, 1996. This book offers a look at the heart, lungs, and blood vessels to find out how the blood keeps flowing and why it is essential to life. P

Scott, Michael. *Ecology.* New York: Oxford, 1996. Illustrated with various photographs, drawings, diagrams, and maps, this book provides readers with a rich first look at Earth's habitats and ecosystems. Readers explore the adaptation of plant and animal life in response to the Earth's changing conditions.

Silverstein, Shel. *Falling Up.* New York: HarperCollins, 1996. An eclectic volume of poems, many scientific, by the master of children's poetry. Sassy and clever, Silverstein's poems and cartoons crackle with rebellious humor.

Simon, Seymour. *Earthquakes.* New York: Morrow, 1991. The nature of earthquakes is explained with the help of photographs.

Simon, Seymour. *The Heart: Our Circulatory System.* New York: Morrow, 1996. Numerous computer-colored micrographs taken by a scanning electron microscope illustrate this magnificent book describing the heart and its functions. Cross-section drawings provide stimulating details.

Sis, Peter. *Starry Messenger: Galileo Galilei.* New York: Farrar/Foster, 1996. A telescopic look at the superlative stargazer, Galileo. The prestige and lunacy surrounding Galileo and his ideas are articulated in brief text and superb illustrations by the author.

Skurzynski, Gloria. *Waves: The Electromagnetic Universe.* Washington: National Geographic, 1996. Spectacular color photographs and easy-to-follow diagrams help children understand basic scientific principles at work in everyday technology. Simple enough for children to understand the link between pure and applied science, yet advanced enough so that children ponder over questions that researchers continue to study today.

Snedden, Robert. *Space.* New York: Chelsea House, 1996. A beautifully illustrated, up-to-date look at space for the elementary school pupil.

Stanley, Diane. *Leonardo da Vinci.* New York: Morrow, 1996. Elegant paintings by the author and captivating text communicate the complex personality and myriad pursuits of one of the most creative individuals of all times.

Taylor, Barbara. *Animal Homes.* New York: DK Publishing, 1996. Typical of the eye appeal in most DK children's books, this beautifully illustrated book shows a variety of animal homes, including those of ants, termites, birds, and small mammals. Embellished with interesting and accurate information about each featured animal.

Taylor, Charles and Stephen Pope. *The Oxford Children's Book of Science.* New York: Oxford University Press, 1996. An excellent and enticing general resource for children in the upper-elementary grades.

VanCleave, Janice. *Janice VanCleave's Guide to the Best Science Fair Projects.* New York: Wiley, 1997. An excellent resource for upper elementary pupils seeking ideas for projects for the school science fair.

Wiese, Jim. *Rocket Science: 50 Flying, Floating, Flipping, Spinning Gadgets Kids Create Themselves.* Toronto: John Wiley and Sons, 1995. This book's sections (mechanics, air power, water power, electricity and magnetism, chemistry, acoustics, and optics) include fun projects with clear explanations of the pertinent scientific principles. Illustrated with perky black-and-white drawings.

Wilson, Janet. *The Ingenious Mr. Peale: Painter, Patriot and Man of Science.* New York: S & S/Atheneum, 1996. This colorful biography explores scientist Charles Peale's spirited personality and assorted pursuits, including his art and scientific discoveries in the field of natural history.

Yolen, Jane. *Welcome to the Sea of Sand.* Illustrated by Laura Regan. New York: Putnam, 1996. The wildlife, weather, and natural wonders of the Sonora Desert are showcased in this book of poetic narrative and splendid paintings. Waves of sand and splashes of color are used to disclose a sea of wonder.

Yount, Lisa. *Antoni van Leeuwenhoek: First to See Microscopic Life.* New York: Enslow, 1996. The story of the life of Antoni van Leeuwenhoek. Not a scientist but a fabric seller, van Leeuwenhoek's life teaches us much about the science processes of observation, persistence, record keeping, and hypothesis. He improved upon a tool of his trade, the magnifying glass, to create quality microscopes. Includes activities using a microscope or magnifying glass.

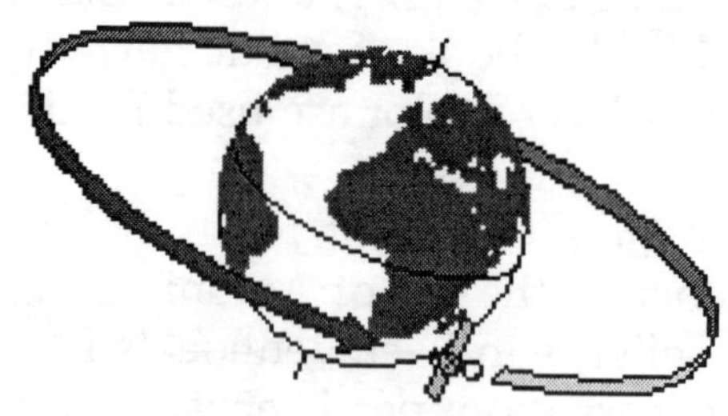

SCIENCE RESOURCES ON THE INTERNET

http://www.stsci.edu/pubinfo/edugroup/stesop-page.html
Space Telescope Science Institute Elementary School Outreach Program. A program designed for pre-service training of teachers in astronomy related areas.

http://www.stsci.edu/
Space Telescope Science Institute. This site is provided by NASA to study the Hubble Space Telescope, a cooperative program of the European Space Agency (ESA) and the National Aeronautics and Space Administration (NASA) to operate a long-lived space-based observatory for the benefit of the international astronomical community.

http://www.stsci.edu/science/net-resources.html
AstroWeb: Astronomical Internet Resources. This site contains pointers to potentially relevant resources available via Internet.

http://www.indiana.edu/~primate/primates.html
African Primates At Home. This site offers images and sounds of East African monkeys and apes recorded by the primatologist M.K. Holder.

http://outcast.gene.com/ae/AE/AEPC/WWC/1991/opposable.html
The Opposable Thumb. The goal is to provide students with various opportunities to understand the physical importance of the opposable thumb among primates.

http://www.miamisci.org/ph/default.htm
The pH Factor. A site designed as a resource to help elementary and middle school teachers introduce acids and bases to their students.

http://tommy.jsc.nasa.gov/~woodfill/SPACEED/SEHHTML/seh.html
The Space Educators' Handbook. Devoted to topics about space.

http://www.acs.org/edugen2/education/ws/wsactiv2/ltolumps.htm
Liquids To Lumps. Everything in the world is made of chemicals! This site is about how chemicals join together to make different, new chemicals.

http://ag.arizona.edu/AES/mac/ahb/ahbhome.html
Africanized Honey Bee Education Project. Africanized honey bees have moved into the Southwest and are here to stay. In addition to the safety issues that need to be addressed because of the defensiveness of these bees, honey bees are also fascinating subjects to study. These lesson plans were developed to familarize pupils with honey bees and bee safety issues through a variety of interesting activities.

http://www.bos.nl/homes/bijlmakers/ento/begin.html
Entomology For Beginners. Entomology is the study of insects. This site provides some basic information on insects.

http://www.ex.ac.uk/~gjlramel/welcome.html
The Wonderful World of Insects. Lots of information about insects, including a glossary of entomological terms, taxonomy, evolution, and care sheets for commonly kept species.

http://www.rfhsm.ac.uk:81/golly/glowworm.html
The Glow Worm Page. Lampyris noctiluca, the glow worm, is not at all worm-like but is a beetle up to 25 mm long. All you could want to know about this interesting little creature is presented on this site.

http://mgfx.com:80/butterfly/
The Butterfly Web Site. Butterfly gardening, raising butterflies, education, and conservation make this the complete one-stop butterfly site.

http://www.tesser.com/minibeast/quiz.htm
Minibeast World of Insects and Spiders. Insects and their relatives (Arthropods) are some of the most amazing animals that inhabit our world, yet most of us rarely give them credit for their incredible abilities. The "Amazing Animal Quiz" can help you and your students "tune in" to the incredible world of arthropods and open their eyes and minds to learning more about them.

http://www.gene.com/ae/AE/AEC/AEF/1996/talbot_observation.html
Cell Observation Excercise. The pupils are required to learn how to use a microscope, know how to determine size of objects, make a wet mount, stain cells, identify large cellular structures, know differences between procaryotic, eukaryotic, plant, and animal cells.

http://www.gene.com/ae/AE/AEPC/WWC/1991/microbial.html
Using A Winogradsky Column to Analyze Microbial Communities. In this investigation, pupils will use easily obtained materials to study ecological succession in a microbiological community. The investigation is appropriate for a variety of age groups. Elementary pupils will be fascinated by the changes occurring over time in their bottles.

http://putwest.boces.org/StSu/Science.html
Educational Standards and Curriculum Frameworks for Science. An annotated listing of science standards by organization and state.

http://seds.lpl.arizona.edu/nineplanets/nineplanets/mars.html
Mars. All about the 4th planet from the sun.

http://raven.umnh.utah.edu/new/teachkits/disease.kit.1.html
The Natural History of Genes: Disease Genetics. From the Utah Museum of Natural History, this site is an electronic curriculum for learning about disease genetics. Includes classroom activities and online resources.

http://www.adler.uchicago.edu/universe/Activities/crater.htm
Create A Crater Activity. Designed for children ages 8-15, this activity allows the participants to experiment with the cratering process by investigating how speed and size of an impacting body influence the shape and depth of craters, and how the surface material is disrupted.

http://weber.u.washington.edu/~chudler/neurok.htm
Neuroscience for Kids. The smell of a flower, the memory of a walk in the park, or the pain of stepping on a nail are experiences made possible by the 3 pounds of tissue in our heads called the BRAIN!! This home page has been created for elementary and secondary school students and teachers who would like to learn more about the nervous system. Enjoy the activities and experiments on your way to learning more about the brain and spinal cord.

http://www.med.harvard.edu:80/AANLIB/home.html
The Whole Brain Atlas. An incredible atlas of views of the brain, both in its healthy stages and when it is invaded by diseases.

http://www.pbs.org/wgbh/pages/nova/einstein/
Einstein Revealed. All about the Genius among Geniuses!

http://www.nalusda.gov/fnic/
Food and Nutrition Information Center. (USDA/FDA). This site includes a wealth of nutrition information.

http://www.brown.edu/Departments/Italian_Studies/dweb/plague/plague.html
The Plague. This site includes contemporary and modern perspectives about the origins, causes, and effects of the plague.

http://falcon.miamisci.org/hurricane/
Hurricane: Storm Science. A five-part resource on hurricanes developed with the (upper) elementary pupil and teacher in mind. Includes a guide for teaching weather in the classroom. Learn about tracking, go inside a hurricane, or read the story of one family that survived a killer storm. Lots of activities, including how to make and use a barometer.

http://www.nsf.gov/
National Science Foundation World Wide Web server. Abundant information on science-related matters as well as extensive links to science areas. The National Science Foundation makes grants and awards in all areas of science.

http://www.carr.lib.md.us/ccps/hose.htm
The Hands-On Elementary Science Program. A complete science curriculum for grades 1-5 that was developed and piloted by teachers and other educators of the Carroll County Public Schools in Maryland.

http://essc.calumet.purdue.edu/
Elementary Science Support Center. The Center supports authentic, problem-based science learning in grades K-8 that is creative, exciting, and intellectually stimulating. Their theme: *If a child cannot learn the way you teach, teach the way he learns.*

http://www.ties.k12.mn.us/~jnorth/
Journey North. An annual Internet-based learning adventure that engages pupils in a global study of wildlife migration and seasonal changes.

http://www.nsta.org/onlineresources/links/resources/
Online Resources. Lesson plans for numerous topics in elementary school science.

http://netnow.micron.net/~bmartini/hots.htm#Science
Bruce R. Martini's Bookmarks for Science. An absolutely awesome set of links to science resources.

http://www.nhm.ac.uk/
The Natural History Museum of London.

http://www.nanothinc.com/NanoWorld/nwtocstandard.htm
Nanoworld. A journey into the world of the small.

http://server2.greatlakes.k12.mi.us/Browser/UNITEResource/Natural_ScienceOutline.html
Natural Science Content. Wonderful site for exploring a vast array of natural science subject areas.

http://www.ngdc.noaa.gov/mgg/image/mggd.gif
Global Relief Map. A great color picture of the Earth, including the sea floor.

http://www.thomson.com/wadsworth/geo/hydrosphere.html#oceans
Earth Science Resource Center. Great links to all sorts of earth science and oceanic resources.

http://www.ncdc.noaa.gov/olimages.htm
Online Images of Storms. Outstanding set of satellite and radar images of almost every hurricane and storm in memory.

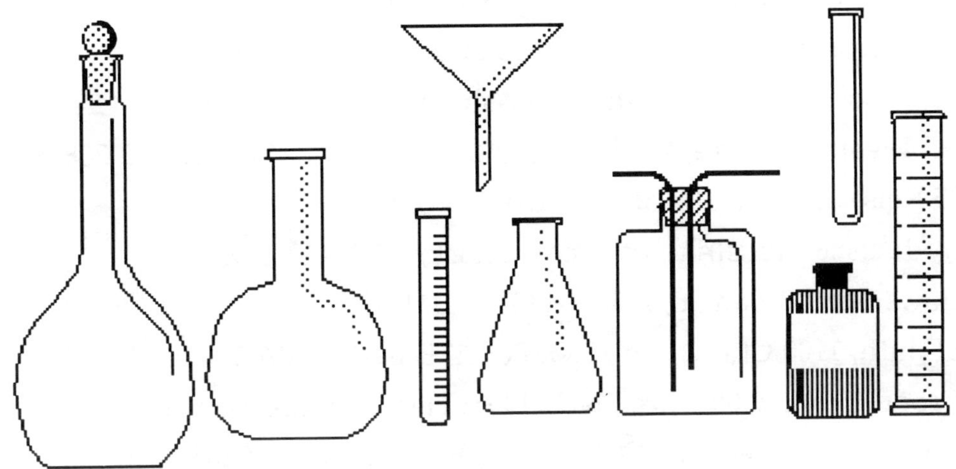

Sources for Science Equipment and Supplies

Life (L), Earth (E), Physical (P), General (G)

A C Supply, 1746 Winding Glen Rd, P.O. Box 1523, St. Charles, MO 63302 (G)

A-L-L Magnetics, Inc., 930 S. Placentia Ave., Placentia, CA 92670 (P)

A.D.A.M. Software, Inc., 1600 River Edge Pkwy., Ste. 800, Atlanta, GA 30328 (G)

AIMS Education Foundation, P.O. Box 8120, Fresno, CA 93747-8120 (G)

Accu-Scope, Inc., 7 Littleworth Ln., Sea Cliff, NY 11579 (P)

Accu-Weather Inc., 619 W. College Ave., State College, PA 16801 (E)

AccuLab Products Group, 614 Scenic Dr., Ste. 104, Modesto, CA 95350 (P)

Acculab Balances, 8 Pheasant Run, Newtown, PA 18940 (P)

Acorn Naturalists, 17300 E. 17th St., Ste. J-236, Tustin, CA 92780 (E)

Adventures Co., 435 Main St., Johnson City, NY 13790 (E)

Air Chek, Inc., P.O. Box 2000, Arden, NC 28704 (P)

American 3B Scientific, 2189 Flinstone Dr., Ste. 0, Tucker, GA 30084 (G)

American Chemical Society, 1155 16th St., N.W., Washington, DC 20036 (P)

American Educational Products, 401 Hictory St., Fort Collins, CO 80522 (G)

American Science & Surplus, 3605 Howard St., Skokie, IL 60076 (G)

American Water Works Assoc., 6666 W. Quincy Ave., Denver, CO 80235 (E)

Apogee Components, Inc., 708 Piedra Dr. Ste. C, Canon City, CO 81212-2253 (P)

Apple Computer, 20525 Mariani Ave., Cupertino, CA 95014 (G)

Arbor Scientific, P.O. Box 2750, Ann Arbor, MI 48106-2750 (G)
Armstrong Medical Industries, 545 Knightsbridge Pkwy., Lincolnshire, IL 60069 (L)
Associated Microscope, P.O. Box 1076, Elon College, NC 27244 (L)
Astronomical Society of the Pacific, 390 Ashton Ave., San Francisco, CA 94112 (E)
Automated Weather Source, 2-5 Metropolitan Ct., Gaithersburg, MD 20878 (E)
Azlon, 205 Kelsey Ln., Ste. I, Tampa, FL 33619 (G)
Bel-Art Products, 6 Industrial Rd., Pequannock, NJ 07440-1992 (P)
Ben Meadows, 3589 Broad St., Atlanta, GA 30341 (G)
Binney & Smith, 1100 Church Ln., P.O. Box 431, Easton, PA 18044-0431 (G)
Bio-Rad Laboratories, 2000 Alfred Nobel Dr., Hercules, CA 94547 (L)
Biology Store, 275 Pauma Pl., P.O. Box 2691, Escondido, CA 92033 (L)
Biospace, 0504 Crystal Cir., Carbondale, CO 81623 (L)
Biosphere 2 & HSP, P.O. Box 689, Oracle, AZ 85623 (L)
Black Forest Observatory, 12815 Porcupine Lane, Colorado Springs, CO 80908-3503 (E)
Boeckeler Instruments, 3280 E. Hemisphere Loop, Bldg. 114, Tucson, AZ 85706 (P)
Boreal Labs, Ltd., 399 Vansickle Rd., St. Catharines, ON CANADA L2S 3T4 (P)
Brinkmann Instruments, 1 Cantigue Rd., P.O. Box 1019, Westbury, NY 11590-0207 (P)
Brock Optical, 414 Lake Howell Rd., Maitland, FL 32751 (P)
Budd Wentz Productions, 8619 Skyline Blvd., Oakland, CA 94611 (G)
Bureau of Economic Geology, P. O. Box X, University Station, Austin, TX 78713 (E)
Burleigh Instruments, Inc., P.O. Box E, Burleigh Park, Fishers, NY 14453 (P)
Burt Harrison & Co., 19 Water St., P.O. Box 732, Weston, MA 02154 (G)
CCS Educational, 24 Rogate Pl., Scarborough, Ontario, CA CANADA M1M 3C3 (G)
CHEM, Lawrence Hall of Science, University of California, Berkeley, CA 94720 (P)
CHEMetrics, Inc., Route 28, Calverton, VA 20138 (P)
CORD Communications, P.O. Box 21206, Waco, TX 76702-1206 (P)
Caley & Whitmore Corp., 18 Highland Ave., Somerville, MA 02143 (G)
Cambridge Physics Outlet, 10 E Green St., Woburn, MA 01801 (P)
Captivation, Inc., 9 Cannongate Dr., Nashua, NH 03063-1943 (P)
Cardboard Carpentry Workshop, 2578 Stape Rd., Penn Yan, NY 14527 (E)
Carl Zeiss, Inc., One Zeiss Dr., Thornwood, NY 10594 (L)
Carolina Biological Supply Co., 2700 York Rd., Burlington, NC 27215 (L)

Carson-Dellosa Publishing Co., 4321 Piedmont Pkwy., Greensboro, NC 27410 (G)
Casio, Inc, 570 North Pleasant Ave., Dover, NJ 07801 (P)
Center Enterprises, Inc., P.O. Box 331361, West Hartford, CT 06133-1361, (G)
Center for Multisensory Learning, University of California, Lawrence Hall of Science, Berkeley, CA 94720-5200 (E)
Central Scientific Co., 3300 CENCO Pkwy., Franklin Park, IL 60131 (G)
Chem Scientific, LLC,67 Chapel St., Newton, MA 02158 (P)
Churchill Media, 6677 N. Northwest Hwy., Chicago, IL 60631 (P)
Coastline Engineering, P.O. Box 26945, Jacksonville, FL 32226 (E)
Connecticut Valley Biological Supply, 82 Valley Rd., Southampton, MA 01073 (L)
Coors Ceramics Co., 16000 Table Mountain Pkwy., Golden, CO 80403 (E)
Corning, Science Products Division, BF-02, Corning, NY 14831 (P)
Cosmos Ltd., 9215 Waukegan Rd., Morton Grove, IL 60053 (E)
Creative Dimensions, P.O. Box 1393, Bellingham, WA 98227 (G)
Creative Teaching Associates, P.O. Box 7766, Fresno, CA 93747 (G)
Crystal Productions, 1812 Johns Dr., P.O. Box 2159, Glenview, IL 60025 (P)
Cuisenaire Co. of America, 10 Bank St., Box 5026, White Plains, NY 10602-5026 (P)
E & L Microscope & Balance Co., 131 N. Broad St., Carlinville, IL 62626 (L)
D & H Distributing Co., 2525 N. 7th St., Harrisburg, PA 17110 (G)
D.C. Heath and Co. School Div., 125 Spring St., Lexington, MA 02173 (G)
DEMCO, Inc./Science Cap, 4810 Forest Run Rd., Madison, WI 53707 (G)
Daedalon Corp., P.O. Box 2028, Salem, MA 01970-6228 (G)
Dale Seymour Publications, P.O. Box 5026, White Plains, NY 10602-5026 (G)
Data Harvest Educational, 349 Lang Blvd., Grand Island, NY 14072 (G)
Davis Instruments, 3465 Diablo Ave., Hayward, CA 94545 (P)
Delta Biologicals, P.O. Box 26666, Tucson, AZ 85726-6666 (L)
Delta Education, 12 Simon ST., P.O. Box 300, Nashua, NH 03061 (G)
Denoyer-Geppert Science Co., 5225 Ravenswood Ave., Chicago, IL 60640-2028 (E)
Design Science Toys, 1362 Rt. 9, Tivoli, NY 12583 (P)
Dinosaur Discovery, 39 Lovering St., Medway, MA 02053 (L)
Discovery Scope, Inc., 15721 Bernardo Hts. Pkwy, St. E401, San Diego, CA 92128 (L)
DuPont NEN Products, 549 Albany St., Boston, MA 02118 (G)

E & L Instruments, 70 Fulton Terr., P.O. Box 1942, New Haven, CT 06509 (P)
EME, P.O. Box 2805, Danbury, CT 06813-2805 (G)
ERIM-Earth Observation Group, P.O. Box 134001, Ann Arbor, MI 48113 (E)
ESE Instruments, 1362 Trinity Dr., Los Alamos, NM 87544 (P)
ETA, 620 Lakeview Pkwy., Vernon Hills, IL 60061-9923 (G)
Eagle Instruments, 20 Adrian Ct., Burlingame, CA 94010 (P)
Earth Science Resource Center, Colorado School of Mines, Golden, CO 80401 (E)
Edmund Scientific Co., 101 E. Gloucester Pike, Barrington, NJ 08007 (G)
Educational Products, 1342 N. 1-35 East, Carrollton, TX 75006 (G)
Educational Rocks & Minerals, P.O. Box 60574, Florence, MA 01060 (E)
Edunetics Corp., 1600 Wilson Blvd., Ste. 710, Arlington, VA 22209 (P)
Edusource, Inc., 252 Snowdon Ave., Toronto, ON CANADA M4N 2B3 (G)
Edvotek, P.O. Box 1232, West Bethesda, MD 20827-1232 (P)
EmCal Scientific, P.O. Box 27105, San Diego, CA 92198-1105 (L)
Emerging Technology Consultants, 2819 Hamline Ave., N., St. Paul, MN 55113 (P)
Encyclopaedia Britannica Ed. Corp., 310 S. Michigan Ave., Chicago, IL 60604-9839 (G)
Entomological Society of America, 9301 Annapolis Rd., Lanham, MD 20706 (L)
Eric Armin Inc. (EAI), P.O. Box 644, Franklin Lakes, NJ 07417 (G)
Eshed Science & Technology, 445 Wall St., Princeton, NJ 08540 (P)
Estes Industries, 1295 H St., Penrose, CO 81240 (P)
Etgens Science Stuff, 3600 Whitney Ave., Sacramento, CA 95821 (G)
Export Science Associates, 36 Lexington Ave., Suffern, NY 10901 (G)
Extech Instruments Corp., 335 Bear Hill Rd., Waltham, MA 02154 (P)
FILETTE KEEZ(r) Corp., 3204 Channing Ln., Bedford, TX 76021-6506 (G)
FJW Optical Systems, 629 S. Vermont St., Palatine, IL 60067 (P)
FOTODYNE, 950 Walnut Ridge Dr., Hartland, WI 53029-9388 (P)
Fairbanks Scales, 821 Locust St., Kansas City, MO 64106 (P)
Fisher Scientific, 485 S. Frontage Rd., Educational Division, Burr Ridge, IL 60521 (G)
Flash Anatomy, 1284 E. Katella Ave., Anaheim, CA 92805 (L)
Flex-O-Models, P.O.Box 844, Everett, MA 02149 (G)
Flight Systems, Inc., 9300 E. 68th, Raytown, MO 64133 (P)
Flinn Scientific, Raddant Road, P.O. Box 219, Batavia, IL 60510 (G)

Flowerfield Enterprises, 10332 Shaver Rd., Dept. 105, Kalamazoo, MI 49002 (G)

Forestry Suppliers, P.O. Box 8397, Jackson, MS 39284-8397 (E)

Freund Publishing House Ltd., P.O. Box 35010, Tel Aviv, ISRAEL (E)

Frey Scientific, Div. of Beckley Cardy, 100 Paragon Pkwy., Mansfield, OH 44903 (E)

GEMS, Lawrence Hall of Science, University of California, Berkeley, CA 94720 (E)

General Supply Corp., P.O. Box 9347, Jackson, MS 39286-9347 (G)

Genesis, P.O. Box 2242, Mt. Vernon, WA 98273 (G)

GeoLearning Corp., P.O. Box 2042, Sheridan, WY 82801 (E)

George F. Cram Co., 301 S. Lasalle St., P.O. Box 426, Indianapolis, IN 46206, (E)

Geoscience Ltd., 410 S. Cedros Ave., Solana Beach, CA 92075-1996 (E)

Grau-Hall Scientific, 6401 Elvas Ave., Sacramento, CA 95819 (P)

HEMCO Corp., 111 North Powell Rd., Independence, MO 64056 (L)

Hach Co., P.O. Box 389, Loveland, CO 80539 (G)

Halsteducate Co., 2140 Lincolnwood Dr., Evanston, IL 60201-2061 (G)

Hampden Engineering Corp., 99 Shaker Rd., E. Longmeadow, MA 01028-0563 (P)

Hands-On Science, 6541 E. 40th St., Unit M, Tulsa, OK 74145-4521 (G)

Harvard Apparatus, 22 Pleasant St., So. Natick, MA 01760 (P)

Hawks, Owls & Wildlife, 701 Groveside Rd., Buskirk, NY 12028 (L)

Health Edco, P.O. Box 21207, Waco, TX 76702-1207 (P)

Holcombs, P.O. Box 94636, Cleveland, OH 44101 (G)

How the Weatherworks, 1522 Baylor Ave., Dept. 97 SES, Rockville, MD 20850 (E)

Howard Minerals, , P.O. Box 10056, Brookyln, NY 11210 (E)

Hubbard Scientific, 401 Hickory St., P.O. Box 2121, Fort Collins, CO 80522 (G)

IBM K-12 Education, P.O. Box 2150-H06B1, Atlanta, GA 30301-2150 (P)

INSIGHTS Visual Productions, P.O. Box 230644, Encinitas, CA 92023-0644 (G)

Ideal School Supply Co., 5623 W. 115th St., Alsip, IL 60482 (G)

Innova Corp., 115 George Lamb Rd., Leyden, MA 01337 (G)

Insect Lore, P.O. Box 1535, Shafter, CA 93263 (L)

Institute for Chemical Education, 1101 University Ave., Madison, WI 53706-1396 (P)

Intelitool, P.O. Box 459, Batavia, IL 60510 (G)

International Optics PLC, 325 Northgate Dr., P.O. Box 2050, Warrendale, PA 15086 (P)

Pelham Ltd., P.O. Box 310, North Stonington, CT 06359 (G)

J T & A, 4 Herbert St., Alexandria, VA 22305 (G)

James International Sales Ltd., 3960 Charles St., Burnaby, BC CANADA U5C 3K8 (G)

Junior Engineering Tech. Society, 1420 King St. Ste. 405, Alexandria, VA 22314 (G)

Kalyx Biosciences, Inc., 20 Camelot Dr., Nepean, ON CANADA K2G 5X8 (L)

Kemtec Educational Corp., 9889 Crescent Park Dr., West Chester, OH 45069 (G)

Ken-A-Vision Mfg. Co., 5615 Raytown Rd., Kansas City, MO 64133 (P)

Kimble/Kontes, 1025 Spruce St., Vineland, NJ 08360 (G)

Knowledge Revolution, 66 Bovet Rd., St. 200, San Francisco, CA 94402 (G)

Kons Scientific Co., Inc., P.O. Box 3, Germantown, WI 53022-0003 (G)

LABO AMERICA, INC., 44775 Aguila Terr., Fremont, CA 94539 (P)

LEGO Dacta, 555 Taylor Rd., Enfield, CT 06083 (E)

LaMotte Co., P.O. Box 329, Chestertown, MD 21620 (E)

Lab Safety Supply, 401 S. Wright Rd, P.O. Box 1368, Janesville, WI 53547-1368 (P)

Lab-Aids, 17 Colt Ct., Ronkonkoma, NY 11779 (L)

Lab-Volt Systems, Inc., P.O. Box 686, Farmingdale, NJ 07727 (P)

Laboratory Craftsmen, Inc., P.O. Box 148, Beloit, WI 53512 (E)

Laboratory Safety Workshop, 192 Worcester Rd., Natick, MA 01760-2252 (P)

Lafayette Instrument, 3700 Sagamore Pkwy., P.O. Box 5729, Lafayette, IN 47903 (P)

Laserpoint, 5629 Omni Dr., Sacramento, CA 95841 (P)

Lasy USA, 1309 Webster Ave., Fort Collins, CO 80524 (E)

L-M Wheaton Coated Products, 5176 Harding Hwy., Mays Landing, NJ 08330-2298 (L)

Learning Alternatives, 2370 W. 89A-Ste. #5, Sedona, AZ 86336 (G)

Learning Technologies, 40 Cameron Ave., Somerville, MA 02144 (G)

Learning Things, 68A Broadway, P.O. Box 436, Arlington, MA 02174 (G)

Leica, 111 Deerlake Rd., Deerfield, IL 60015 (P)

Let's Get Growing!, 1900 Commercial Wy., Santa Cruz, CA 95065 (G)

Leybold, Inc., 7050 Telford Way, Unit #5, Mississauga, On CANADA L5S 1V7 (G)

Life Technologies, P.O. Box 6009, Gaithersburg, MD 20884-9980 (L)

Lyon Electric Co., 2765 Main St., Chula Vista, CA 91911 (P)

MICRO-VID, P.O. Box 1517, Huntington Beach, CA 92647 (L)

MISONIX, 1938 New Highway, Farmingdale, NY 11735 (G)

MMI Corp., 2950 Wyman Pkwy., P.O. Box 19907, Baltimore, MD 21211 (G)

Magnet Source Master Magnetics., 607 S. Gilbert, Castle Rock, CO 80104 (P)

Magnetic Way, 80 Pineview Dr., A division of Creative Edge, Amherst, NY 14228 (P)

Math/Science Nucleus, 4009 Pestana Pl., Fremont, CA 94538-6301 (P)

Medical Plastics Laboratory, P.O. Box 38, Gatesville, TX 76528 (L)

Meiji Techno America, 2186 Bering Dr., San Jose, CA 95131 (E)

Merlan Scientific Ltd., 247 Armstrong Ave., Georgetown, ON CANADA L7G (E)

Metrologic Instruments, P.O. Box 307, Bellmawr, NJ 08099-0307 (P)

Mettler-Toledo, P.O. Box 71, Hightstown, NJ 08520 (P)

Mico-Optics, 68-21 Fresh Meadow Ln., Fresh Meadows, NY 11365 (P)

Micro Mole Scientific, 1312 N. 15th, Pasco, WA 99301 (P)

Microbix Education System, 341 Bering Ave., Toronto, ON CANADA M8Z 3A8 (L)

Microcosmos, Boston University, 605 Commonwealth Ave., Boston, MA 02215 (G)

Midwest Products Co., School Division, P.O. Box 564, Hobart, IN 46342 (G)

Model A Technology, 2420 Van Layden Wy., Modesto, CA 95356 (G)

Modern School Supplies, Inc., P.O. Box 958, Hartford, CT 06143 (G)

Mohon International, P.O. Box 550, Paris, TN 38242 (G)

Monroe Systems for Business, 1000 The American Rd., Morris Plains, NJ 07950 (G)

Moritex U.S.A., 6440 Lusk Blvd., Ste. D-105, San Diego, CA 92121 (G)

Mtn. Home Biological, P.O. Box 1142, White Salmon, WA 98672 (L)

Museum Products Co., 84 Route 27, Mystic, CT 06355 (L)

NADA Scientific Ltd., P.O. Box 1336, 39 Butternut St., Champlain, NY 12919 (L)

NAGAWTIS Software Research, 1801 Gouldin Rd., Oakland, CA 94611 (G)

NASCO-Modesto, 4825 Stoddard Rd., P.O. Box 3837, Modesto, CA 95352 -3837 (G)

NEN Life Sciences, 549 Albany St., Boston, MA 02118 (L)

NYSTROM Div. of Herff Jones, 3333 N. Elston Ave., Chicago, IL 60618 (E)

Nakamura Scientific Co., P.O. Box 1336, Champlain, NY 12919-1336 (P)

Nalge Nunc International., P.O. Box 20365, Rochester, NY 14602 (P)

Nasco, 901 Janesville Ave., P.O. Box 901, Fort Atkinson, WI 53538-0901 (G)

National Association of Conservation, 408 E. Main, League City, TX 77574-0855 (E)

National Earth Science Teachers, 2000 Florida Ave., NW, Washington, DC 20009 (E)

National Gardening Association, 180 Flynn Ave., Burlington, VT 05401 (E)

National Geographic Society, 1145 17th St., NW, Washington, DC 20036 (E)

National Learning Center, 800 3rd St. N.E., Washington, DC 20002 (G)

National Optical Instruments, 12000 Crowpoint Dr., #100, San Antonio, TX 78233 (P)

National School Products, 101 E. Broadway, Maryville, TN 37804 (G)

National Teaching Aids, 1845 Highland Ave., New Hyde Park, NY 11040 (G)

Nature Discoveries, 389 Rock Beach Rd., Rochester, NY 14617 (E)

Nature Store, 455 Cedar St., West Barnstable, MA 02668 (E)

Naturesaver, P.O. Box 457, La Jolla, CA 92038 (E)

Nebraska Scientific, 3823 Leavenworth St., Omaha, NE 68105-1180 (G)

New Omni Inc., P.O. Box 450448, Atlanta, GA 30345 (G)

Newbury Hydraulics, Ltd., Box 1173, Gibsons, BC CANADA V0N 1V0 (P)

Newport Corp., 1791 Deere Ave., Irvine, CA 92714 (G)

Newton's Apple, 172 E. 4th St., c/o KTCA TV, St. Paul, MN 55101 (P)

NightStar Products, 695 Mistletoe Rd., Ste. D, Ashland, OR 97520 (E)

Nikon Instrument Group, 1300 Walt Whitman Rd., Melville, NY 11747-3064 (P)

Northwest Laboratory Supply, 5510 Nielson Rd., #B, Ferndale, WA 98248 (G)

Northwest Scientific, 171 Cooper Ave., Tonawanda, NY 14150 (G)

Novostar Designs, 317 S. Main St., P.O. Box 1328, Burlington, NC 27216-1328 (E)

Nurnberg Scientific Co., 6310 SW Virginia Ave., Portland, OR 97201 (P)

Ocean Biologics, Inc., 5315 139th Pl., SW, Edmonds, WA 98026 (E)

Ohaus Corp., 29 Hanover Rd., Florham Park, NJ 07932 (P)

Omni Resources, 1004 S. Mebane St., P.O. Box 2096, Burlington, NC 27216-2096 (G)

Omnion, P.O. Box O, Rockland, MA 02370 (G)

Orbix Corp., 6329 Mori St., McLean, VA 22101 (G)

Other Worlds Enterprises, 2029 Sunshine Circle, Woodland Park, CO 80866-6193 (E)

Owls, Etc., 15 Riviera Ct., Great River, NY 11739 (L)

Oxford Instruments, P.O. Box 2560, Oak Ridge, TN 37831-2560 (P)

PASCO Scientific, 10101 Foothills Blvd., Box 619011, Roseville, CA 95678-9011 (P)

PEPCO, 10206 Rosewood, Overland, KS 66207 (G)

Parco Scientific Co., 316 Youngstown-Kingsville Rd., SE, Vienna, OH 44473 (G)

Patio Garden Pond, 7919 S. Shields, Oklahoma City, OK 73149 (L)

Pellets, P.O. Box 5484, Bellingham, WA 98227-5484 (L)

Pitsco, 1002 E. Adams, Pittsburg, KS 66762 (L)

Play-Tech, 139 Harristown Rd., Capsela Division, Glen Rock, NJ 07452 (L)

Polaroid Education Program, 575 Technology Sq., Bldg. #4, Cambridge, MA 02139 (P)

Polydron USA, 9874 Red River, Fountain Valley, CA 92708 (P)

PowerLab Studios, Inc., 616 Ramona St., Ste. 20, Palo Alto, CA 94301 (L)

Prentice Hall, 1 Lake St., Upper Saddle River, NJ 07458 (G)

Protein Solutions, Inc., 6009 Highland Dr., Salt Lake City, UT 84121 (L)

Putnam/Northern Westchester, 200 Boces Dr., Yorktown Heights, NY 10598-4399 (G)

Quantum Technology, 30153 Arena Dr., Evergreen, CO 80439 (E)

Quest Aerospace Education, 519 W. Lone Cactus Dr., Phoenix, AZ 85027-2921 (E)

RCR Scientific, 206 W. Lincoln Ave., Goshen, IN 46526 (L)

Rainbow International Distributors, 237 Fairgate Dr., Vacaville, CA 95687 (E)

Ranaco, 4345 E. Irvington, Tucson, AZ 85714 (E)

Resolution Technology, 26000 Avenida Aeropuerto #22, San Juan Capistrano, CA 92675 (P)

Right Before Your Eyes, 136 Ellis Hollow Creek Rd., Ithaca, NY 14850 (P)

Rocket Age Enterprises, 9 Lance Rd., Lebanon, NJ 08833 (P)

SCI-MA Education, 325 S. Westwood, #4, Mesa, AZ 85210 (G)

Saddleback Educational, 3505 Cadillac Ave., Building F-9, Costa Mesa, CA 92626 (E)

Sargent-Welch/VWR Scientific, 911 Commerce Ct., Buffalo Grove, IL 60089-2375 (G)

Sarut, 107 Horatio St., New York, NY 10014 (G)

Satellite Data System, P.O. Box 219, Cleveland, MN 56017-0219 (E)

Schoolmasters Science, 745 State Circle, P.O. Box 1941, Ann Arbor, MI 48106 (G)

Sci Space Craft International, P.O. Box 61027, Pasadena, CA 91116-7027 (E)

Sci Tech, 200 Innovation Blvd. Ste. #236, State College, PA 16803 (P)

Science Fair Supply Co., 6117 Bradley Manor, St. Louis, MO 63129 (G)

Science First, 95 Botsford Pl., Buffalo, NY 14216 (G)

Science Inquiry Enterprises, 14358 Village View Ln., Chino Hills, CA 91709 (G)

Science Instruments Co., 6122 Reisterstown Rd., Baltimore, MD 21215 (P)

Science Kit and Boreal Laboratories, 777 E. Park Dr., Tonawanda, NY 14150 (P)

Science Museum of Minnesota, 30 E. 10th St., Saint Paul, MN 55101 (L)

Science Source, P.O. Box 727, Waldoboro, ME 04572 (L)

Science Supply Co., P.O. Box 836, Yarmouth, ME 04096 (G)

Science, Math & Gifted Products, Inc., N7513 537th St., Menomonie, WI 54251 (P)
Scientific Universe Products, 5715 Sunset Ln., Mukileteo, WA 98275 (E)
Scope, Sequence & Coordination, 1709 Dryden, Ste. 519, Houston, TX 77030-2404 (L)
Scott Resources, 401 Hickory St., P.O. Box 2121, Fort Collins, CO 80522 (L)
Seiler Instrument Co., 170 E. Kirkham Ave., St. Louis, MO 63119-1791 (P)
Sellstrom Manufacturing Co., P.O. Box 355, Palatine, IL 60078-0355 (G)
Sharp Electronics Corp., Sharp Plaza, Box G, Mahwah, NJ 07430 (P)
Shasta Visions, P.O. Box 990, Mt. Shasta, CA 96067 (G)
Sheldon Laboratory Systems, 102 Kirk St., P.O. Box 836, Crystal Springs, MS 39059 (L)
Silver Burdett Ginn, 299 Jefferson Rd., P.O. Box 480, Parsippany, NJ 07504 (G)
Skilcraft, 328 N. Westwood, Toledo, OH 43607 (G)
Skullduggery, 624 S. B St., Tustin, CA 92680 (L)
Skulls Unlimited International, P.O. Box 6741, Moore, OK 73153 (L)
Sky Publishing Corp., P.O. Box 9111, Belmont, MA 02178-9111 (E)
Southern Precision Instruments, 3419 E. Commerce St., San Antonio, TX 78220 (G)
Southland Instruments, Inc., P.O. Box 1517, Huntington Beach, CA 92647 (P)
Spectronic Instruments, 820 Linden Ave., Rochester, NY 14625 (P)
Spectrum Educational Supplies, 125 Mary St., Aurora, ON CANADA L4G 1G3 (G)
Stokes Publishing Company, 1292 Reamwood Ave., Sunnyvale, CA 94089 (G)
Summit Learning, P.O. Box 493, Fort Collins, CO 80522 (G)
Sunburst Communications, 101 Castleton St., Pleasantville, NY 10570 (L)
Sunny Ideas, 4412 Huron, Midland, MI 48642 (G)
Suntrak, 2350 E. 91st St., Indianapolis, IN 46240 (G)
Swift Instruments, P.O. Box 562, San Jose, CA 95106 (P)
Synthephytes, P.O. Box 1032, Angleton, TX 77516-1032 (P)
Syracuse Pulp and Paper Foundation, 1 Forestry Dr., Syracuse, NY 13210-2778 (E)
TEDCO, 498 S. Washington St., Hagerstown, IN 47346 (G)
Tandy Corp./Radio Shack, 1600 One Tandy Center, Fort Worth, TX 76102 (P)
Tangent Scientific, 10-261 Martindale Rd., St. Catharines, ON CANADA L2E 1A2 (G)
Tasco Sales, 7600 N.W. 26 St., Miami, FL 33122-1494 (G)
Teacher Video Production Corp., P.O. Box 1531, Wailuku Maui, HW 96793 (L)
Teachers Laboratory, P.O. Box 6480, Brattleboro, VT 05302 (L)

Team Labs, 6390B Gunpark Dr., Boulder, CO 80301 (L)

Texas Instruments, P.O. Box 650311, M/S 3908, Dallas, TX 75265 (P)

The Scope Shoppe, Inc., 113 Read St., P.O. Box 1208, Elburn, IL 60178 (L)

Thorn Smith Laboratories, 7755 Narrow Gauge Rd., Beulah, MI 49617 (E)

Thornton Educational Products, P.O. Box 2566, Naples, FL 33939 (G)

Tri Space, P.O. Box 7166, McLean, VA 22106-7666 (E)

Triarch, P.O. Box 98, Ripon, WI 54971-0098 (E)

Triops, P.O. Box 10852, Pensacola, FL 32524 (L)

Trippensee Planetarium Co., 301 Cass St., Saginaw, MI 48602-2097 (E)

Tyris Environmental, L.C., P.O. Box 64514, Tucson, AZ 85728-4514 (E)

U.S. Fish & Wildlife Service, 9720 Executive Center Dr., St. Petersburg, FL 33702 (E)

Ulrichs Fossil Gallery, Fossil Station #308, Kemmerer, WY 83101 (E)

Unilab, 1604 Walker Lake Rd., Mansfield, OH 44906 (L)

United Products & Instruments, 605 Montrose Ave., South Plainfield, NJ 07080 (G)

Unitron, Inc., 170 Wilbur Pl., Bohemia, NY 11716-0469 (G)

Uptown Sales, 33 N. Main St., Chambersburg, PA 17201 (G)

Vee Gee Scientific, 13600 NE 126th Pl., Ste. A, Kirkland, WA 98034 (L)

Vernier Software, 8565 SW Beaverton-Hillsdale Hwy., Portland, OR 97225-2429 (L)

VideoLabs, 10925 Bren Rd., E., Minneapolis, MN 55343 (P)

Vital Technologies Corp., 670 Hardwick Rd., Bolton, Ontario CANADA L7E 5R5 (L)

WARDs Natural Science Est., 5100 W. Henrietta Rd., Rochester, NY 14692-9012 (L)

WESCO, 1577 Colorado Bl., Los Angeles, CA 90041 (L)

WR Hellman Co., 2451 SE Clover Ct., Hillsboro, OR 97123 (G)

West Coast Aquatics, 906 Calle Collado, Thousand Oaks, CA 91360 (E)

Wikki Stix Co., 2432 W. Peoria, #1188, Phoenix, AZ 85029 (G)

Wild Goose Co., 375 Whitney Ave., Salt Lake City, UT 84115 (L)

Wildlife Supply Co., 301 Cass St., Saginaw, MI 48602-2097 (L)

Wind & Weather, P.O. Box 2320-ST, Mendocino, CA 95460 (E)

Women in Mining Ed. Foundation, 1801 Broadway, Ste. 400, Denver, CO 80202 (E)

World Class Learning Materials, 111 Kane Street, Baltimore, MD 21224-1728 (G)

Young Entomologists Society, 1915 Peggy Pl., Lansing, MI 48910-2553 (L)

Young Naturalist Co., 1900 N. Main, Newton, KS 67114 (L)

Ztek Co., P.O. Box 1055, Louisville, KY 40201-1055 (G)

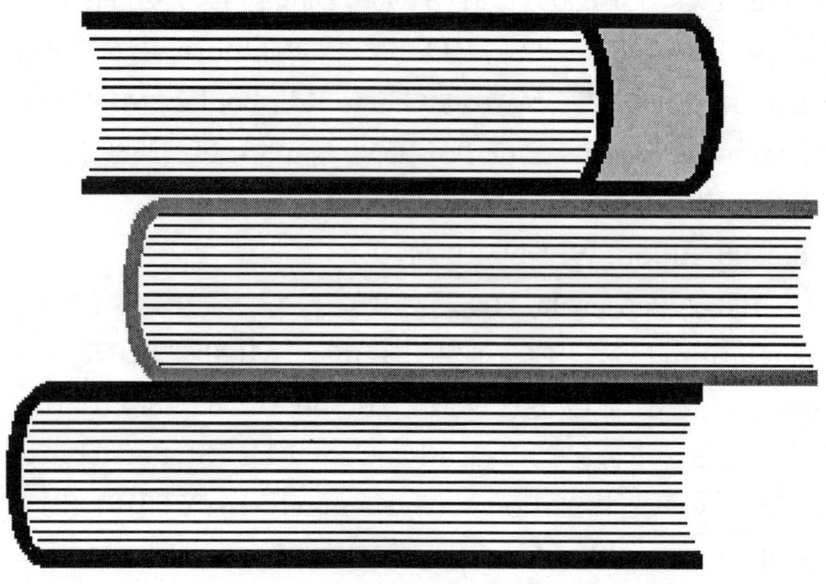

References for Further Reading

Bereiter, C., and M. Scardamalia. 1989. Intentional learning as a goal of instruction. *In Knowing, Learning, and Instruction: Essays in Honor of Robert Glaser,* L.B. Resnick, ed.: 361-392. Hillsdale, NJ: Lawrence Erlbaum and Associates.

Brown, A. 1994. The advancement of learning. Presidential Address, American Educational Research Association. *Educational Researcher, 23*: 4-12.

Brown, A.L., and J.C. Campione. 1994. Guided discovery in a community of learners. In *Classroom Lessons: Integrating Cognitive Theory and Classroom Practice,* K. McGilly, ed.: 229-270. Cambridge, MA: MIT Press.

Bruer, J.T. 1993. *Schools for Thought: A Science of Learning in the Classroom.* Cambridge, MA: MIT Press.

Carey, S. 1985. *Conceptual Change in Childhood.* Cambridge, MA: MIT Press.

Carey, S., and R. Gelman, eds. 1991. *The Epigenesis of Mind: Essays on Biology and Cognition.* Hillsdale, NJ: Lawrence Erlbaum and Associates.

Champagne, A.B. 1988. Science Teaching: Making the System Work. In *This Year in School Science 1988: Papers from the Forum for School Science.* Washington, DC: American Association for the Advancement of Science.

Cohen, D.K., M.W. McLaughlin, and J.E. Talbert, eds. 1993. *Teaching for Understanding: Challenges for Policy and Practice.* San Francisco: Jossey-Bass.

Darling-Hammond, L. 1992. *Standards of Practice for Learner Centered Schools.* New York: National Center for Restructuring Schools and Learning.

Harlen, W. 1992. *The Teaching of Science.* London: David Fulton Publishers.

Leinhardt, G. 1993. On Teaching. In *Advances in Instructional Psychology,* R. Glaser ed., vol. 4: 1-54. Hillsdale, NJ: Lawrence Erlbaum and Associates.

Loucks-Horsley, S., J.G. Brooks, M.O. Carlson, P. Kuerbis, D.P. Marsh, M. Padilla, H. Pratt, and K.L. Smith. 1990. *Developing and Supporting Teachers for Science Education in the Middle Years.* Andover, MA: The National Center for Improving Science Education.

Loucks-Horsley, S., M.O. Carlson, L.H. Brink, P. Horwitz, D.P. Marsh, H. Pratt, K.R. Roy, and K. Worth. 1989. *Developing and Supporting Teachers for Elementary School Science Education.* Andover, MA: The National Center for Improving Science Education.

McGilly, K., ed. 1994. *Classroom Lessons: Integrating Cognitive Theory and Classroom Practice.* Cambridge, MA: MIT Press.

NBPTS (National Board for Professional Teaching Standards). 1991. *Toward High and Rigorous Standards for the Teaching Profession: Initial Policies and Perspectives of the National Board for Professional Teaching Standards, 3rd ed.* Detroit, MI: NBPTS.

NCTM (National Council of Teachers of Mathematics). 1991. *Professional Standards for Teaching Mathematics.* Reston, VA: NCTM.

NRC (National Research Council). 1994. *Learning, Remembering, Believing: Enhancing Human Performance,* D. Druckman and R.A. Bjork, eds. Washington, DC: National Academy Press.

NRC (National Research Council). 1990. *Fulfilling the Promise: Biology Education in the Nation's Schools.* Washington, DC: National Academy Press.

NRC (National Research Council). 1987. *Education and Learning to Think,* L.B. Resnick, ed. Washington, DC: National Academy Press.

Schoen, D. 1987. *Educating the Reflective Practitioner: Toward a New Design for Teaching and Learning in the Professions.* San Francisco: Jossey-Bass.

Shulman, L.S. 1987. Knowledge and teaching foundations of the new reform. *Harvard Education Review, 57* (1): 1-22.